MARTIN COHEN

I THINK, THEREFORE I EAT

Turner Publishing Company

Turner Publishing Company
Nashville, Tennessee
New York, New York
www.turnerpublishing.com

Cover design: TK
Book design: David Reed

Library of Congress Cataloging-in-Publication Data

Names: Cohen, Martin, 1964- author.
Title: I think therefore I eat : the world's greatest minds tackle the food
  question / by Martin Cohen.
Description: Nashville, Tennessee : Turner Publishing Company, [2018] |
  Includes bibliographical references and index. |
Identifiers: LCCN 2018014598 (print) | LCCN 2018016655 (ebook) | ISBN
  9781684422005 (ebook) | ISBN 9781684421985 (pbk. : alk. paper) | ISBN
  9781684421992 (hardcover : alk. paper)
Subjects: LCSH: Food--Philosophy. | Food preferences. | Food--Psychological
  aspects. | Nutrition. | Health behavior.
Classification: LCC B105.F66 (ebook) | LCC B105.F66 C64 2018 (print) | DDC
  641.3001--dc23
LC record available at https://lccn.loc.gov/2018014598

Printed in the United States of America
17 18 19 20 10 9 8 7 6 5 4 3 2 1

PRAISE FOR *I THINK THEREFORE I EAT*

"Is it a recipe book? Is it a socio-political manifesto? Cohen sets out to uncover the 'truth' behind food. What he has achieved is a comprehensive book on matters food, chemistry, beliefs and history, without dictating on any of these. Cohen put logicians beside chocolate cakes: a refreshingly light, yet expansive read.
— Lina Ufimtseva, Blogger, *Philosophical Investigations*

"I Think Therefore I Eat is a journey towards self-discovery, an objective and witty analysis of historic and current food trends. In a fun and easy way to read, he helps you to understand that at the end, the only one you should listen to, is your very own body. Because it all depends, and detail matters!"
— Tania Biral, Web Content editor

"From Nietzsche on broth to the Marxist theory of snacks, Martin Cohen lays on a veritable banquet of thoughtful dishes for all tastes."
– Professor Constantine Sandis, philosopher and author of *The Things We Do and Why We Do Them*

"An immensely informative and entertaining narrative about the intersection between deep thinkers of philosophy and our contemporary specialists of food and nutrition. A book for everyone who eats."
— Keith Tidman, public policy and science editor

"What I loved about this book is that Martin Cohen provides much food for though via studying the thoughts and opinions of many great philosophers. He doesn't state what is the right path to follow. Rather, he provides a vast wealth of info that leads the reader to make up their own minds and create a habit of seeking out the answers for ourselves. I can't view food the same way and I consider myself better off for it."
– Charlene Martel, *The Literary Word*

"Witty and readable, I Think Therefore I Eat will shock food experts of all kinds but the rest of us will think carefully before we eat. We'll improve our life styles and extend our life expectancy as a result."
— Colin Kirk, author of *Life in Poetry*

"Cohen's suggestions are delicious and furiously contemporary, as the Inspectors of the Michelin Guide also once put it, writing about my own restaurant."
— Jeremy Laze, Chef at La Villa Eugène, Caen

If you hunger for a fresh taste of food truth then you'll find Martin Cohen's I Think, Therefore I Eat will serve up an insightful culinary feast that will nourish your mind.
– Karen A. Stephenson @EdibleWildFood.com

"But perhaps the real reason why relatively few philosophers analyze food is because it's too difficult. Food is vexing. It is not even clear what it is. It belongs simultaneously to the worlds of economics, ecology, and culture. It involves vegetables, chemists, and wholesalers; livestock, refrigerators, and cooks; fertilizer, fish, and grocers.... It is much easier to treat food as a mere case study of applied ethics than to analyze it as something that poses unique philosophical challenges."

—From *The Philosophy of Food*, ed. David M. Kaplan

Contents

Introduction: The Crystal Vase

In 1881, in search of better conditions, not only for his stomach but for his thinking, the strange German philosopher Friedrich Nietzsche traveled to Lake Sils in the shadow of the Alps. Here, he would rise at 5:00 a.m., wash his whole body in cold water, and then meditate for an hour. Breakfast would be two raw eggs with bread rolls and aniseed rusks, washed down with tea. The morning would be spent walking and thinking, and lunch would be steak and macaroni, washed down with beer.

Where his illustrious predecessor, Immanuel Kant, had insisted that company was essential for the enjoyment of food, Nietzsche detested such chatter and insisted on eating alone. More walking and philosophizing in the afternoon were followed by similar food to what he had eaten at breakfast, with the addition of *polenta*, the local delicacy. Polenta is a Central European dish made by boiling cornmeal into a thick, solidified porridge, and eaten baked, fried, or grilled. Healthy? I wouldn't think so. Even more ominously, his regimen included no fruit or vegetables. Nietzsche called Sils his "rescue place." His bodily ailments became worse, if anything, but (for the first time in many years) Nietzsche felt calm and contented.

The story illustrates three important things: One is that food shapes us and defines us, both in terms of *what* we eat and *how* we eat it. The second, perhaps less appreciated, is that we are almost uniquely passive in our acceptance of other people's judgments about food. And the final, third thing is that philosophers are the *original* food gurus.

Surprised? You shouldn't be. Philosophy is a subject with an unparalleled tradition of trying to get body and mind in harmony—and of tackling insoluble questions. Plus, as anyone who's tried a diet or consulted a nutritionist will know, the question of "what to eat" really is a deep one.

Mind you, if you went by TV and the newspapers, you could be forgiven for thinking that celebrities, be they chefs or models, have more of a handle on the key food issues than qualified doctors and nutritionists—let alone philosophers. And you might well be right. Because the worst thing about food science, the elephant in the room, is that it's not just the opinions that are changing—the "facts" themselves shift too. That's why, for thirty years, snacking on sugar was supposed to be the way to *lose* weight, and that's why millions of people are even now on low-cholesterol diets that fail to lower their cholesterol and instead increase their risk of heart disease. Yet nothing in the past is as weird as the current orthodoxy, which says that natural foods, from beef to cheese, from bread to orange juice, can be deconstructed and re-created by food scientists using cheap, junky ingredients and chemicals.

Weird, and dangerous too—dangerous for your health. Which is why in this book I tease apart the strands of diet science and biochemistry, along with an ounce of economics and a dash of human psychology, to get to the bottom of the food question. But you don't need to be a serious student of Socrates to read *I Think Therefore I Eat*. You just need to acknowledge that some important food questions haven't been answered yet. Or, maybe they have. Perhaps we've simply gotten lost, because we've been following profiteers and TV personalities instead of those wise souls devoted to truth, ethics, and reason—the philosophers.

There's more than one way to eat badly. You can eat too much (which we hear a lot about now), you can eat too little—and you can eat the wrong stuff. You can eat (like Nietzsche) what *seem* to be the right things, but aren't, and you can eat what may (to parents, for example) seem to be unhealthy foods—but actually provide a better mix of nutrients than seems possible.

If the response to "what to eat" for many of us is quite simple, and depends on what is at the back of the fridge, the answer to the more important question of how to eat healthily is that, well, it's complicated. There's plenty of advice around, but it's often contradictory—and even where there is a consensus, it clearly works better for some people than for others. That's why the question really requires individual answers, and it's also why I think this book could play a small part in helping people to find their own unique solutions. In this book there's no one strategy pushed, no one-size-fits-all solution suggested. Instead there's something better. Remember that old saying about giving someone a fish and you feed them for a day, but teach the same person to fish and you feed them for a lifetime? Well, that's the idea here. Instead of offering a one-size-fits-all piece of advice that won't actually work, instead, I'll outline three guiding principles, which you can then actively use to suit your needs and concerns. Plus, I'll illustrate the ideas and arguments in the great food debate with a whole range of examples both from history and from recent, cutting-edge research. At intervals I'll bring in some very human stories—but not ones like you've heard before. These are eating stories and strategies drawn from philosophical history, because the great philosophers make equally great case studies.

Here are the three principles having to do with food and how to eat wisely:

1. *Detail matters.*

2. *Everything connects.*

3. *Don't mess with the crystal vase.*

Principle 1, "Detail matters," is about resisting easy solutions and short-cuts to thinking. Because, yes, fruits contain sugar, but no, their effects on the body are *not* the same as, say, the effects of a glass of Coca-Cola, which also contains sugar.

Principle 2, *Everything connects*, is why food debates can go on and on and after a while even seem to contradict themselves.

And it is also why dieters have such problems: you cut out one food, and somewhere along the line there will be a consequence. Maybe you cut out too much fat while forgetting that your brain—a much neglected part of the body when thinking about diets!—needs a steady supply of dietary fats to create the myelin that wraps around your nerve cells so they can send electrical messages.

And that third guiding principle, "Don't mess with the crystal vase," is both the most important one and the one most often ignored. Another way to put it might be "Don't perform DIY repair on Swiss watches." The point is that the human body is a very delicate arrangement of intricate parts that (creationist theories notwithstanding) seems to have taken an unimaginably long time to evolve. Presumably, it started with just one cell; now we are made up of an estimated 37.2 trillion cells! Many of them (as I explain in chapter 16) are not even human ones—yet they all play a role in keeping us alive and well. The body is so incomprehensibly complicated that it defies logic that people—not least experts—seek to reduce to simple rules and linear "cause and effect" explanations. This is a central, guiding theme in this book: acknowledge complexity, and don't take a hammer to the crystal vase (or the Swiss watch) by, for example, drastically restricting your diet, whether as part of a weight-control regimen or, conversely, by indulging in just one or two favorite (or convenient) foods—like pizza and chips.

If you're hungry for the truth, you can read *I Think Therefore I Eat* in one sitting. However, the book is divided into bite-size sections for convenient "snacking." You'll also notice that the chapters contain sidebars—some of which highlight interesting asides and others that provide extra detail about a topic—as well as diet tips and recipes. It is a "dip in and out" book, with a central thread: the quest for healthy food. Although the book is structured in a way to be easily comprehensible to busy readers, the techniques that make information accessible and interesting—that make sense of complex material—are, in a deep sense, philosophical.

The Idea Behind this Book

I've encountered public health, ethical, and environmental issues connected to food for many years, but for me it all began to fall into place when I was assigned to a research post that took me to sun-soaked, sub-tropical Australia. There, every day, on my way to work, I would drive through the pineapple fields of Queensland, in the shadow of the exotically shaped Glass House Mountains. I was astonished to see that the pineapples could be grown in the dry, sandy soil that seemed too poor to support much. They don't grow pineapples in the Sahara, and this environment was not much better! Australia, however, has vigorously embraced the scientific addition of nutrients to the land.

In the case of the Aussie pineapple farms, some of the farmers were spreading industrial and domestic waste—from refrigerators to engine oil—on the fields. *And all those substances went into the pineapples too.* With this simple discovery came a slightly unsettling proof of an old saying about food: you are what you eat—but you are whatever *it* eats too.

You see, boring old soil is a universe of tiny bacteria and fungi—and so are our stomachs. Modern farming poisons this highly evolved blend and replaces it with a chemical brew that is extremely toxic to humans. Science—and philosophy—excels at breaking down complexity but is less good at appreciating it. The moral is: we should all try to eat better stuff. Yes, easy to say—but harder to put into practice.

And that's why lots of people buy cookbooks written by celebrities, or subscribe to healthy eating plans, and still others queue up to visit qualified nutritionists (or consult doctors) before coming away with official, government-sanctioned lists of good and bad foods. And then, for many, there's plan B, the fallback strategy. Which is to give up the struggle of trying to eat healthily and just eat miserably instead. But whatever particular option one chooses, too often the question of what to eat becomes a pressured one, and dieting a task and burden.

So, this isn't a diet book. At least, not in *that* sense. You see, there are many ways the word *diet* can be used, and the one that we've become used to—a self-imposed straitjacket of what we can and cannot eat—is a recent interloper: restrictive, judgmental, value-laden. Food, let alone philosophy, shouldn't be like that. Both should be part of a celebration of life and its myriad possibilities. Because food is above all about pleasure and making fun choices—which is why we don't actually eat government-prepared packs of nutrients and vitamin pills, but instead have long aisles of brightly packaged foods in the modern food temples called supermarkets.

My idea in this book is not to tell you what to eat but rather how to make better, more informed decisions about food. It's a book for people who actually *like* food, but who have other priorities too. That's why in this book I'm not telling you to change your lifestyle. I'm not presenting myself as some kind of personal trainer, let alone a medical advisor. Instead my plan is to share ideas and information about food to increase your autonomy. Only then, yes, maybe you'll feel inspired to make changes to your menu and lifestyle. Those changes might help you to become healthier and happier, and even (if you want to) lose some weight.

Distilling complex information carefully into a concise form is my specialty. Of course, I always attempt to make my work eminently readable, practical, and entertaining as well. As a result, *I Think Therefore I Eat* reads more like a lunchtime conversation between friends than a textbook or scientific tome—an unexpected mix of modern science, ancient lore, and real stories to satisfy a broad range of palates. It also provides a buffet of fascinating food-related tidbits—like the worrisome fact that white bread turns to fat as quickly as a sugary drink, and that eating real chocolate is not only useful for keeping your weight down but can also provide a considerable dose of substances that are "cousins" to cannabis and amphetamine! And lastly, *I Think Therefore I Eat* offers an entertaining and somewhat sideways introduction to some of the great philosophers and to philosophy itself.

There's plenty of good news about food too. To start with, foods like cheese and dairy, Mediterranean dishes with olive oil, and even pasta don't have to be avoided as part of a healthy diet! You *can* eat after seven and drink wine as well. Plus, you *can* salt your food liberally, and doing so will certainly help you to stay away from junk food and eat less. You can eat bread and butter and even enjoy chocolate cake—if you make it with "real" ingredients, because one slice contains only about the same amount of sugar as a couple of apples.

This book contains lots of ideas for anyone who must fit cooking into a busy lifestyle—people who, in the past, have been forced down the "convenience" route, and ended up with cupboards of ready-made food after quick trips to the supermarket. The TV gourmets who have the time—and money—for exotic ingredients and leisurely food preparation can certainly offer tips, but their recipes are unlikely to be of much use to the rest of us. Both eating and buying food that is healthy requires definite strategies, and this is what the book offers above all.

Exploring Nutrition

Although there are plenty of diet tips here, I stress that this book is more of a general, educational *exploration*. On the way, I will tell you about some of the ideas about food and healthy eating of the philosophers over the centuries. There are two very good reasons to go back to them. These are people who thought deeply not only about subjects like the nature of the universe, the difference between truth and opinion, and the principles of the good life, but also about food. Their ideas on food may not be definitive, not game changers, but they are perceptive and often surprisingly practical. Take, for example, the most famous philosopher of them all, Plato. He recommended a diet based on fresh fruit and nuts (with honey for treats) while pointing out, 2000 odd years ago, that if everyone wants to eat meat with every meal, there won't be enough food to go around, and the ensuing competition for resources will inevitably lead to environmental degradation and wars. Or take the flamboyant French political philosopher Rousseau. He wrote, about three hundred years ago, that a meal of brown bread and a slice of cheese is both very convenient and rather delicious. Both thinkers also offer detailed menus for what they call a more "balanced" life, a more philosophical diet.

The second reason to talk about the philosophers, however, is that they're ordinary people. They're real individuals who often struggled with health issues, just like the rest of us.

But there are also reasons to consult philosophy in a broader sense, because philosophy provides us with some powerful conceptual tools for making sense of food issues. The key philosophical tools are the "Three C's": spotting *contradictions* and looking for *consistency* in advice, all while applying *common sense*. Now, people like to sneer at common sense, and indeed it is easy to come up with funny examples where it leads to ridiculous consequences, but the alternative to it—uncritical acceptance of what we are told—is often worse. Common sense says that crops should be grown in the soil using sunlight, not in sheds using chemicals. Common sense suggests that injecting animals with powerful drugs and growth hormones that would be dangerous to us if we directly ingested them also makes their flesh dangerous to eat. But in many such cases, powerful economic interests push a contrary "reassuring" message, couched in scientific language, even as the health statistics of people show a resolutely adverse trend.

And there are other powerful box-openers in the philosophical toolbox alongside the Three C's, like the concept of reductionism. *Reductionism* may sound like a ten-dollar term, but here's a rather simple example from food science: The fact that diets high in fruit seem to reduce the risk of certain diseases can be explained simply in terms of the fruits' vitamin C content; therefore, eating food products containing added vitamin C or taking vitamin C tablets can provide the same function. Thus, Kellogg's famous cornflakes "with added vitamins" are promoted as a healthy and balanced meal, despite, in reality, being a dried sludge of crushed maize. Reductionism in food science means that the language of chemistry—*polyunsaturated, amino acids, antioxidants*—takes over, too often without any evidence, without even the pretense of any evidence, that food and its ingredients can really be simplified in this kind of way.

Often, only philosophy is left to remind us to be skeptical when food is reduced to its chemical ingredients in such a way that processed foods start to seem pretty good and "real foods" look suspicious.

Another lesson from philosophy is more of a cautionary tale than a conceptual tool. The thousand-year quest of the philosophers to search for eternal truths also sheds light on today's diet gurus. For Plato, the search was for things like Truth, Beauty, and, well, Unicorns. For many modern nutritionists it is for things like Calories and Nutrients. These are for them the "real foods," the eternal and unchanging essences that lie behind the surface appearances that humble mortals buy in supermarkets. To the reductionists who cling to this mind-set, it is not the fruit that's good for us, but the vitamin C; it's not whole grains we need, it's the vitamin B complex; it's not salmon steak with pine nuts we crave, but nitrogen. (Nitrogen, you ask? Yes, because this element is the "master nutrient" that makes us grow—just as it does the wheat in the fields.)

Add to which, nutritional science, just like philosophy, loves its *Manichean dualisms*, its competing forces of good and evil. Fat is bad; low-fat is good. Vitamins are virtuous, and sugar is just plain wicked. Our love of binary divisions means that today, there's a state of war between saturated and unsaturated fats, between omega-3 and omega-6 fatty acids. We don't even know what these things are, but we're happy to put one into the evil category and the other in the virtuous, and then support the good fight of the one against the other.

Of course, smart people like *us* wouldn't do simplistic things like that, would we? But then what about the idea that margarine is the healthy option to wicked butter? Or that low-fat milk is better for you than—ugh!—whole milk? The truth is that both of the supposedly more modern, healthier alternatives are produced in factories using ingredients that are not only quite alien but, quite possibly, poisonous to the human body.

In fact, the entire edifice of "low fat" dietary advice is shot through with holes and seems to only remain standing because of the reluctance of people to think for themselves in health matters but instead to rely on "expert" advice. It's a reluctance that's really self-defeating because (of course) the experts do not agree on anything in food matters. Illustrating this, two large and extremely expensive surveys in recent years have dealt blows to the dietary orthodoxies of the twentieth century—yet the official advice given out has hardly changed. In 2005 and 2006, research convincingly demonstrated that the claimed health advantages of dietary fiber (preventing certain cancers and heart disease) seemed to be bogus, and that even more extraordinarily, "low fat" diets actually increased the individual's risks of heart disease and, wait for it, made people put on weight!

As one TV diet guru, the implausibly named Xand van Tulleken of the so-called Definitive Diet, admits, "look into dieting in any depth and you will find not just a total lack of consensus about what works and what doesn't but wild, angry arguments." Similarly, the British author and celebrity personal trainer, Joe Wicks, makes his main selling point that his book "is not a diet book" and trashes other experts' approaches and advice—even as he unveils what looks like a very traditional approach of strict calorie controls and "high intensity exercise."

Such diet gurus are benefiting from the fact that opinions on diet issues keep see-sawing from side to side to impose their own narrow perspective. But there's no getting away from the fact that (as I explain in chapter 35, titled "The Method of Doubt") a willingness to review current orthodoxies and consider alternative hypotheses is not only the hallmark of the true philosophical spirit but the key to keeping ahead of changing food advice.

So this book is also a kind of course in critical thinking and skeptical science. It's my aim and intention here to offer an objective, bird's-eye view rather than a narrow, partisan recommendation for this or that approach, and to provide arguments and not just assertions.

It's also for me part of a general philosophical quest we might call Mission Objective Truth—because there is so much contradictory advice circulating in the food industry, not to mention deception and special pleading, from hidden ingredients to cynically mis-described health claims.

As the food writer and journalist Michael Pollan says in a barnstormer of a book called *In Defense of Food* (Penguin 2008):

> We are up against a ferocious and implacable opponent: a worldwide food marketing machine that has bottomless pockets. (In the US alone it is estimated to access $30 billion.) Disgracefully running alongside it is a mini industry of nutritional science—the links between which can be seen most clearly if you consider the strange "safety recommendations" of food authorities, such as that of the US Food and Drug Administration, that eating chips is good for your

heart or of the American Heart Association for
Coco Puffs cereals and Caramel Swirl Ice Cream.

That's a pretty radical agenda, but only one that as you'll see, maybe with some surprise, the philosophers have been pushing and debating for thousands of years. Nonetheless, I think a renewed interest in the philosophy of food is particularly needed now. Why? Because the world has two great food crises. In the developing world, there is chronic poverty and malnutrition, along with multiple environmental threats from deforestation in the Amazon to desertification in Africa and Asia—all driven by our taste for meat and the anonymous multinational food giants' thirst for cheap crops like corn oil and soy. If, in the West, attention is focused on largely hypothetical changes driven by increases in average global temperatures, in much of the world, environmental changes linked to food production are very immediate and practical—not to say disastrous.

But the other crisis, which affects the rich world every bit as much as it does the developing countries, is even more pressing. This is the so-called obesity epidemic.

Obesity is estimated to cost the global economy around $2 trillion a year. Call it a thousand dollars a year for every family in the world. Or, put another way, for a medium-sized country like the UK, there's a bill of over $70 billion a year. Which explains why, in the industrialized world, countries like the United States are spending around 20 percent of their health-care funds on problems linked to obesity, along with huge social costs counted in lost working days and increased benefit payments. Diseases related to unwise eating include cardiovascular disease, type 2 diabetes, and some cancers.

Obesity is defined in the United States as corresponding to a waist size in women of 35 inches or higher, and in men a waist size of 40 inches or higher. If those waistlines could be even slightly reduced, the cost of health insurance programs like Obamacare could have come easily and painlessly from the existing health budget. And yet, at the same time, in these same countries, billions of dollars are spent encouraging fast food. I'm not plucking figures from thin air: $4.6 billion was spent just on *advertising* by American *fast food* restaurants in 2012, for example. It's the kind of public policy contradiction that has philosophers tearing their hair out!

Looked at in terms of either the health costs or the advertising budgets, these are huge issues. Only slightly less remarkable is how little attention economists, much less politicians, give to the "epidemic." Part of this is because the root causes of obesity and unhealthy eating are complex—ranging from the social sciences to biology and technology. There are many other contributing factors, like, for example, the shift toward urbanization and car transport.

Let's go back to Australia. Australia is home to many unique and specially adapted plants, including the tree the Aboriginals called the Bunya Bunya. These trees, with their cones full of juicy nuts, were revered so much by the original Australians that everyone born was assigned a tree. They became its guardian, and the rights to its fruit were matched by a duty to guard it—even, if necessary, to die for it! A ruthless element among the first European settlers chopped down the forests and killed the indigenous people—and sent to extinction many of the local species too—because they wanted to turn the country into cattle ranches and wheat fields. Both the settlers and the Aboriginals, in their different ways, were defined by what they ate.

The central theme in this book is the following: hundreds of thousands of years of evolution have not *really* disposed us to pile on lots of extra pounds, develop diabetes, and die of heart disease. On the contrary, we are born with bodies that are a miracle of self-regulation and efficiency. The trick today is how to get the mind and the body in agreement on what needs to be done to re-establish the ancient balance. And this book is a practical guide to doing just that.

Part I
Separating Food Fact from Food Fiction

Chapter 1

Searching Out Imitation Foods

Public enemy number 1 is... bread.

Ah, bread! It's hard to find a simpler, more basic food. It has a special place in social life, with the planting of wheat leading to both the first fixed settlements and a spiritual reverence for the cycle of life and death. It is spikes of wheat, watered by a priest, that adorn the temples of Ancient Egypt, alongside scenes of the baking process. At the time of Plato and Socrates, that is 2400 years ago, the ancient Greeks were already producing more than eighty types of bread. Humble bread dominates Christian iconography from the "breaking of" rituals to full-blown miracles, as in the Bible story of Jesus feeding the multitudes with loaves and fishes. There's even a hidden message in the otherwise implausible selection of Bethlehem as Jesus' birthplace, because the settlement's name can be translated as "house of bread"! So, it's not really surprising to discover, if still not widely appreciated, that perhaps two of the greatest philosophers, John Locke and Jean-Jacques Rousseau, waxed positively *lyrical* on the virtues of brown bread, with the latter enthusiastically singing its praises as part of a rustic repast "with tolerable wine."

Tall and thin, with a long nose like a horse and what one biographer has called "soft, melancholy eyes," John Locke was no kind of seventeenth-century culinary expert, but he will be forever counted as one of the great political philosophers on account of his ringing endorsement of the doctrine of natural rights: "All being equal and independent, no one ought to harm another in his life, health, liberty, or possessions," Locke declares, firmly. The English philosopher is celebrated for his political philosophy of fundamental human rights and freedoms and is credited with inspiring both the American and the French Revolutions. His paw prints are all over the American Declaration of Independence, the U.S. constitutional separation of powers, and the U.S. Bill of Rights. His ideas lie at the heart of the American *Declaration of the Rights of Man*. But less well known is that he had a philosophy of food and strong views on what to eat. These are set out in the form of advice to young people in a little-known essay called "Some Thoughts Concerning Education," penned in 1692: "I should think that a good piece of well-made and well-bak'd brown bread, sometimes with, and sometimes without butter or cheese, would be often the best breakfast.... I impute a great part of our diseases in England, to our eating too much flesh, and too little bread."

Locke's pronouncements have thundered down the centuries, but his ones on food seem to have been treated rather casually! Indeed, the first thing you will notice today about many popular diets is that they actually try to rule out bread. Take the currently very popular Paleo, or "Stone Age Man," diet, for example (discussed in detail in chapter 4). It claims that not only bread but everything made from cereals and grains is bad for the human body and must be banned.

Now the argument that the human metabolism cannot cope with grains is factually challenged, as you can find out in chapter 4. But there *is* actually a problem with many breads today, which is simply stated: they are not really bread. How can something both *be* bread and yet, at the same time, *not be* bread? It is, in a sense, a profoundly philosophical matter. But it's also a very practical one. Here's a little personal story that throws light on why bread, as John Locke intuited, is something of a benchmark for many dietary issues.

When I was very small, about eight or nine, my school departed from its usual routine of reading, writing, and arithmetic, to have the children make bread rolls and butter. The butter was made by shaking milk in a bottle. Both the butter and the bread rolls tasted delicious, and I was particularly puzzled as to why the bread I had at home tasted completely different. Only years later did I find out that in the United Kingdom in those days, the early 1970s, "bread" had become almost completely controlled by a stock market–listed company called Premier Foods that inflicted the evil Mothers Pride brand on innocent consumers. "Crumbs so smooth and crumbs so white, with freshness baked inside," as the slogan ran. A similar story was being told all over the industrialized world. In the United States, Continental Baking had long been thumping out countless brightly colored packages of mass-produced Wonder Bread under the slogan: "It's Slo Baked." Which, evidently, it wasn't. Doubtless playing on bread's long association with things divine, during the 1940s, Wonder Bread even began to call itself the "Quiet Miracle," on the basis of all the added goodness that it contained.

This chapter is indeed about all the extra things that today go into bread—and it makes for a long chapter. However, it's far from a miracle—more of a quiet scandal. But let's start with practical things; coincidentally, one of Mothers Pride's centers of operations was in the hills near my house, a squat aircraft hangar of a factory that churned out three kinds of bread: thin, medium, and thick cut—all three, of course, made from white flour. The thick bread was for toast, likely with some sugary topping, and it lasted about one week before going moldy. The bread we made that day in school, by comparison, came out of the oven as little loaves that you broke open, and only needed the butter melted into it. Rousseau described this simple pleasure very well. (See chapter 8.)

You see, real bread is made of ground-up wheat (flour), a bit of water, yeast, and a pinch of salt. That's it! No need for added sugar or oils, as have become ubiquitous. The only trick is the magic of the spoonful of yeast that makes it rise and become soft. But what are shop breads like Wonder Bread or Mothers Pride made of? Remember my Rule 1 of food: *Detail matters.* And I'm sure it is a question that Locke himself would have been keen to investigate, with his lifelong strategy of seeking to understand "the whole" by looking at the minutest particles it consisted of. So, here's a closer look at some of the kinds of things we're normally too busy to think about when we choose our bread—but which just might have very real implications for our food choices if we did know about them.

My omniscient line-editor, Kelley suggested that we should include a basic bread recipe. If so, it could go about here?

A Very Authentic Bread

Jean-Claude Papon, a venerable French *épicier* and baker, shared his tips for making a basic bread with me. This is enough to make little rolls for a whole class of children, we think.

flour: 18oz / 500 g

Baker's yeast: 0.3oz / 8 g

salt: 10 pinches

water: 32 cl / 10 fl.oz

Okay, so what do you do? First of all, mix the salt and the flour. Then dissolve the yeast in a cup with the warm water. Next, make a little pit in the center of the flour. Poor the yeast, and the rest of the water and slowly add the flour by hand. Mix until you get a very soft pastry. Now put this on the flat surface. Here's what Jean-Claude says is the crucial bit: knead the mix for 5 to 7 minutes (folding the pastry on itself), so that it becomes more and more elastic.

A Very Authentic Bread (cont.)

Then place the pastry in a bowl, cover it with a tea-towel and leave to rest for at least half an hour. The volume of the pastry must double. Then 'back to work'! Flour your fists and beat the pastry to empty it of its air. And then lightly flour the surface and start to make little rolls.

Put the rolls on an oven rack but before cooking let them rest another half hour. Then place in a very hot oven (Gas Mark 9, 475°F, 240°C) for 12-15 minutes. Humidify the top of the rolls by very lightly sprinkling with water.

Cook in a very hot oven (240 degrees), for 12 to 15mns. Check the cooking by taping the base of the bread, it must sound hollow.

In the United Kingdom, which is typical of all the optimistically classified "developed" economies, most industrial bread is now made using something called the Chorleywood bread process (CBP). This was invented in 1961 not, alas, by some earnest gourmet or even a homely figure called Mrs. Chorleywood, but by the British Baking Industries Research Association. CBP uses high-speed mixers and a witch's brew of chemicals to make a very white loaf out of budget-grade grain in double-quick time. Additional magic is achieved by adding fat, emulsifiers, and enzymes to the traditional ingredients, all of which are then pounded to death in about three minutes by the mixers. Is this wise? Rest assured, as the firm's slogan ran: "Mother knows best!" (And if you fondly imagine that you don't eat it anyway, skip to chapter 38 and then be prepared to be appalled to find out what goes into the typical American burger bun.)

In the 1970s, not counting the supposedly healthy added minerals, industrial bread included a long list of chemical additives, but since the 1990s the list has been dramatically shortened. This is because nowadays manufacturers prefer to use "flour improvers," which they don't need to even let you know are there, because the law says that "processing aids" do not need to be declared on the label. But if tiny quantities of such additives can do subtle things to the bread, they may equally well be doing something to our bodies.

So, to get to the point, what are the ingredients of a modern loaf? An American organization dedicated to "real foods," called Fooducate, recently analyzed the ingredient lists of over 2,000 breads. Their survey found that the average mix had around twenty ingredients! Below is an examination of them, which, although long, is very revealing. In fact, it might put you off eating bread—but that's not the right response. Hopefully, it motivates you to spend a bit more time (and money) buying "real bread," as many people now are.

Ingredient number 1 is *flour*. Even Mothers Pride was made with flour, because, of course, this is the key to bread. Indeed "control of the flour market" was something that the giant food companies almost achieved in Britain—thereby preventing small companies from selling real bread. Fortunately, their iron grip was broken, but today, less than half of breads include whole-wheat flour; the rest use refined or enriched flours.

Essential ingredient number 2 is *salt*. These days, manufactured bread often does not have enough salt in it, owing to a strange and misguided perception that "salt is bad." However, it's not going anywhere quickly as salt has a special function in bread-making of balancing the fermentation by the yeast. Salt remains a key factor in whether or not bread is tasty.

Ingredient number 3 is *water*. It's marvelously cheap, so "real water" is still used.

And then, of course, there's the famous *yeast*, ingredient number 4. The yeast ferments the carbohydrates in the dough, producing carbon dioxide. (Yes, eating toast is helping to overheat the planet! But that's another story...) It is yeast microorganisms *reproducing* that make the dough expand and rise. Manufacturers often add extra wheat gluten, which is naturally present in flour, to speed up the process and reduce the amount of kneading required. A lot of people today worry that they may be allergic to gluten, and this manufacturing trick won't help, but in fact research has found that barely 10 percent of those who think they have a gluten intolerance really do.

Coming in at my number 5 are *vitamins and iron*. Actually, this sounds okay, but when products have vitamins and iron added, it often implies someone has removed them first. Wholegrain flours do not need the addition of these nutrients because they already contain them—and more—in the bran and germ. Typically, Vitamin B1 (thiamin), Vitamin B2 (riboflavin), Vitamin B3 (niacin), folic acid, and iron are added to the mix for a very modern bread. Vitamin C (ascorbic acid) is also added not for your benefit but to help feed the yeast. A big question mark over all such supplements is whether they work in the same way once abstracted from their original chemical and physical context. Put another way, when you see vitamins and iron being added to a product, it really means you are *not* getting them in the natural way that your body is best able to benefit from—or indeed cope with. One of those briefly newsworthy studies by health research organizations, in this case the U.S.-based Environmental Working Group in 2014, found that additives were actually themselves a potential health risk—especially for children and pregnant women or when taken along with vitamin supplements. It warned that nearly half of U.S. children under the age of 8 were at risk of ingesting potentially harmful amounts of Vitamin A, zinc, and niacin due to excessive food fortification.

But now we start to get to ingredients you might not expect—or want—to find. Unexpected bread ingredient number 6 is *soybean oil or some other variety of fat*. These are used to make the texture of the bread more smooth and tender, as well as extending the shelf life slightly (so the bread doesn't go stale so quickly). Adding olive oil has a similar positive effect, but soybean oil is much, much cheaper. Just a pity that it is also more fattening, and researchers fear it may even be cancerous.

At place number 7 is *calcium sulfate*. Also known as... plaster of Paris. This is literally ground-up pieces of the white rock. Natural, in a sense! Bread companies use it to speed up the fermentation process, to increase shelf life, and to make the dough stick less to their machinery. But is it really something you want to eat?

Ingredient number 8 is *mono- and di-glycerides, ethoxylated mono- and di-glycerides*. These strange-sounding chemicals are added to make the dough blow up bigger (which means the dough requires less of the other ingredients, making it cheaper) as well as for practical purposes like making it easier to get the bread out of the baking pan.

Slithering in at number 9 is *high-fructose corn syrup (HFCS)*. Even "real" breads sometimes use a sweetener to improve taste and help the dough rise (because yeast loves sugar). In fact, bread often contains a dash of honey, and although manufacturers prefer to play down the sugar content of their breads, in the case of a spoonful of natural honey, *shhh...* it might even be good for you! However, HFCS is the cheapest sugar, and that is why manufacturers love it more than almost anything else. It's just a detail, then, that along with soybean oil, corn syrup seems to be a good way to kill yourself! This is what one contemporary food writer, Joseph Mercola, says about such syrups:

> Completely unnatural man-made fats created
> through the partial hydrogenation process cause
> dysfunction and chaos in your body on a cellular

level, and studies have linked trans-fats to health problems ranging from obesity and diabetes to reproductive problems and heart disease.

But if you think that sounds bad, trust me, you haven't heard anything yet. Ingredient number 10 is *calcium propionate*. Think fungicide. It is added to the bread to inhibit mold and bacterial growth. It's considered safe for mice, and it seems that we're supposed to trust that what's true for mice is also true for humans. (See the sidebar "Why You Can't Rely on Safety Tests.")

Why You Can't Rely on Safety Tests

Although in the U.S. and elsewhere all prescription drugs must at some point be tested on humans, the vast bulk of medical and therapeutic testing is in practice carried out on mice. Testing on people is much more useful, but it is complicated, expensive—and dangerous. So specially bred rodents are used instead. This is despite the fact that there is no reliable or predictable correspondence between how a mouse reacts to, say, an antibiotic, and how a human does. The human body is just too complicated to be easily imitated. Nonetheless, just like the proverbial drunk searching for the dollar in the wrong street (because the light's better there), pharmaceutical companies test drugs on these long-suffering animals, hoping to find out, say, their bacterial or inflammatory response properties. But, like that drunk, they're looking in the "wrong street." Mice, for example, unlike humans, tolerate millions of live bacteria in their blood before the induction of severe inflammation or shock, and are thousands of times more resistant to most inflammatory stimuli than humans. Perhaps we should be pleased that neither food supplements nor foods in general need to be tested at all.

Ingredient number 11 is *soy lecithin*. This is generally used as an emulsifier, usually to keep ingredients—like oils and fats—from separating or simply to improve texture and shelf-life. Soy itself may be genetically engineered and grown using the controversial pesticide Roundup, which some research studies have found has toxic effects even in almost infinitesimal proportions. Whether it is soy itself, the way it is grown, or the way it is processed, soy in any form today is accused of upsetting the hormonal balance and thereby confusing the body into putting on weight! Ingredients like this are in direct contravention of Food Principle 3: *Don't Mess with the Crystal Vase*. Don't poke around in Swiss watches with hammers. We'll return to the subject of soy in chapter 19 ("The Economics of Obesity"), where we'll see just why it may be the "farmer's friend" but it certainly shouldn't be ours.

Item number 12, *sodium stearoyl lactylate*, brings us firmly into the industrial age—and further away than ever from John Locke's seventeenth-century bucolic dream. Lactylates are organic compounds that are used everywhere! In foods from pancakes and waffles to vegetables and ice creams—and in packaging and shampoos too. When used in bread, they increase the volume of the loaf by increasing the ability of the mix to absorb more water—and remember, water is the cheapest ingredient! At least, I suppose, it could be said that dieters should welcome this as making every ounce of bread a bit less fattening. But it's a very far cry, and a sad departure, from John Locke's simple staff of life. Locke—who fondly recalls how the Roman emperor Augustus, "when the greatest monarch on the earth," chomped a bit of dry bread in his chariot, as well as how Seneca, in his 83rd Epistle, gave an account of allowing himself in old age, when "his age permitted indulgence," to eat a piece of dry bread for dinner—would struggle to even find a bread prepared to dry out obediently these days.

Unsung bread ingredient 12 is positively a poster boy compared to number 13: *monocalcium phosphate*. Phosphates, which farmers value as fertilizers, are usually made from ground-up bones. Okay, bakers use them merely as a leavening agent and preservative, but still... ground-up bones! Funnily enough, only it's not really so funny, ingredient number 14 is also an agricultural fertilizer. *Ammonium sulfate* is a chemical that pops up in the most unexpected places! Here, it is used as extra food for the yeast.

Also dangerously trashing Food Principle 3, the don't-mess-with-the-delicate-balance-of-the-body one, is ingredient 15—*enzymes*. These are added to speed up the time it takes dough to rise. Time is money! The two most often used are amylase and protease. Amylase can be produced from three different sources: bacteria, fungus, and pigs! In other contexts, enzymes like these come with numerous health warnings about unexpected side effects.

At least ingredient 16 is half-okay. *Azodicarbonamide* is added to make the dough easier to handle and because it bleaches the flour (makes it whiter). Why only half-okay? Because, curious to say, it is considered safe in the United States, but is banned from use in Europe, where it is accused of causing allergic reactions and asthma attacks. Some would say that makes it completely un-okay. Similar doubts surround ingredient 17: *DATEM,* also known as Diacetyl Tartaric Acid Esters of Monoglycerides. This is another dough conditioner used to improve volume and uniformity. KILLEM, correction, DATEM actually failed a safety study in 2002, after it was found to cause "heart muscle fibrosis and adrenal overgrowth" in rats. But then, as I say, what is true for rats is not necessarily true for humans—so just keep your fingers crossed while eating your sandwiches!

So now you know there's a lot of weird stuff being added to food, and now you're going to check the ingredient labels more carefully. At least for the next week. But what you can't do much about and what you can't check very easily is what's not mentioned on the ingredient labels. And that's exactly what the next chapter is about.

Chapter 2

Don't Forget to Check What's *Not* in the Ingredients

That much under-appreciated work of philosophical fiction, *Alice in Wonderland,* is full of jokes about nobody and nothingness, the point being that nothing is a slippery concept. Or rather, that *nothing* is a slippery concept.

"Take some more tea," the March Hare said to Alice, very earnestly.

"I've had nothing yet," Alice replied in an offended tone, "so I can't take more."

"You mean you can't take LESS," said the Hatter: "it's very easy to take MORE than nothing."

Indeed, when it comes to consuming packaged foods, it's very easy to take too much of what, according to the ingredients label, isn't there. Too much carrageenan (which, in the EU, is identified as E407), or modified starch (E1422) or gelatin or.... Here is why.

Suppose you pop into the supermarket to grab a bite for lunch and are tempted by something not particularly healthy looking for dessert. You'd check the ingredients, of course, and take a look at the detailed dietary information provided on the label. Perhaps it all looks perfectly reasonable—with the possible exception of one new thing: "functional flour."

Now, you couldn't get much more harmless than flour. It must be one of the oldest processed foods around, made by grinding golden wheat between large grey millstones. Well, maybe. But that was long ago, and today things have moved on!

Nowadays, functional flour is rather different from the flour of old, and it's very high-tech. Get this: the market for functional flours is projected to exceed $800 billion by 2019. This is serious money! *Something* is going on—and yet consumers are not being told very much about it.

In fact (and this is straight from the horse's mouth of Markets-and-Markets, a market research firm that provides data to many of the world's biggest companies and brands), the functional flours market is propelled by and intertwined with the rise in consumption of processed and packaged food products.

Take one company that specializes in making the flour, Ingredion. Here is what that company's website has to say about their star product, Novation®:

> Our Ingredion NOVATION® product line helps you create satisfying, wholesome foods *with clean ingredients labels*... [emphasis added]

That's right, the key thing about functional flour is to remove off-putting terms from the ingredients lists. It's kind of the latest move in the endless three-way chess game between consumers and public health authorities and huge food businesses. Don't imagine you're immune because you buy organic or opt only for wholesome, natural foods, because Ingredion (or a similar company) has likely gotten there before you.

> Today, the NOVATION® family of functional native starches includes waxy maize, tapioca, rice and potato bases, along with organic varieties and the PRIMA line for added freeze/thaw and cold storage stability. The result: You now have the option to make a "natural," "organic" or "wholesome" claim without compromising end-product quality or sacrificing in-process performance.

All of which goes to show that there's a lot going on below the surface in food these days. But it doesn't show why it really matters. However, if you suffer from allergies or asthma, or if you are averse to contracting cancer or suffering liver failure later—or if you just want your body to regulate itself (including, of course, its own weight) those hidden ingredients certainly might matter. After all, manufacturers aren't stupid, or even if they are, market forces soon correct them, and the ingredients being hidden are precisely the ones consumers are worried about: the ones that have been publicly linked to weight gain, to cancer, to liver failure, and so on.

Recall my Three Principles of food:

1. *Detail matters.*

2. *Everything connects.*

3. *Don't mess with the crystal vase.*

Functional flour is part of an alternative ideology that says detail doesn't matter, nothing connects, and the vase can be glued together again. And sure enough, many of the hidden ingredients are things that in the European Union used to appear as "E numbers" on labels—until the media frightened everyone by highlighting links to cancer and so on. Two "undesirable" E numbers, for instance, that embarrassingly were found in products containing flour were carrageenan (E407), a thickening agent derived from seaweed, and modified starch (E1422). Another ingredient manufacturers are shy about publicizing is gelatin, which is not dangerous as far as I know, but being made from pork or beef, it is a big no-no for many Muslims, Jews, and vegetarians. And then there's benzoyl peroxide, which is sold very openly under its actual name—but in drugstores, where it's offered as a powerful drying agent for skin prone to spots. What's it doing in flour? Well, it sucks the color out of everything it touches, meaning those substances go whiter. And that's why it turns up doing similarly useless things in whey and milk, and in many cheeses including homely-sounding favorites like Gorgonzola, Parmesan, and Swiss Emmental. The science magic of modern food links these great cheeses to chemicals that come with health warnings when sold as external ointments.

Or take another stealth ingredient waiting to subvert your body: bromate. It comes in several "flavors," as it were, such as calcium, potassium, and sodium. Actually, bromates are not totally unnatural; they form in lakes and reservoir water when sunlight causes the element bromine to react with ozone in the atmosphere. That said, bromate in drinking water is undesirable because it is a suspected human carcinogen; other effects include kidney failure. In 2014, the discovery of tiny amounts of bromate in Coca-Cola's Dasani bottled water forced an embarrassing recall of half a million bottles of the newly launched product in the UK.

Yet, at the same time as Coke's water was being poured down the drain, bromates were being used in baked goods to produce stronger dough and cause higher rising. A survey by the Environmental Working Group in 2016 found them present in a long list of everyday supermarket products from pizzas to hot cross buns (a bread roll sweetened with vine fruit and spices traditionally served in England around Good Friday and Easter). Just fancy that!

Even odder is that bromates are supposed to be banned as "flour improvers" in the United Kingdom, Canada, Sri Lanka, China, Nigeria, Brazil, and Peru. In the U.S., the FDA has only *urged* bakers to voluntarily stop using it. It seems that modern flours are so complex that regulators can't keep up. The moral is, if you want to cook with a traditional, whole-meal flour, with no pesticides, no additives, *no tricks*—you may just have to grow and grind the wheat yourself!

Why We're Eating Azodicarbonamide

When a truck carrying azodicarbonamide overturned on a Chicago highway in 2001, it prompted city officials to issue the highest hazardous materials alert and evacuate people within a half-mile radius. People on the scene complained of burning eyes and skin irritation.

Yet, despite being so scary and even banned in some contexts, the imposing sounding chemical is another ubiquitous food additive. It is used in the baking industry to bleach flour, as a dough conditioner, and as an aging ingredient. It turns up in products served by chains like Starbucks (in their croissants) and fast-food restaurants in the form of hamburger and hot dog buns.

Regulators accept that azodicarbonamide can be a "respiratory sensitizer" that can trigger an allergic reaction. When azodicarbonamide breaks down, it can form semicarbazide (SEM), which is considered to be a weak carcinogen and thus is banned in the European Union, Australia, New Zealand, and Singapore. In the United States, though, the ever-cautious (about banning things) Food and Drug Administration counts the additive as safe in small amounts.

Chapter 3

Eat Like a Horse

Horses know there's a lot more to grass than just grass.

You can learn a lot from animals because, even if pets can be fussy eaters, by and large animals don't have complicated tastes. In fact, the Scottish philosopher David Hume described humans as being just like animals only with the additional facility of a sophisticated language. Compare a plump little pony grazing in a paddock with a glistening, sinewy racehorse. What do you think the dietary difference is between the two animals?

The answer is not in the diet. Both animals eat grass, oats, and carrots. Racehorses do not eat lots of chicken and tuna washed down with protein shakes, nor do they spend the week before the race on half rations trying to get "ripped." After all, they're herbivores.

And yet, according to horse specialist Karen Briggs, for years, the racing community labored under the misconception that more protein in a racehorse's diet equaled more energy. Fortunately, she says, owners now know that isn't the case. I say "fortunately" because not only is protein a poor energy source, but too much of it can actually be harmful, leading to respiratory and heart rates that go too high during exercise, and also to excessive sweating. You won't have heard that about the protein shakes that you're encouraged to drink before going to the gym. *Remember, don't mess with crystal vases*—they're harder to put back together than they are to break.

Horse trainers, unlike many "personal trainers" of humans, seem to understand these days that the thing that really matters is to make sure their clients—in this case, the racing thoroughbreds—get the right balance of amino acids. And that requires very different strategies from those based on the supposition that (almost magically) "protein builds muscle."

In fact, all those animals that seem to get by on grass—cows, rabbits, deer, even kangaroos!—are actually getting a more balanced diet than we might imagine. Because, along with their...*ahem*... common or garden grass, the hay that they're tucking into contains a good proportion of legumes—such as alfalfa or clover. Good-quality hay generally contains between 14 and 25 percent crude protein! Even rabbits nibbling your weed-free lawn get a diet that includes about 6 to 14 percent protein. Of course, such parallels can't be taken too far. One of the main differences, of course, is that horses and other herbivores can break down and absorb nutrients, including protein, from plant cellulose, whereas humans can't.

And yet racehorses still offer a good parallel to the over-enthusiastic dieter. In unenlightened stables, instead of roaming in lush pasture, the horses are confined to a stall for twenty or more hours a day. Instead of eating delicious, fresh, sweet grass they are forced to eat dry hay and copious (a little is good) amounts of grain—the "protein." Like gym-rats fitting in fitness sessions before or after a day in the office, these horses spend their days in barns with poor ventilation and little chance for natural exercise, only a programmed workout. The consequence is that they become stressed, lose muscle, and even develop health problems like ulcers.

Diet Tips: Straight from the Horse's Mouth

- Eat fresh vegetables and salads.
- Graze—have lots of small meals.
- Make sure you get plenty of fresh air and sunlight.

Horses also provide another diet parallel for humans: like us and all other animals, they need certain minerals and vitamins. But again, for horses and other herbivores, most of these needs are met naturally through fresh hay or grass and sunshine. Old hay, like old prepackaged salad or other vegetables, loses most of its goodness and vitamins. And there's one more shared truth: nutrients are most effective when taken in many small meals throughout the day—grazing—rather than in a few large ones.

What is the most horsey food we humans eat? Is it lettuce? Carrots? (I had a friend who lived mainly off carrots—shredded, sliced, boiled, in soup.... She overdosed on carotene and her skin went yellow—not a healthy diet at all. *Don't mess with the crystal vase.*) No, the correct horsey meal for humans is good old muesli: the almost tasty source of natural oats. And it can be made fully tasty if you top it with large amounts of nuts, dried

Raw Food

The art of "cooking" with uncooked raw ingredients is necessarily a subtle one. In cooking, after all, the heat allows the chemicals in the foods to circulate and blend with each other. Too often, raw food tastes plain and watery. In a way, that's not surprising, as the kinds of food we eat raw tend to have a high water content.

However, done right, raw dishes can be both tasty and attractive, even if, done wrong (as alas is normally the case), those same foods taste bland and boring. Salad dressing was invented not so much to make salads tasty as to disguise the failure to make a decent salad in the first place. Uncooked dishes like a mix of tomato, arugula, thinly sliced parmesan or cubes of feta cheese, and black olives with a dressing of extra virgin olive oil plus a dash of honey and mint are examples of easy ways to combine various raw ingredients and extra flavors to good effect.

and fresh fruit, and whole milk. But beware the many varieties that have sneaked in extra sugars. *Detail matters.*

There's a revealing story about what happens if you follow the horsey approach, and it concerns perhaps America's greatest philosopher, Henry David Thoreau. He is famous for having spent two years living in a small cabin by a pond and living off not so much the fruits of the woods but his own field. Naturally, Thoreau was a vegetarian. He remarks how one farmer said to him: "You cannot live on vegetable food solely, for it furnishes nothing to make the bones with," even as the farmer "religiously devoted a part of his day to supplying himself with the raw material of bones, walking all the while behind his oxen, which, with vegetable-made bones, jerk him and his lumbering plow along in spite of every obstacle."

That's irrational because the mighty ox shows how a vegetarian diet can work, at least for animals accustomed to it. Mind you, many of the philosophers whom we rely on to provide little oases of good sense and rationality in a disorganized world disappointingly also turn out, on closer inspection, to be not only rather eccentric, but downright irrational. Thoreau, an anarchist who eked out a living by making pencils while living in a shed by a pond, appears at first glance to be completely weird. Yet, despite being short, shabby, wild-haired, and generally rather unprepossessing, he nonetheless seems to have anticipated much of the ecological renaissance that today's philosophers (and diet gurus) have only just begun to talk about. Oh, and yes, he was always rather thin.

In his journal entry for January 7, 1857, Thoreau says of himself:

> In the streets and in society I am almost invariably
> cheap and dissipated, my life is unspeakably
> mean. No amount of gold or respectability would
> in the least redeem it—dining with the Governor
> or a member of Congress! But alone in the distant

woods or fields, in unpretending sprout-lands or
pastures tracked by rabbits, even in a bleak and,
to most, cheerless day, like this, when a villager
would be thinking of his inn, I come to myself, I
once more feel myself grandly related, and that
cold and solitude are friends of mine.

I suppose that this value, in my case, is equivalent
to what others get by churchgoing and prayer.
I come home to my solitary woodland walk as
the homesick go home. I thus dispose of the
superfluous and see things as they are, grand and
beautiful… I wish to… be sane a part of every day.

Thoreau cultivated a small bean farm of two and a half acres,
which provided the bulk of the food he ate—peas, corn, turnips,
potatoes, and above all green beans, the last of which crop he
sold for extra cash. During the second year, he reduced the
range of his crops, if anything, writing:

… that if one would live simply and eat only the
crop which he raised, and raise no more than
he ate, and not exchange it for an insufficient
quantity of more luxurious and expensive things,
he would need to cultivate only a few rods of
ground, and that it would be cheaper to spade
up that than to use oxen to plow it, and to select
a fresh spot from time to time than to manure
the old, and he could do all his necessary farm
work as it were with his left hand at odd hours in
the summer.

He drank mainly water, echoing his ancient predecessor,
Diogenes, by writing that it was "the only drink for a wise man;
wine is not so noble a liquor." He worried about the temptations
of a cup of warm coffee or a dish of tea!

Thoreau's diet tips, gained from his life in the woods, included, among other things, that it "cost incredibly little trouble to obtain one's necessary food" and that "a man may use as simple a diet as the animals, and yet retain health and strength." These insights are from his most famous book, *Walden* (1854). He continues to make his case for simple foods by arguing:

> I have made a satisfactory dinner, satisfactory on several accounts, simply off a dish of purslane (*Portulaca oleracea*) which I gathered in my cornfield, boiled and salted. I give the Latin on account of the savoriness of the trivial name. And pray what more can a reasonable man desire, in peaceful times, in ordinary noons, than a sufficient number of ears of green sweet corn boiled, with the addition of salt? Even the little variety which I used was a yielding to the demands of appetite, and not of health. Yet men have come to such a pass that they frequently starve, not for want of necessaries, but for want of luxuries; and I know a good woman who thinks that her son lost his life because he took to drinking water only.

Purslane, by the way, is one of those almost completely forgotten natural wild foods that we have all around us without noticing. It grows unappreciated in shady corners of your garden, or more likely on patches of rough ground, as it prefers a poor soil. As Karen Stephenson, curator of the wonderfully alternative website ediblewildfood.com has noted purslane can be eaten as a cooked vegetable and used in salads, soups, stews, or indeed almost any dish that you wish to sprinkle it over. Plus, it is antibacterial, antiscorbutic, depurative, diuretic, and febrifuge, and the leaves contain more omega-3 fatty acids (which prevent heart attacks and strengthen the immune system) than any other plant, indeed more than some fish oils.

All the parts of the plant are edible too, the thick green leaves, the yellow flowers, and black seeds.

Alas, these days, as Google will reveal, people don't eat much purslane. Instead they ask the search engine things like: "Can you eat the weed purslane?" and "Can dogs eat purslane?" and even "How do you get rid of purslane?" I've not even had it myself, to be honest, although I like the idea.

But back to the cabin in the woods of Walden, where, following in the footsteps of the great John Locke, or perhaps just thinking of something to accompany his weedy soup, Thoreau describes the unique pleasure of homemade bread rolls:

> Bread, I at first made of pure Indian meal and salt, genuine hoe-cakes, which I baked before my fire out of doors on a shingle or the end of a stick of timber sawed off in building my house; but it was wont to get smoked and to have a piney flavor, I tried flour also; but have at last found a mixture of rye and Indian meal most convenient and agreeable. In cold weather it was no little amusement to bake several small loaves of this in succession, tending and turning them as carefully *as an Egyptian his hatching eggs.*

But in a chapter of *Walden* titled simply "The Bean Field," Thoreau records how, above all:

> I came to love my rows, my beans.... They attached me to the earth, and so I got strength like Antæus. But why should I raise them? Only Heaven knows. This was my curious labor all summer—to make this portion of the earth's surface, which had yielded only cinquefoil, blackberries, johnswort, and the like, before, sweet wild fruits and pleasant flowers, produce instead this pulse. What shall I learn of beans or beans of me? I cherish them, I hoe them, early

and late I have an eye to them; and this is my
day's work.

For Thoreau, buying beans, or allowing others to grow them
for him, would have disconnected him from the land, from
direct contact with nature, the source of both his bodily and
spiritual nourishment. It was not enough to just have something
to eat; he also wanted the experience of growing it. *That's* the
real difference between horses and humans.

Diet Tips: From Thoreau

Food that you've grown has a special quality.

You don't need to eat a huge range of things to be healthy.

Chapter 4

The Caveman Diet

One of the most popular diet regimens today is something called the Paleo diet, or sometimes rather less flatteringly the Caveman diet. Talk about "back to nature"! The whole approach is built upon the assumption that what is natural is what is best. It's such a common assumption that philosophers even give it a name: the "appeal to nature"—but they count it as a fallacy, an example of flawed reasoning. After all, it's not natural to cook food, but that doesn't prove it is a bad idea. That said, many of the great philosophers, from Plato to Friedrich Nietzsche, can't resist appealing to something very similar in their writings on food, and I've already alluded to it several times with my talk of the "unnaturalness" of food additives and keeping horses cooped up in barns. So it's an approach that can't be disregarded, but has to be treated with caution, particularly as ideas about what is actually "natural" are amongst the most debatable there are.

The most prominent of many experts today supporting the Paleo approach is Loren Cordain, an academic at Colorado State University whose website uncompromisingly describes him as "the world's leading expert on the evolutionary basis of diet and disease." Since his PhD is in Exercise Physiology, his expertise seems to have extended well beyond his formal background, but philosophers can hardly complain about that!

In any case, behind him is one Dr. Walter Voegtlin, who wrote a book called *The Stone Age Diet*, published in 1975 and generally forgotten. The book was part of the "fat is bad" debate that had raged in the U.S. for some twenty years, and Dr. Voegtlin was pitching firmly *for* fat and *against* the then-prevailing dietary advice by arguing that the Stone Age diet would have been a mix of fats and protein, with only small amounts of carbohydrates. (Carbohydrates, proteins, and fats are the three *macronutrients* that provide energy—in the form of calories—from food. See "Know Your Three Energy Sources," in chapter 5, for more about them.)

Walter Voegtlin contends that countless eons of evolutionary adaptation have left the digestive systems of *Homo sapiens* quite different from herbivorous animals and thus unable to successfully adapt to a diet based on plant foods. Our teeth, our stomachs, our gall bladders all point, he says, to eating meat. And so, in his ultra-thorough cupboard clear-out, into the garbage can go not just processed white flour but all of our modern-day mainstay cultivated grains, because they're stuffed with carbohydrates. While you're at it, throw out all milk products, packed as they are with lactose (a type of sugar found in dairy products), and, of course, anything sugary.

Voegtlin says that, with the exception of vitamins C and K, all essential nutrients can be derived from animal foods, and argues that an essentially carnivorous "caveman" diet is actually richer in vitamins and minerals than modern omnivorous diets, let alone herbivorous ones.

The idea behind both Dr. Voegtlin's diet and all its Paleo successors (the word *Paleo* is short for *Paleolithic*, which means "Stone Age") is that some of the mainstays of modern diet, such as grains and milk products, are unnatural, and that the human body is ill-suited to digest them. Hence the resulting health problems affecting many millions of people. Instead of eating sandwiches, pizzas, and muesli, people should eat more vegetables, fruits, nuts (yes, yes yes!)—and lots and lots of lean meat. Many of the ancient philosophers held a special veneration for "wild foods," particularly plant ones, but also eggs and milk, seen as the "fruits of nature" there to be gathered and peacefully enjoyed. Fish, too, can be "gathered."

But not meat. This seems invariably to disturb the serenity of an imagined Arcadian idyll.

However, websites supporting the Paleo approach recommend recipes like Slow-Cooked Paleo Pork Ribs and Roots or Red Meat and Sage-Infused Mushroom Paleo Burgers. Even snacks are meaty: left-over chicken with mayo, canned tuna, or the American treat known as beef jerky.

Some Paleo enthusiasts have tried to leaven the mix with nibbles like pork rinds and hard-boiled eggs, but basically the Paleo snack is not going to be something your office colleagues are going to ask you to share.

Dr. Cordain's 2002 book, *The Paleo Diet*, suggests that over half of your daily calorie requirement is supposed to be supplied from lean meat and fish, with merely one-sixth coming from fruits, vegetables, and nuts. Cordain's cavemen are very modern in that they avoid salt and sugar almost entirely. Inasmuch as the diet emphasizes the benefits of fresh fruits and vegetables, and frowns on processed food, it is harmless advice. But other aspects of the diet are controversial. The British Dietetic Association warns, for example, that many versions of the diet exclude key food groups, "raising the potential for nutritional deficiencies at least unless careful substitutions are made."

That's the nutritional critique, but biologist and author Marlene Zuk criticizes the Paleo diet and similar regimens on broader methodological grounds: for trying to create rules about what people *should* do from assertions about what people used to do, and from what is supposed to be in some sense "natural." Zuk, like Loren Cordain, is an academic, but she is an actual specialist in the area of evolutionary biology. In email exchanges with me about the science of diet, she told me that she was surprised at how much attention her rebuttals of the Paleo approach have attracted. She instead saw her critique as only a small part of a wider debate about human adaptation. Yet, maybe she should not have been *too* surprised, as arguments about what to eat are far more attention-grabbing than those about historical events.

As the conclusion to her book *Paleofantasy*, Zuk writes, "'Paleofantasies' call to mind a time when everything about us—body, mind, and behavior—was in sync with the environment… but no such time existed." She adds, "We and every other living thing have always lurched along in evolutionary time, with the inevitable trade-offs that are a hallmark of life."

Zuk argues, for example, that Paleo diets tend to deprive people of many sources of calcium, which could lead to health problems affecting the skeleton and teeth. And while it is true that milk and milk products (cheese, cream, yogurt) are a relatively recent human innovation—in terms of evolutionary timescales—it is not true that the human body is slow to adapt.

Today, the digestive systems of many people, particularly those of European descent, have adapted to eating dairy by

How rational are our food choices?
How rational is the Paleo diet?

Well, not very. But then human beings are a lot less rational than we are often led to believe—especially by philosophers. In a classic work that looks at the real drivers of human behavior, *Animal Spirits: How Human Psychology Drives the Economy, and Why It Matters for Global Capitalism* (Princeton University Press, 2009), George Akerlof and Robert Shiller examine some of the implications of research in behavioral economics for economic booms, crises, and busts. In a splendid demonstration of dedication to exploring consumer choices, Professor Shiller once even ate several varieties of cat food on TV, explaining that this was the only way to definitively disprove the grand claims made for one brand over another!

> ### How rational are our food choices? How rational is the Paleo diet? (cont.)
>
> Now, cat food certainly raises cat spirits, but the phrase *animal spirits* is actually a term used by the great economist John Maynard Keynes to describe the gloom and despondence that led to the Great Depression and later to the "exuberance" that accompanied recovery. The financial crash of 2008 that started with a mass rush to buy overpriced houses in America is a textbook example of "animal spirits" being allowed to drive decision-making—but so too is the everyday trip to the supermarket. When we buy food, we are heavily influenced by what's on the label—the claims that what we are getting is wholesome, luxury quality, and so on.
>
> Big Ag, grocery chains, even celebrity chefs on TV all appeal to our *irrational* side—alternately promising to boost our self-esteem and sense of well-being or undermining our confidence and playing on our fears. Professors Akerlof and Shiller argue, as Keynes did decades before, that managing the animal spirits requires the steady hand of government. They also warn that relying on consumers to be more rational, let alone on market forces to produce optimal outcomes, simply won't *cut the mustard!*

developing lactose tolerance via a gene that encodes instructions for making the enzyme lactase, which breaks down lactose. In humans who are lactose tolerant, the gene doesn't shut down after infancy but instead keeps manufacture of the enzyme turned on and available throughout adult life.

Zuk also warns that in targeting natural grains, Paleo diets do away with good sources of natural fiber and of minerals and vitamins. (Refer back to my Principle 2: *Everything Connects*.)

The central claim made by Paleo adherents that our bodies are ill-suited to digest such foods belies the fact that our stomachs rely on a vast collection of bacteria which are far from fixed but rather vary all the time. No one really knows which bacterial species thrived in Paleolithic intestines, but we can be pretty sure that whatever they were, today's microbial communities are very different.

So it seems that what's good (or bad) for a caveman is by no means what is right or wrong for you. And when vocal supporters of the Paleo diet, such as Mark Sisson, a fitness trainer in Malibu, California, proclaim on their websites that "while the world has changed in innumerable ways in the last 10,000 years (for better and worse), the human genome has changed very little and thus only thrives under similar conditions," they ignore the detail and appeal to popular myths rather than scientific facts.

Another rather large hole in the theory undergirding the Paleo diet is that the phrase "Stone Age man" is a misleading terminological shortcut. Groups of ancient peoples actually ate very differently from one another, depending on the food resources of the region they lived in. In some parts of the world, yes, lean meat was a major source of nutrients—but in others it would have been fish, and in still others an almost vegetarian diet of fruits and nuts.

And although archaeological discoveries of mammoth or bear skulls make for better headlines, the remains of plant foods—seeds, berries, roots, leaves, and bulbs—have also, in fact, been found at many Paleolithic sites. At digs in the Rocky Mountains, for example, sunflower seeds, prickly pear seeds, amaranth seeds, and limber pine seeds have been discovered.

Of course, we don't tend to eat our veggies like that now, which underlines the other important point about the idea that our stomachs are fixed in an evolutionary framework created millions of years ago. Humans are not determined within one rigid blueprint; we can and do adapt to circumstances—and so do plant species. The plant foods people have eaten over the last ten thousand or so years are very different from those available to Stone Age people.

Christina Warinner, professor of Microbiome Sciences in the Department of Archaeogenetics at the Max Planck Institute for the Science of Human History, in Germany, has researched in detail just about every single species commonly consumed by humans today—whether a fruit, vegetable, or animal—to see if it is different from its Paleolithic predecessor. She has traced out how we have bred cows, goats, and chickens to provide as much meat, milk, and eggs as possible, and how we have selected natural mutations from plants or cross-fertilized them to produce species with the traits we desire: the sweetest fruits, the largest grains. Corn, for example, was originally a straggly natural grass known as *teosinte*, while tomatoes, so important for many Mediterranean dishes (even pizza) were originally rather small berries! Over thousands of years, single species have been adapted by humans to produce a whole range of foods—to the extent that we forget they were ever not natural. Cabbage, broccoli, cauliflower, Brussels sprouts, and kale are all different human creations drawn from a single species, *Brassica oleracea*. Considered in this light, the veggies that Paleo dieters adorn their factory-farmed meat with start to look pretty unnatural too.

The popularity of Paleo-style diets belies expert opinion and specialist warnings against such shortcuts. In an article in 2013, the *Scientific American* was moved to recall the stern warning of anthropologist William Leonard, who wrote in the same magazine a decade earlier, "Too often modern health problems are portrayed as the result of eating 'bad' foods that are departures from the natural human diet.... This is a fundamentally flawed approach to assessing human nutritional needs."

Chapter 5

The Energy Balance

The central idea in ancient advice about health is the importance of balance, and the central myth of dieting is that how much you eat and how much you exercise have gotten out of kilter. Taoism, and Eastern philosophy in general, is all about the notion of maintaining equilibrium and finding harmony—with the concepts directly applied to eating. Physical exercise too was approached with this in mind. Over in the West, the original Olympic ideal was rooted in the idea of the all-around athlete, which is why, during the Olympics, there are still otherwise rather strange combinations of activities such as the pentathlon. This is the sport of which Aristotle wrote:

> Beauty varies with each age. In a young man, it consists in possessing a body capable of enduring all efforts, either of the racecourse or of bodily strength, while he himself is pleasant to look upon and a sheer delight. This is why the athletes in the pentathlon are most beautiful, because they are naturally adapted for bodily exertion and for swiftness of foot.

Today, however, medal winners come in a range of bodies, most of which are anything but "balanced" and may indeed be deformed in the pursuit of short-term goals.

That the virtues of balance have been espoused by doctors for thousands of years is revealed by ancient texts such as the one describing the time that the Yellow Emperor, of ancient China, asked his chief minister, Qi Bo, why it was that "people nowadays" did not live as long. His wise counselor replied that it was because in the past people practiced the Tao and appreciated the flow of *yin* and *yang* and the principle of balance in all things. But "these days," Qi Bo warned,

> People have changed their way of life. They drink wine as though it were water, indulge in destructive activities, drain their *jing* and deplete their *qi**... Seeking emotional excitement and monetary pleasures, people disregard the natural rhythm and order of the universe. They fail to regulate their lifestyle and diet, and sleep improperly.[1]

This is wise advice. However, today there's also a misleading sense in which we suspect any health problem as having been caused by an excess or a deficiency of something. "Too little magnesium causes Alzheimer's." "Too little iron causes anemia." And the problem of excess weight, a problem that is so multifaceted and so complex, is often reduced to the following advice: reduce the amount of food you eat each day by 500 calories and you will lose a pound of fat a week.

That's paraphrasing livestrong.com, to take just one popular website example. The site even offers tidy ways to "save" the calories each day, like cutting out one tablespoon of mayonnaise in your sandwich (like dieters do that?) or one ounce of cheese.

Obviously, if this were true, we could all be thin! Just make this small effort, and over a year you would lose 52 pounds. In metric figures, you would lose a tad under half a kilo a week or nearly 24 kilos a year. Dieting just got really easy!

How unfortunate then, that actual trials have convincingly shown that calorie intake fails to predict weight, and vice versa. It just isn't that simple. Take some of the statistics gathered by a large American research initiative called the Healthy Eating

---

1   In traditional Chinese medicine, *jing* is the body's essence and *qi* is the life energy.

Index. Their research shows that adults with a body mass index of 20 or less and those with a BMI of more than 30 (which is the line for being clinically obese) have similar caloric intakes.

You can't believe it? Then consider the evidence available from looking at particular groups. In men who, according to the energy-balance model, regularly undereat, it turns out that yes, 3 percent of them have a thin to rather anorexic BMI of 15 to 20. But far more, 17 percent, are managing to stay officially obese on the same—apparently inadequate—energy inputs. So those plump friends who insist that they eat sensibly quite possibly *are*.

The statistic I started with, that one pound of body weight lost or gained corresponds to 3,500 calories eaten or not eaten, was originally conjured up in 1958 by a New York doctor named Max Wishnofsky. Decades later, his result has been cited thousands of times in the media and scientific literature despite being little more than an opinion based on implausible assumptions.

For example, behind every dieter's optimistic belief that cutting out the cheese or the mayo will make you thin lies the big assumption that at present they are eating exactly what they need—i.e., that their body is in perfect energy balance. Otherwise the reduction would not result in weight loss, but merely in slower weight gain.

Of course, this leads to the evergreen idea of a calorie-controlled diet designed to deliver just the correct daily input of energy and not a calorie more.

As to what that amount is, websites are quite happy to tell you that men need about 2000 to 3000 calories a day and women need 1600 to 2400. That's actually a pretty big range and is supposed to cover people of different sizes, of different ages, with different mixes of fat and muscle, and engaging in different amounts of physical activity. The figures do not reflect the fact that they were calculated in the era before widespread use of cars and when jobs were much more physically demanding.

The figures also do not reflect the degree to which the amount you eat is converted by the body into energy—which is by no means fixed. Some people may convert food at a high efficiency, others at a low efficiency. Put another way, if you are cutting 500 calories from your daily diet, you may be chronically undereating or still overeating. Chronically undereat and your body suffers permanent damage. Overeat and ... well, the evidence is in front of you.

Diets that focus on reducing carbohydrate intake decrease the amount of glycogen stored in the liver and in muscles, which in turn decreases the retention of water. This, of course, causes a rapid drop in weight—but it may have little to do with burning fat. A big complication in the energy equation is that body fat is not just fat, but a mix of things, including water and protein. Water is a huge issue in weight measurement: many apparent reductions in weight (particularly speedy ones) are actually temporary dehydration of the body.

Know Your Three Energy Sources

The body has three energy sources: carbohydrates (stored as glycogen in the muscles and liver), protein, and fats. It burns them preferentially in that order because of the energy requirements (based on thermodynamics) to both store and break them down. Glycogen is depleted rapidly, and once the body has run short of this energy source, it switches to utilizing protein, the next most efficient energy source. Fat, despite being the most energy dense of the three sources, is harder for the body to convert into energy.

The second part of the energy equation (*calories in* minus *calories expended* equals *fat gained*) is that bit about exercise. It's mind-boggling to discover that 90 percent of the ten thousand weight-conscious members of the U.S. National Weight Control

Registry were exercising for an average of one hour every day in their bid to burn off extra calories.

Nonetheless, it's tempting to think that, as long as caloric input has been capped at the right level through dieting, every extra calorie burned in physical activity will eventually result in less excess weight. But there are problems even with this calculation. First of all, it has been estimated that the normal, lean adult human body contains 130,000 calories of stored energy made up of about 38 percent muscle, 20 percent fat, and everything else as the balance. An obese adult often has twice as much energy stored: around a quarter of a million calories, and anyone who is ten stone (64 kilograms) overweight is looking at a stock of half a million. It'll take some time on the treadmill to burn any noticeable proportion of that off!

When we talk about eating too much and "getting fat," we are really talking about cause and effect—or in the slightly grander language of the philosophers, "causation." And that brings us to another of philosophy's greatest thinkers, David Hume, whose radical debunking of not only everyday notions but the fundamental science of cause and effect upturned the whole philosophical world. Hume has the reputation of being philosophy's freest, most iconoclastic thinker, so much so that the great Immanuel Kant credited him with awakening Kant from his "dogmatic slumbers." Hume acquired his reputation for thinking the unthinkable by claiming that certain truths we all take for granted—like the idea that the past will resemble the future, that there really are scientific laws, that there is some important difference between right and wrong—are all merely hand-me-down assertions based on emotion rather than logic. Think of debates over food and health—how often does someone trot out a tidy "if you do this, then that will happen" argument? If you eat nitrogen (in the form of protein), you will grow big and strong. If you walk briskly, you will get thin. And yet life is more complicated than that, and most of these prescriptions are false promises. Hume is forever important for highlighting that issue in general.

In the kitchen, though, Hume's thinking ran along very traditional lines. In a letter to a friend in 1769, he jokes of his "great talent for cookery, the science to which I intend to addict* the remaining year of my life." But judging from his famous girth, he had left this interest in cooking science rather late. "Ye ken I'm no epicure, only a glutton," he once admitted.

Indeed, if he was otherwise a very canny philosopher, Hume seems not to have known what was good for him, since his forays into the kitchen produced mainly beef and cabbage, and "sheep's-head broth." If food really does "maketh man," surely no one would knowingly choose to become either beef and cabbage stew, or sheep's-head broth. Actually, on the face of it, these are both very slim-making dishes and yet, in later years, Hume steadily ballooned to the extent that he became something of a figure of fun, unkindly depicted in numerous cartoons. This in itself illustrates another very good scientific point: calories, which are essentially a measure of energy, do not seem to come in different flavors. A calorie is just the energy needed to raise the temperature of one gram of water by one degree. This kind of scientific regularity, heat the water by x and it goes up by y, flies directly against Hume's theory—but then as he willingly admitted, he aimed to produce ingenious arguments, not practical life strategies. And actually, how water behaves depends on many subtle things, like its exact chemical components (i.e., what's present in the sample of water besides its pure chemical components, H_2O), air pressure, whether you're looking at it.... (That last factor is a bit controversial, I admit.)

Indeed, theories and strategies do seem to operate in different realms. When a team of researchers at Harvard University in 2009 specifically looked at the effects of different kinds of calories and weight loss, they found a complete mismatch. The researchers assigned some 811 overweight adults to one of four diets, each composed of different proportions of fat, protein, and carbs (low-protein; high-protein/low-fat; high-fat/low-carb; or high-carb). After 6 months of dieting, all the participants lost an average of 13 pounds (6 kg). They began to regain weight after 12 months, and by 2 years, total weight loss averaged out to 9 pounds (4 kg), with no meaningful differences found between the different groups.

Similarly, another study by researchers at Arizona State University found that an eight-week high-carbohydrate, low-fat, low-protein diet was equally effective (or, if you like, ineffective) in terms of weight loss as a low-carbohydrate, low-fat, high-protein diet of the kind that many people are optimistically following.

There really don't seem to be simple rules. Consider another unfortunate strategy that many would-be weight-watchers fall for, which is to look at their personal energy calculation in terms of meals rather than longer periods like days or weeks. We tend to eat erratically, and if we skip one or two meals, over the whole day we almost invariably eat a bit extra at some point to "catch up." Similarly, if we do a strenuous activity one day, we tend to rest the next day or two, while still "rewarding" ourselves with extra food. In fact, when energy inputs and outputs are averaged over longer periods (weeks), we tend to find that a balance is struck between intake and expenditure—and it is hard to shift that balance by much. It's really only possible to change the body's "feed me" signals little by little—if that!

Even when diets are linked to supervised exercise sessions— and the lurking suspicion that anyone who's still not getting thin has maybe not been doing their exercise is eliminated—it turns out that there is still a tremendous variation in response. Food Rule 1: *Detail matters.* Maybe people have different stomach bacteria, different sleep patterns—different levels of stress! Anyway, the research is unambiguous and to this extent follows Hume's warnings about cause and effect being less than reliably linked. Put on the same diet regimens, some individuals will lose significant amounts of weight and some will actually gain weight. The only thing that seems clear is that the impact of exercise alone on the energy equation is...negligible.

All of which goes to emphasize that health really is a holistic issue. In terms of the supposed need for "energy balance," the second of my food principles, *Everything connects*, means that all the components that make up said energy balance interact with one another. To take a simple example, if you want to lose weight, increasing your amount of exercise activity won't work if the amount you eat and drink increases at the same time. Nor will increased exercise alone work if your body changes the way it burns energy due to passive compensatory changes in energy expenditure. You can't stop *that*—it's called getting fit.

Recall Principle 1: *Detail matters*. Other things being equal, your body, being a well-designed machine, will quietly burn fat to power itself. *But not immediately after eating*. The story is a bit complicated, but basically, when you eat carbohydrates (which are contained in almost everything but particularly in sugary and snack foods), the resultant rush of glucose into the blood stream (the process that gives you a very nice feeling of being well-fed and even of having lots of energy) also causes the body to secrete the hormone insulin. This is because excessively high blood glucose levels are toxic to many tissues in the body, and the body needs insulin as a first step in reducing the excess.

Insulin has two main functions:

1. To switch the body from metabolizing fat for energy to metabolizing glucose for energy so that it can burn off the excess glucose more speedily

2. To store glucose away in the muscles and liver as glycogen

The key thing for dieters to know is that when you eat carbohydrates, for a while afterward, fat cells are prevented from releasing their energy stores into the bloodstream. And the effects of a typical carbohydrate-laden meal can last for several hours until the blood glucose level has stabilized back down to normal, with a further time lag for the insulin level to return to normal.

When insulin levels are elevated, the body cannot burn fat for energy, so it must instead get energy from other resources. Its first choice is to use the glycogen stored in the muscle and liver. Depending on how fit you are, and how often you raid those glycogen reserves, they may contain enough to cover the digestion gap. But when they are not, then the body's next choice is to break down muscle and convert the protein they contain into glucose. (When the body is stressed by too strict a diet, too much exercise, or illness, then the destruction of muscle—called "wasting"—is all too obvious.) In other words, if you're trying to burn fat and retain muscle, the worst thing that you can do is to snack on carbohydrates. Doing so means that your insulin levels remain elevated, preventing the fat cells from releasing energy, and forcing the breakdown of muscle instead. This is why athletes guzzle protein. The protein doesn't magically turn into muscle, but it reduces the risk of existing muscle being broken down. And it temporarily fills the tummy nicely too.

Speaking of which brings us to the all-important "I've had plenty, thank you" mechanism.

Knowing when you have eaten enough is (like most things) more complicated than it seems. In fact, it depends on several physiologic and molecular mechanisms. One is a physical signal related to the distension of the gastrointestinal tract that is communicated to the brain. Another is the secretion of gut peptides (small chains of amino acids, which are also the building blocks of proteins) that interact with receptors in the brain. A third mechanism is the hormone ghrelin, which is produced by the stomach. Ghrelin levels are high when we have not eaten for a while, and they drop after meals.

And then there's the hormone leptin, which was first identified in 1994, with the media soon excitedly nicknaming it "the obesity hormone," the "fat hormone"—and even the "starvation hormone"! Certainly, leptin plays a role in how the body regulates appetite. In the early years of the twenty-first century, Sadaf Farooqi, professor of metabolism at Cambridge University, studied patients with severe, early-onset obesity. Her team (trampling David Hume's warnings) delightedly obtained a direct correspondence between leptin and obesity concerning mutations in genes relating to the body's management of the hormone. They even delightedly "cured" one patient previously unable to control their appetite via injections of leptin.

But other researchers stress that leptin is nearly always part of a wider picture—with its failure to function linked to insulin resistance. (This is a condition in which the body's cells respond poorly to insulin, resulting in blood glucose levels that remain high. It is often a precursor to type 2 diabetes.) And the amount of insulin your body produces is linked to how much sugar you consume. *Again, everything connects.*

Chapter 6

The Salt Paradox

To salt or not to salt? For thousands of years sodium chloride has been highly valued and sought after—but now it is shunned as a wicked, body-disrupting additive. We're told to cut down on it—yet the body can't actually work without it. That's paradoxical. As is the fact that the latest research clearly shows that if people reduce how much salt they eat, the body responds by hoarding its supplies more carefully as a way of guarding its quota. That's pretty significant, yet the lesson doesn't seem to have penetrated to the public health authorities yet.

Today, anyone who consumes too much salt faces health warnings as dire as anything directed at the nicotine industry. Salt is said to be linked to high blood pressure, heart attacks, and kidney failure—and it may be bad for bones too. That's the considered opinion of many experts and government health bodies. Lastly, for those merely watching their weight, conventional dietary advice is to avoid salt because it encourages water retention.

The smarter advice may be to eat plenty of salt, in case your body finds worse ways to make up for its salt cravings. Indeed this could be your best defense against junk foods. In his barnstorming book *Salt Sugar Fat: How the Food Giants Hooked Us* (Random House 2013), the American food writer and investigative journalist Michael Moss highlights how the food industry today uses salt as a kind of weapon of mass control—adding it to things that, well, just shouldn't be salty. He writes: "without salt, processed food companies cease to exists." And Moss points out that manufactured salts take on all kinds of forms as a smorgasbord of sodium chemicals are added by manufacturers, not merely to add taste to food but to delay spoilage, bind ingredients, et cetera, et cetera. These "unnatural salts" appear on food labels as monosodium glutamate, sodium nitrite, sodium saccharin, sodium bicarbonate, sodium benzoate, sodium citrate, sodium phosphate...

These are what I think might be called unnatural salts. But there are still natural salts. They often come with valuable extra minerals and, as King Lear's daughter, Cordelia, knew, are really a great gift to the human race. Should we be cutting back on them too? Well, not so fast.

"There is a distinct and growing lack of scientific consensus on making a single sodium consumption recommendation for all Americans," says Sonja L. Connor, a professor of health science and president of the Academy of Nutrition and Dietetics. Professor Connor cites research indicating that the low sodium consumption recommended by the government actually turned out to be associated with "increased mortality for healthy individuals." She's not alone. A report commissioned by the Institute of Medicine in 2010, for example, found that there was no scientific reason for anyone to aim for sodium levels below 2,300 milligrams a day, and a study published in the *Journal of the American Medical Association* in 2011 found that low-salt diets actually *increased* the risk of death from heart attacks and strokes. In May 2015, the Academy of Nutrition and Dietetics, the largest U.S. organization of food and nutrition professionals, issued a statement expressing their concern about the science behind the federal government's salt advice.

Dr. Niels Graudal, a senior consultant at Copenhagen University, in Denmark, summed it all up, saying, "I can't really see, if you look at the total evidence, that there is any reason to believe there is a net benefit of decreasing sodium intake in the general population." Graudal and his team had reviewed no less than 167 salt studies that all linked salt to blood pressure, but additionally looked at other factors related to heart health. What did they discover? That, yes, reducing salt intake could lower blood pressure, but that it *also* resulted in a 2.5 percent increase in cholesterol and a 7 percent increase in triglycerides—both important measures of heart health. *Detail matters, everything connects.*

The researchers also found that dietary salt reduction caused kidneys to produce more of the enzymes and hormones that regulate the body's salt levels, with the result that the body started to retain more salt. All these increases were considered significant, and potentially harmful for cardiovascular health. The bottom line? "I cannot see why the society should spend billions on sodium reduction," Professor Graudal said. *Don't mess with the crystal vase.*

Okay, so the salt issue is far from black and white…but is there a smart, middle course to be taken? If so, certainly it would be useful to know, if only for visiting salt-obsessed relatives and friends. And as we've just seen, opinions differ, and not only among the general public. Experts even disagree on things that you might think could be known, like how many people actually die from salt-related illnesses. According to the New York City Department of Health (and Mental Hygiene, one should note), a shocking 150,000 Americans perish each year from too much salt. This is an incredible toll—some thirty times that in the U.S. from all other kinds of food "poisoning." If sugar weren't already holding that position, the little white crystals would now be considered Public Health Hazard No. 1.

However, it turns out that such statistics may be more literally "incredible" too. Another paper, published around the same time, in the *New England Journal of Medicine*, equally firmly announced a salt-related toll of 44,000 lives a year, thereby saving 106,000 lives with the stroke of a pen, or more precisely the pressing of some keys on a calculator. A later editorial (dated August 14, 2014) concluded that the research linking salt consumption to adverse health effects rested largely on *statistical correlations* and needed to be taken, *ahem*, with a pinch of salt.

But that's not how salt research is being taken. For governments everywhere, salt consumption presents another health crisis, and the view is firmly that "something must be done." In the UK, for example, the government has already moved to forcibly reduce its citizens' daily salt intake; indeed, British authorities are congratulating themselves for having reduced consumption by about 10 percent between 2000 and 2008. How many lives have been saved? The government didn't claim to know precisely, of course, but the authorities were keen to let it be known that Britain had once again led the world in a virtuous campaign.

However, even measuring the initiative by the miserly standard of reduced salt consumption, and not by actual health results, the UK government's achievements were soon disputed. Researchers at the Universities of California and Washington accused the British authorities of cherry-picking their salt surveys to produce the reduction, while ignoring other studies that found no change in people's consumption.

It seems that the human body has evolved over millions of years to maintain its salt reserve at a certain level, and government guidelines be damned. Which is probably why, when American "pro-salt researchers" analyzed surveys from over thirty countries and cultures, they found that despite wide differences in diet and medical opinion, people all consumed about the same amount of salt!

Part 11
Philosophical Eating Strategies

Chapter 7

Nietzsche on the Nutritional Excellence of Industrial Meat Brothe

Friedrich Nietzsche was always obsessed with meat—his *charcuterie*—and drew inspiration and strength from an assortment of hams and sausages. The infamous philosophical architect of the "Superman," or *Übermensch*, (sometimes translated as "Over-man," which always sounds to me more like a kind of Wellington boot) also dabbled in vegetarianism but decided pleasure should come before health in such things. In a letter to a friend he writes:

> It is clear that occasional abstention from meat, for dietetic reasons, is extremely useful. But why, to quote Goethe, make a "religion" out of it? … anyone who is ripe for vegetarianism is generally also ripe for socialist "stew."

Nietzsche specialized in ancient philosophy and even made Zarathustra the hero of one of his books. But his Zarathustra is very different from everyone else's. That's because Friedrich Nietzsche is philosophy's *enfant terrible*—the thinker who threw away all the discipline's treasured conventions and norms, and produced instead strange, violent declarations railing against God, morality, and humanity in general. Nietzsche's book *Ecce Homo*, "behold the man," (the title itself being an irreverent reference to Christianity), includes a lengthy account of his own dietary choices, which he explains as prompted by a life plagued by ill health.

For Nietzsche, nutrition was part of a desperate effort to stave off illness. He writes:

> My experiences in regard to this matter have been as bad as they possibly could be; I am surprised that I set myself this question so late in life and that it took me so long to draw "rational" conclusions from these experiences... But as to German cookery in general—what has it not got on its conscience! Soup before the meal... meat boiled to shreds, vegetables cooked with fat and flour; the degeneration of puddings into paper-weights! And if you add to this the absolutely bestial drinking habits during meals of the ancients and not only of the ancient Germans you will understand the origin of the German spirit—that is to say, in bad stomachs. German spirit is indigestion; it can digest nothing.

The English and even the French are no better though, Nietzsche continues. The English diet seems to him to constitute a "return to Nature"— which he (obscurely) says is akin to cannibalism. "It seems to me to give the spirit heavy feet— the feet of English women."

Much of Nietzsche's philosophy is concerned with the philosophical problem of free will, and whether or not we really have any. Food choices were for him a good example of how we may have less freedom than we imagine, for many of us cannot eat what we want but instead have to bend toward what our body tolerates.

Nietzsche offers some examples. First of all, water is as good as wine, because wine is not as delightful as it is always supposed to be—instead it gives you headaches. Secondly, a heavy meal is to be preferred to a light one, as (he says) the stomach digests food better when full. (I haven't heard that one before: supersize it!) At the same time:

> A man ought therefore to know the size of his stomach. For the same reasons all those

interminable meals should be avoided which I call
interrupted sacrificial feasts and which are to be
had at any *table d'hôte*.

Another of Nietzsche's food principles is that nothing
should be eaten between meals, and coffee in particular should
be avoided because it makes people "gloomy." Tea, on the other
hand, he allowed might have beneficial properties—but only
in the morning. Then, it should be taken very strong, in small
quantities. "It may be very harmful and indispose you for
the whole day if it be taken the least bit too weak," he warns.
Perhaps because he took his tea so strong, he advises drinking
some milk beforehand, or even a cup of thick, oil-free cocoa.

Plagued himself by painful stomach disorders, he says:
"Remain seated as little as possible, put no trust in any thought
that is not born in the open whilst moving freely about—nor
when the muscles are not in festive mood. All prejudices
originate in the intestines."

Related to all this is the question of locality and the weather.
Nietzsche writes that "the climate of Germany alone is enough
to discourage the strongest and most heroically disposed of
stomachs," and that great thoughts ultimately depend upon
and arise out of out of these organic digestive functions.

Let anybody make a list of the places in which
men of great intellect have been found and are still
found; where wit, subtlety and malice constitute
happiness; where genius is almost necessarily at
home: all of them rejoice in exceptionally dry air.
Paris, Provence, Florence, Jerusalem, Athens—
these names prove something—namely: that
genius is conditioned by dry air, by a pure sky—
that is to say by rapid organic functions, by the
constant and ever-present possibility of procuring
for one's self great and even enormous quantities
of strength.

He adds in a weak attempt at self-deprecating humor: "I have a certain case in mind in which a man of remarkable intellect and independent spirit became a narrow, withdrawn, a grumpy old crank simply owing to a lack of subtlety in his instinct for climate."

In *Ecce Homo* (which bears the subtitle *How One Becomes What One Is*), in a chapter titled characteristically "Why I am so clever," Nietzsche asks, "Why do I know a few things more than other people? Why in fact am I so clever?" He has answers, of course: "I have never pondered over questions that are not really questions. I have never wasted my strength."

Where traditional philosophers dispute over God, the immortality of the soul, salvation, and "the beyond," he says that "even as a child" he had no use for such notions. "I do not waste any time upon them—maybe I was never childish enough for that? I have not come to know atheism as a result of logical reasoning and still less as an event in my life: in me it is a matter of instinct. I am too inquisitive, too questioning, too high spirited to be satisfied with such clumsy answers." No, Nietzsche explains that he is much more interested in another question— "a question upon which the 'salvation of humanity' depends to a far greater degree than it does upon any piece of theological curiosity": the issue of *nutrition*. He blames "the absolute worthlessness of German education" for having so failed to highlight the importance of the topic that he only realized in later life what great issues there are in food.

Over the years, Nietzsche experimented with a wide variety of diets. As a young man he had stayed at a clinic in the Black Forest where a Doctor Weil put him on a special regimen of four small meals consisting almost entirely of meat, bracketed by fruit salts first thing and a glass of claret before bed. As the great philosopher explained to a friend, the diet allowed "no water, no soup, no vegetables, no bread." Yet innovative though it was, it did not seem to help with his stomach problems. Nietzsche next experimented with vegetarianism before being put off by one of the few people he admired, the famous composer of grand operas, Richard Wagner. Then, at a particularly low point in his health, he tried living on milk and eggs, also to no avail. Finally, he tried eating hardly anything at all, but as we might expect, this was unsuccessful too. At this point, Nietzsche came across a new invention—something called Liebig's meat extract. This impeccably scientific food consisted of a thick, pasty substance that was supposed to be mixed with water to produce a beef broth. Think bouillon (or maybe Oxo) cubes.

Bouillon cubes are little blocks of extra-strong flavoring often added to stews and sauces. They are usually made from a base of a meat, like beef, but these days they come in chicken or even mushroom and mixed vegetable varieties. They are a terrible idea whatever they are made of, and worse, they often come with a fairly suspect cocktail of extra ingredients, including so-called flavor enhancers like monosodium glutamate. I'm always horrified by how many people crush these cubes into their cooking—usually in the belief that doing so "adds taste." They might better be described as "taste destroyers."

The publicity for Dr. Weil's original beef stock explained that it took about thirty-four pounds of South American beef to produce just one pound of extract, and that it was renowned for being both digestible and nourishing. Alas, the reputation was undeserved. Like many a processed meal, Liebig's meat extract had few nutrients left in it, if any.

Liebig eventually became the company known today as Oxo, a prominent maker of bouillon cubes (or stock cubes, as they're called in the UK). Many years later, when Oxo became the official sponsor for the 1908 Olympics, people thought it made perfect sense for the marathon runners to be guzzling the "fortifying drink."

Nietzsche's central philosophical thrust goes against conventional thinking and values. His diet was essentially guided by his sense of exceptionality, and a suspicion of fruit and vegetables as the foods favored by intellectual enemies.

With his migraines, his stomach upsets, and his early death, he paid a high price for his beliefs.

Chapter 8

Blessed Are the Cheese-makers

Forget complicated recipes: eat simply. Here, Jean-Jacques Rousseau, the great French "romantic" philosopher—and for some the first ecologist and environmentalist—sets the scene with characteristic style:

> Though I lived with the strictest economy, my purse insensibly grew lighter. This economy was, however, less the effect of prudence than that love of simplicity, which, even to this day, the use of the most expensive tables has not been able to vitiate. Nothing in my idea, either at that time or since, could exceed a rustic repast; give me milk, vegetables, eggs, and brown bread, with tolerable wine and I shall always think myself sumptuously regaled; a good appetite will furnish out the rest, if the *maitre d' hotel*, with a number of unnecessary footmen, do not satiate me with their important attentions.
>
> Five or six *sous* would then procure me a more agreeable meal than as many *livres* would have done since; I was abstemious, therefore, for want of a temptation to be otherwise: though I do not know but I am wrong to call this abstinence, for with my pears, new cheese, bread and some glasses of *Montferrat* wine, which you might have cut with a knife, I was the greatest of epicures.

Actually, Rousseau's rural lunch looks rather like the traditional British farmer's lunch—a roll of bread with a bit of cheese and pickle. The British think they add a touch of luxury with a tomato (and a pint of beer)—but it all only goes to show (once again) that foods that countries claim as peculiar to them are actually more international. However, since the British have so few claims to fame in food matters, the few they do have are cherished. And it seems likely that it was the British, and not the Americans, who *really* invented fast food, at least in the form of the sandwich. This bread-enclosed snack is attributed to the eighteenth-century aristocrat John Montagu, Earl of Sandwich—which was then, and indeed still is, a place rather than a food. Montagu was a politician and a gambler and was apparently so committed to his work that he would not leave his gaming table to eat. But forget bread for a moment and think about the cheese.

Milk, and all its associated products, notably cheese, cream, and butter, scarcely rates in philosophy books, let alone political treatises. Where alcohol, hunting, and meat eating are regularly brought into public debate, the dairy cow is left quietly chewing the cud and trying to mind its own business.

Apart, that is, from the writings of Jean-Jacques Rousseau. Recall that Rousseau is no obscure ancient Greek or soporific academic. On the contrary, he is the voice, as well as a bit of the inspiration, behind the revolutions that swept away the French monarchy and created the new republican government in the United States. Put short, Rousseau is one of the most influential philosophers of them all. We can surely learn from him, and certainly when making a snack.

Rousseau was forever praising the nutritious and psychological properties of milk and its ability to reconnect people with nature. Throughout his writings, from *Émile, or On Education* to his *Confessions*, dairy is depicted not only as a building block of humanity but also as a vegetal fruit-like figure within his idealised bucolic literary scenes. According to this philosophy, dairy products have a special place in creating the human character and determining our connection with our environment.

> Our first food is milk. We get accustomed to strong flavors only by degrees; at first they are repugnant to us. Fruits, vegetables, herbs, and finally some meats grilled without seasoning and without salt constituted the feasts of the first men. The first time a savage drinks wine, he grimaces and throws it away; and even among us whoever has lived to twenty without tasting fermented liquors can no longer accustom himself to them. We would all be abstemious if we had not been given wine in our early years. In sum, the simpler our tastes, the more universal they are.
>
> The most common repugnances are to composite dishes. Has anyone ever been seen to have a disgust for water or bread? That is the trace left by nature; that is, therefore, also our rule. Let us preserve in the child his primary taste as much as is possible. Let his nourishment be common and simple; let his palate get acquainted only with bland flavors and not be formed to an exclusive taste. I am not investigating here whether this way of life is healthier or not; that is not the way I am looking at it. For me to prefer it, it suffices to know that it conforms most to nature and is the one most easily adaptable to every other. Those who say that children must be accustomed to the foods they will use when grown do not reason well, it seems to me.

Rousseau's Rocket Salad

Pears, cored and thinly sliced

Walnuts, coarsely chopped

A bowl full of rocket leaves, also known as roquette (arugula)

Parmesan cheese, grated

In a large bowl, toss all ingredients together.

I don't know how much rocket or arugula Rousseau actually ate, but it certainly fits the philosopher very well. (The cheese, pears, and nuts he does speak highly of.) The tangy green herb has been widely grown throughout the Mediterranean area since Roman times and was reputed to be a great aphrodisiac, most famously by the ancient poet Virgil, who, in one of Rousseau's favorite reads, explains that the herb "excites the sexual desire of drowsy people."

Rousseau liked to teach. In *Émile*, he explains how to bring up children, in the *Discourse on Inequality* he says how to order society, and in the *Confessions* he talks about personal morality and family values. In this book, an otherwise unedifying work in which the great philosopher details exactly how much of a scoundrel he really was—from peeing in supper dishes to "taking advantage" of young women servants to later abandoning all his children to orphanages—appears a scene which is very revealing even in its apparent simplicity. In it, he imagines a utopian countryside with an abundance of agriculture that brings him absolute joy. "The trees were loaded with the choicest fruits, while their shade afforded the most charming and voluptuous retreats to happy lovers; the mountains abounded with milk and cream; peace and leisure, simplicity and joy, mingled with the charm of going I knew not whither, and everything I saw carried to my heart some new cause for rapture."

Rousseau considers the profound impact of breast-feeding on infants, affirming that it intensifies the mother-child bond, and therefore the overall harmony of the family, which he views as a fundamental unit of civilization. Indeed, *Philosophia-Sapientia*, the ancient personification of wisdom, suckled philosophers at her breasts with the milk of knowledge and moral virtue. Breast milk, thought to have particular health properties, was variously prescribed as a cure for earaches, fevers, and even sores. While today this notion of women and milk seems anti-feminist and conservative, during Rousseau's time period, it was remarkable and radical. Middle-class women were rarely allowed to breast-feed their own babies, and they had little to do with rearing them.

The eighteenth century was the hey-day of wet-nursing. Royalty first used wet nurses, and soon breastfeeding attracted a stigma. Small, firm breasts were considered more attractive than large ones, and breasts should get larger as they fill with milk. The French Revolutionaries showed Lady Liberty bare-breasted, but the policy was for women to stay at home, and their monopoly on breast milk was one of the reasons given. In a bizarre public demonstration of national renewal on the site of the Bastille in Paris, in 1793, some eighty-six male deputies drank milk from a specially constructed fountain intended to represent the breasts of Isis, symbol of new beginnings.

Breast Milk

It's not by mere chance that Rousseau starts off his masterpiece on the "art of education," *Émile, or On Education*, with a tribute to breast milk and maternity (still a modern concept in the eighteenth century).

When, in 1758, Swedish botanist Carl Linnaeus came up with a new way to categorize animals by grouping together those that fed their children on milk, he not only reconnected humans with their four-legged cousins but also added to a sense of male superiority over women. Rousseau, however, perceives a mother's milk as having a revolutionary capacity to stimulate a "natural feeling" of compassion. "When mothers deign to nurse their own children, then will be a reform in morals; natural feeling will revive in every heart; there will be no lack of citizens for the state; this first step by itself will restore mutual affection," he says. In essence, he is arguing that the mother's milk awakens in the baby its innate gift of empathy. He writes, "The first education is the most important, and this first education belongs incontestably to women; if the Author of Nature had wanted it to belong to men, He would have given them milk with which to nurse the children."

Rousseau's Romantic Dessert

Strawberries

Whipped cream

Put the strawberries in a bowl. Add whipped cream. You got it!

Strawberries, "perfect little red hearts," are edible Valentines. Today, we know that the humble strawberry has extraordinary properties on the circulation of the blood, but the fruit has long been counted as a natural aphrodisiac: the ancient Romans used it as a symbol of Venus, the goddess of love. Rousseau praises strawberries highly, and they have, since ancient times, invariably been associated with love and passion.

Rousseau's Strawberry Soup

Rousseau would also have been aware of a French rural tradition of serving newlyweds strawberry soup to help promote amour, and, being an unscrupulous sort of chap, he may have served it to his lady friends. Today, the ingredients for a soup like this might be: a generous portion of strawberries, a cup of orange juice, another cup of plain yogurt, and a half teaspoon vanilla extract. Puree all ingredients in a blender until smooth. Top with whipped cream and add some mint as a garnish, if you like. And yes, this is a cold soup. Continentals do stuff like that!

Chapter 9

The Paracelsus Principle:
Eat Fat to Get Thin

In a stern sidebar titled "The Fat Factor," food writer Selene Yeager warns that a half-cup serving of oats includes over one gram of fat. She continues: "Much of a grain's fat is found in the bran and grain layers. In most grains, these layers are stripped away during processing, but in oats they're retained. So when you're trying to limit the amount of fat you eat in your diet, a bowl of oatmeal may not be your best choice."

That's from *The Doctors Book of Food Remedies* (2007). Yeager speaks to an audience who is already sure that, well, fat is bad— an audience "softened up," as it were, by years of browsing books like the *Reader's Digest* tome *Foods that Harm, Foods that Heal: An A-Z Guide to Safe and Healthy Eating* (1996). The book counsels against frying vegetables in oil, as doing so causes them to "soak up" "substantial amounts of fat." Instead readers are advised to boil their veggies or eat them raw. This is triply worrying advice as veggies not cooked in oil or butter (a) taste pretty awful, thus (b) tempting people toward junk food whose tastes have been augmented by ingenious application of chemicals, and (c) certain nutrients are vulnerable to destruction by heat.

Where did the lingering perception that fat is Public Enemy No. 1 come from? Well, it seems that the notion can be traced back to a single researcher, Ancel Keys, who published a paper saying that Americans were suffering from "an epidemic" of heart disease because their diet was more fatty than their bodies were used to after thousands of years of evolution. In 1953, Keys added additional evidence from a comparative study of the U.S., Japan, and four other countries. Country by country, his research impressively demonstrated that a high-fat diet coincided with high rates of heart disease. It turned out that Keys' country-by-country comparison had been skewed, as he'd discarded countries that did not fit his theory, such as France and Italy with their oily, fatty cuisines. That's not even counting the so-called Inuit Paradox, which concerns the question of just how can the Inuit people (Eskimos), who gorge on animal fat and rarely see a vegetable, be healthier than many people today who, on the face of it, have done the right thing by constructing their diet around a balanced mix of grains, fruits, vegetables, meat, eggs, and dairy?

Equally unfortunate for the hypothesis is the fact that, on closer investigation, prehistoric "traditional diets" were not especially low-fat after all. Indeed, if the hunter-gatherers of yore relied on eating their prey, they would have had a lot more fat in their diet than most people do today. In reality, as *Science* magazine pointed out, during the most relevant period of 100 years before the supposed sharp upturn in heart disease, Americans were more likely to be consuming large amounts of fatty meat, so the epidemic followed a *reduction* in the amount of dietary fat Americans consumed—not an increase. No wonder the American Heart Association (AHA) issued a report in 1957 stating plainly that the fats-cause-heart-disease claims did not "stand up to critical examination."

The case for there being any such epidemic was dubious too—the obvious cause of higher rates of heart disease was that people were living longer, long enough to develop heart disease. But it was too late: the cascade of misinformation had already begun. And three years later, the AHA issued a new statement, reversing its view and abandoning its doubts. It had no new evidence, but it did have some new members writing the report, in the form of Keys himself and one of his friends. Their new report made the cover of *Time* magazine and was picked up by non-specialists at the U.S. Department of

Agriculture, who then asked a supporter of the theory to draw up "health guidelines" for Americans.

Soon, scarcely a doctor could be found who was prepared to speak out against such an overwhelming consensus, leaving only a few specialized researchers to continue protesting. And all this was good enough for the highest medical officer in the U.S., the Surgeon General, to issue a doom-laden warning about fat in foods, insinuating that ice cream was a health menace on par with smoking tobacco. It was the high point of a pretty feeble theory, and a triumph of preference over evidence. Only many years later, after large-scale studies were conducted in which comparable groups were put on controlled diets (low-fat and high-fat), would a correlation be found. However, it was not what was expected. It turned out that the low-fat diet seemed to be unhealthy. Even today, no one is quite sure why.

The solemn warnings about eating too much fat underline how skeptical you need to be when reading apparently authoritative food advice. The pursuit of low-fat foods sounds like it ought to be a really good idea, but often it leads people away from healthy foods toward over-processed and fattening junk ones. What the apparently unbalanced Inuit diet illustrates, says Harold Draper, a biochemist and expert in Eskimo nutrition, is that there are no essential foods—only essential nutrients, and these nutrients are obtainable in more ways than we imagine. So, could it be that hunting out fatty foods could bring us to good health after all? Indeed, could eating fat be a way to stay thin? It sounds paradoxical, but there's a good philosophical and indeed biological precedent for such an approach.

The story starts with Paracelsus, who was a brilliant but controversial thinker. He lived in Germany in the first half of the sixteenth century and is credited (amongst other things) with founding the modern fields of pharmacology and toxicology. Certainly, his thinking was revolutionary for its time, including, as it did, new treatments using specially mixed chemicals rather than traditional remedies involving plants or ground-up minerals. And where the ancients explained illness in terms of imbalances that needed a dose of the opposite to restore health, his therapeutic principle was "like cures like." Appendix A of this book explores this interesting theory further, using the example of some everyday foods, but Paracelsus explored—and demonstrated—the idea by distributing bread contaminated with minute amounts of human *excrement* to residents of the small town of Stertzing during the plague. This sounds not so much odd as plain awful, but in effect it was an early form of vaccination.

Anyway, to the point. Many nutritionists now (contra the diet tips of Ancel Keys described above) accept that eating fat does not actually make you fat, but it's quite another step to argue that it might make you thin. Yet this is what the Mediterranean diet today is, in effect, all about, and it is also Paracelsus's idea in practice. The food writer and practicing family physician Mark Hyman stresses that fat is one of the body's most basic building blocks. He maintains that fat consumed in the food that you eat not only plays absolutely vital roles in the body, like building cell membranes and protecting against disease, but that eating the "right fats" (crucial distinction!) can speed up metabolism, stimulate fat burning, and even reduce hunger.

We've been told so many nasty things about fat that we tend not to realize that in the form of olive oil or in a "real" cheese, for example, it is an excellent energy source, supplying almost two and half times as much energy, gram for gram, as carbohydrate. Yes, cheese and olive oil actually make you thin. At least, that is, eaten in moderation and in the context of a well-balanced diet that includes plenty of fruits and vegetables and minimizes processed foods. Check out the traditional Mediterranean diets of France, Greece, and Italy! The fats found in cheese (I would stress, in *real* cheese, not processed) are high-quality natural fats, packed with those omega-3 fatty acids that are normally associated with fish oil and are also important for helping the brain philosophize!*

Paracelsus Warns Against Believing the Experts

Paracelsus argued against the notion of authority as a basis for the tenets of medical practice, and instead advocated observation and research with empirical evaluation of results. Paracelsus (which means "above and beyond Celsus") was not his real name (it was Philippus Aureolus Theophrastus Bombastus Von Hohenheim), but one he adopted because he regarded himself as even greater than Celsus, the renowned first-century Roman encyclopedist and medical writer. He alienated other physicians by openly ridiculing their thinking and accusing them of greed. Their revenge includes the continued usage of his real name in the word bombastic—which the dictionary defines as high-flown; inflated; pretentious.

Consider, again, the example of the racehorse. Breeders know that there are special benefits afforded by increasing the amount of fat in a thoroughbred's diet. Trainers add corn or soy oil to horses' feed. They do so because fat plays a very useful role in activities that involve the muscles—in technical language, it allows better glycogen utilization during anaerobic activities (like races), with less fluctuation in blood glucose and blood insulin levels. Plus, by reducing the amount of glucose the muscles must raid from the blood, the high-carbohydrate diet helps delay the onset of fatigue. *Everything connects.* Snack on a small bag of organic potato chips or a cheese sandwich at lunchtime, and you really can stave off feeling tired at work! If people stare, just say Dr. Cohen told you.

The bottom line is that it is the type of fat that counts rather than the amount of fat. The fats found in things like olive oil, nuts, and seeds actually protect a person from many chronic diseases. And the Mediterranean diet emphasizes foods rich in omega-3 fatty acids, whole grains, fresh fruits and vegetables, fish, garlic—and wine. As I say, that's my advice—but it's based on reading the evidence. Fat in the diet is far from all bad. Your body needs a certain amount of it every day for the functioning of the brain and nervous system, to keep your skin and hair healthy, and to aid in the absorption of fat-soluble vitamins from the foods you eat. Plus, to avoid the dreaded "gym face," (sunken cheeks, wrinkles, and hollow eyes) you need to keep supplying the cells of your body with enough fat.

That said, you need to have the right proportion of fats in your diet, not too much. (Too much fat is bad. But then, Mae West's views notwithstanding, too much of anything is bad.) How much is good then? Nutritionists generally say that about one third of your calories each day should be in the form of fats.

Diet Tips: Olive Oil

Drizzle olive oil over everything. It is a wonder food.

You can even apply it directly to your skin for its wonderful emollient effects!

Chapter 10

Banquet Like a Pythagorean

"Oh, my fellow men!" exclaimed Pythagoras, a philosopher so ancient that he is even older than Plato and Socrates. Indeed, he is in many ways the father of Western philosophy. And he is a philosopher who had strong views about what to eat.

> Do not defile your bodies with sinful foods. We have corn. We have apples bending down the branches with their weight, and grapes swelling on the vines. There are sweet flavoured herbs and vegetables which can be cooked and softened over the fire. Nor are you denied milk or thyme-scented honey. The earth affords you a lavish supply of riches, of innocent foods, and offers you banquets that involve no bloodshed or slaughter.

Pythagoras, by the way, was a vegetarian. But even if you hanker after "sinful foods' and do not stick to veggie stew and milk and honey puddings, you probably follow more of Pythagoras's dietary advice than you realize. In particular, have you ever wondered why you eat three meals a day, and why a traditional meal has three courses?

The answer has less to do with nutrition, let alone common sense, and more to do with philosophy than you might imagine. In particular, it has to do with the significance attached to the number three by one of history's most influential, if at the same time least celebrated, philosophers.

For the Pythagoreans, the number one is the source of all things. It is both even and odd, and perpetually combines and recombines to create the world. The number two is imperfect, as it creates the possibility of division. Geometrically speaking, it is a line. The number three was called "the whole" because it combines one and two, and because it allows for a beginning, middle, and end. Three is the first shape—shall we say the first *form*—a triangle.

After learning all the secrets of the world through extensive travel, Pythagoras came to believe that everything in nature was divisible into three parts and that no one could become truly wise without being able to see every problem as being fundamentally triangular. He said, "Establish the triangle and the problem is two-thirds solved"; further, "All things consist of three."

The Power of Three

Maybe it's psychology, but one way or another the "power of three" shows itself in the most unexpected places—including hard-boiled nutritional science. It was an English doctor, William Prout, who decided that food consists of three main elements: protein, fat, and carbohydrates, the terms that have stalked food debates ever since. A German scientist, Justus von Liebig (whom we met in chapter 7), discovered that three chemicals—nitrogen, phosphorous, and potassium—seem to be pretty much all that plants need to grow, ignoring a handful of additional elements necessary for animals to grow and flourish. Liebig also developed the first baby formula, consisting of three substances: cow's milk, wheat, and malted flour—and a dash of sodium bicarbonate. (Okay, four.) Of course, since real milk contains a great many more things than this (such as vitamins, certain essential fats, and amino acids, not to mention bacteria and immune-enhancing compounds), Liebig's formula left babies severely malnourished.

It's no coincidence that we obediently place ourselves in one of three classes (upper, middle, and working), that schools and universities in most of the world have three terms (spring, summer, and autumn), and that the American system of higher education grants one of three degrees (bachelor, master, or doctor). (In some American universities, the trimester system hangs on within what often seems a very ad-hoc arrangement.) The triangle reappears in Plato with his recommendation that the rulers of society divide people into "Gold, Silver and Bronze," and even Aristotle obediently concludes Book VIII of his *Politics* by saying, "Thus it is clear that education should be based upon three principles: the mean, the possible, the becoming, these three." G. W. F. Hegel and Karl Marx reproduce Pythagoras's triangle with their theories of society: *thesis* and *antithesis* combine to form *synthesis*.

"Pythagoras is one of the most interesting and puzzling men in history," writes Bertrand Russell, in his *History of Western Philosophy*. "Not only are the traditions concerning him an almost inextricable mixture of truth and falsehood, but even in their barest and least disputable form they present us with a very curious psychology. He may be described, briefly, as a combination of Einstein and Mrs Eddy*. He founded a religion, of which the main tenets were the transmigration of souls and the sinfulness of eating beans."

If Bertrand Russell correctly observes that, in the phrase of his collaborator, Alfred North Whitehead, that the whole history of Western philosophy consists of "footnotes to Plato," he also ruefully has to concede that much of Plato consists of footnotes to Pythagoras. Russell then says (with unusual generosity) that if Pythagoras's theory that "all things are numbers" is literally nonsense, that "what he meant is not exactly nonsense." He concludes:

> I do not know of any other man who has been as
> influential as he was in the sphere of thought. I say
> this because what appears as Platonism is, when

analysed, found to be in essence Pythagoreanism. The whole conception of an eternal world, revealed to the intellect but not to the senses, is derived from him. But for him, Christians would not have thought of Christ as the Word: but for him, theologians would not have sought logical proofs of God and immortality.

Diet Tip: Triples All Round

Pythagoras thought everything in the universe was guided by numbers, and today's cosmologists are inclined to agree. So maybe we should take a leaf from his book and whenever we eat, however simple the meal, structure it as three courses, ideally with three elements to each course.

It's a remarkable tribute. Of course, people do not really fit into three social classes, it would make more sense to have four school terms per year, and only prisoners eat three meals a day. But, with meals at least, we think we ought to! *That's* influence.

However, rejecting or more likely completely ignorant of Pythagoras's advice, in recent years Dr. Xand van Tulleken has made rejecting the tyranny of three meals a day the central idea of his so-called Definitive Diet. As well as being a doctor, as we see, Xand van Tulleken is also one of a pair of twins, and he apparently devised the diet after his weight shot up by over 50 percent and horrified his slim twin. Having a slim identical twin is a cruel way to see damning evidence every day that you are eating too much. So Xand tried various conventional diets and soon found, as he puts it, that the advice was contradictory, and based on not very much evidence. This much is correct, but all the diet gurus say the same thing—about *everyone else's* diets.

Anyway, Xand tried various regimens, including a low-carb diet, where he solely ate meat, fish, eggs, and cheese. But he found it boring and unhealthy and any weight lost was soon put back on again. So, at last he decided to use his own judgment (aided by his medical training, of course) to work out for himself a diet regimen that might work. And his first conclusion was that to lose weight you should actually...eat less. No, there's more to it than that! To be precise, he says to try having just one meal a day to start the diet off. What's more, this one meal is strictly calorie controlled: he recommends making it less than 800 calories, which is about one third of what you would eat normally over the day. But, and this is the clever bit, since you are eating only one meal instead of three, he says that you can still have a decent meal. And he recommends making your meal the last one of the day, which is surely pragmatic.

The second stage in the diet is to eat two meals a day, skipping either breakfast or lunch. Dr. Xand says Definitive Dieters can enjoy two healthy meals, but they should still total only around 1,200 calories a day, a pretty minimal intake. One meal consists of 800 calories and the other of 400 calories. The final stage of the plan—luxury!—allows a third meal although it is only some 300 calories or so, which is about what you might chomp through in a couple of chocolate cookies. But Dr. Xand certainly doesn't recommend those, of course; he wants you eating food that is high in fiber, low in carbs, and rich in healthy fats.

Certainly, the overall plan sounds sensible as a way of eating less without missing it too much, but what does, *ahem*, Dr. Cohen (admittedly not an M.D.) think of the Definitive Diet? Well, yes, it does seem plausible that diets drastically reducing your food intake will make you thin. However, as explained elsewhere in this book, such regimens also risk damaging your health—mending the Swiss watch with a hammer, messing with the crystal vase—for example, by depriving your muscles and bodily organs of nutrients and energy, your nerves and brain of fat, your liver of glucose. It also means you lose the pleasure of eating and have to put up with being hungry for most of the day and having energy dips. Diets like this are ones that most people seem to be unable to stick to for very long.

So, recall instead the similar but different advice of another philosopher, Diogenes of Sinope, who lived on the Ionian coast in the fourth century BCE. Among other rather sensible practices, Diogenes always waited until he was thirsty before he drank anything and hungry before he ate. He thought that waiting until you were actually hungry was the best way to make sure that your food would be enjoyed, explaining that hunger was the most satisfactory and pungent of appetizers. Sometimes, people who struggle to control their body weight say that it is partly a reflection of the fact that they enjoy eating "too much," whereas (by implication) thin people do not.

Diogenes's advice not to drink except when thirsty would really make social life rather dull, not to mention that drinking water or tea is a very good way to regulate those pangs of hunger. That said, his brainy advice that you can get more enjoyment from food by waiting to actually be hungry before you eat is surely worth a try. With his method, we can have our cake and eat it too, so to speak!

Chrysostom, the ancient Greek historian, records his style thus:

> … he used to partake of a barley cake with greater
> pleasure than others did of the costliest of foods,
> and enjoyed a drink from a stream of running
> water more than others did their Thasian wine.
> He scorned those who would pass by a spring
> when thirsty and move heaven and earth to find
> where they could buy Chian or Lesbian wine; and
> he used to say that such persons were far sillier
> than cattle.

The bottom line is: there's not much new, much less "definitive," about the Definitive Diet, so move along, folks. Did I mention that the good Dr. Xand was also a TV announcer (along with Chris, his identical twin)? So not quite the dedicated nutritionist quietly investigating public issues that we might imagine. Or that he is a specialist in tropical medicine rather than anything diet related? And yet, even so, I think Dr. X does provide one valuable piece of dietary advice: "If you are eating way more food than you actually need each day (as most of us are), the easiest way to tackle that is not so much to worry about what goes into your meals, but to simply drop the number of meals you take a day."

Mary Baker Eddy was the founder of Christian Science, a new religious movement in the United States that appeared in the latter half of the nineteenth century and evidently particularly annoyed Russell.

Chapter 11

Jean-Jacques Rousseau and the Importance of Eating Fruits in Season

At age thirty-eight, rather late by the standards of many *thinkers*, but at the sweet point in terms of philosophers, Jean-Jacques Rousseau underwent a profound period of sudden insights. The catalyst was seeing an advertisement offered by the Academy of Dijon for a prize essay on the subject "Have the arts and sciences benefited mankind?" In the essay he submitted to the competition, Rousseau warns that scientists, far from being our saviors, are ruining the world, and any notion of progress is an illusion that spreads even as we move further and further away from the healthy, simple, and balanced lives of the past. Instead, he salutes the kind of society advocated by Plato, two millennia earlier, or indeed the "simple life" of ancient Sparta.

The essay, usually known as the "Discourse on the Arts and Sciences," was like a breath of fresh air in the stale debates of the time, and what is rather more surprising, Rousseau won the prize. Propelled thus from obscurity to celebrity, he began to adopt new patterns of behavior more fitting to his essayist views: he developed a love for long walks and quite contemplation of the countryside; he eschewed all sophistication and technology. He even sold his watch, saying he no longer needed to know the time.

However, it is to his book *Emile, or On Education* (1762) that we need to turn to see Rousseau's description of the ideal diet. Naturally, he disagrees with the fashion of the time for exotic ingredients and dishes and instead stresses the unique character of everyday foods.

In the service of my table and the adornment
of my dwelling I would imitate in the simplest
ornaments the variety of the seasons, and draw
from each its charm without anticipating its
successor. There is no taste but only difficulty to
be found in thus disturbing the order of nature; to
snatch from her unwilling gifts, which she yields
regretfully, with her curse upon them; gifts which
have neither strength nor flavor, which can neither
nourish the body nor tickle the palate. Nothing is
more insipid than forced fruits.

A wealthy man in Paris, with all his stoves and
hot-houses, only succeeds in getting all the year
round poor fruit and poor vegetables for his table
at a very high price. If I had cherries in frost,
and golden melons in the depths of winter, what
pleasure should I find in them when my palate
did not need moisture or refreshment. Would the
heavy chestnut be very pleasant in the heat of the
dog-days; should I prefer to have it hot from the
stove, rather than the gooseberry, the strawberry,
the refreshing fruits which the earth takes care to
provide for me.

In egalitarian style, the philosopher of the French and
American Revolutions promises that every meal will be a
feast, "where plenty will be more pleasing than any delicacies."
Somewhat trampling underfoot my Food Principle 2, *Detail
matters*, he continues:

There are no such cooks in the world as mirth,
rural pursuits, and merry games; and the finest
made dishes are quite ridiculous in the eyes of
people who have been on foot since early dawn.
Our meals will be served without regard to order
or elegance; we shall make our dining-room

anywhere, in the garden, on a boat, beneath a tree; sometimes at a distance from the house on the banks of a running stream, on the fresh green grass, among the clumps of willow and hazel; a long procession of guests will carry the material for the feast with laughter and singing; the turf will be our chairs and table, the banks of the stream our side-board, and our dessert is hanging on the trees; the dishes will be served in any order, appetite needs no ceremony…

No tedious flunkeys to listen to our words, to whisper criticisms on our behavior, to count every mouthful with greedy eyes, to amuse themselves by keeping us waiting for our wine, to complain of the length of our dinner. We will be our own servants, in order to be our own masters. Time will fly unheeded, our meal will be an interval of rest during the heat of the day.

This all struck a great contrast to the view, over in England, of Francis Bacon, who had argued in his *New Atlantis* a century earlier that it is man's duty, as an act of charity, to transform nature for the "benefit and use of life." Rousseau instead warned that human manipulations of nature create monstrosities, a view with added resonance today in the age of genetically modified plants and animals. And although he was Swiss-French rather than Italian, Rousseau is in many ways the true precursor to the twentieth century's Slow Food Movement (which originated in Italy and which you can read about in chapters 23 and 24).

However, Rousseau was not *entirely* innovative in praising fruit. In England, his fellow political visionary and indeed bread lover, John Locke, had offered a few decades earlier some very particular views about fruit. Where Rousseau loved to shock, Locke hated to be radical, and instead describes the topic, with characteristic timidity, as "one of the most difficult chapters in the government of health":

> Our first parents ventured Paradise for it; and 'tis no wonder our children cannot stand the temptation, tho' it cost them their health. The regulation of this cannot come under any one general rule; for I am by no means of their mind, who would keep children almost wholly from fruit, as a thing totally unwholesome for them; by which strict way, they make them but the more ravenous after it, and to eat good or bad, ripe or unripe, all that they can get, whenever they come at it. Melons, peaches, most sorts of plums, and all sorts of grapes in England, I think children should be wholly kept from, as having a very tempting taste, in a very unwholesome juice; so that if it were possible, they should never so much as see them, or know there were any such thing. But strawberries, cherries, gooseberries, or currants, when thorough ripe, I think may be very safely allowed them, and that with a pretty liberal hand, if they be eaten with these cautions.

Where Rousseau would eat strawberry soup for starters and no doubt other things too, all in the wrong order ("our meals will be served without regard to order or elegance"), the Englishman comes nearer to endorsing my three food principles, and certainly offers three key rules for eating fruit:

- *Rule 1.* Fruit should not be eaten after meals, as people usually do, when the stomach is already full of other food, but rather before or between meals, and children should have them for their breakfast.

- *Rule 2.* Bread eaten should be taken with them. (*Remember, I told you he was keen on bread!*)

- *Rule 3.* They should only be consumed when perfectly ripe.

However, in a spirit of liberalism and tolerance, John Locke concedes, "Apples and pears, which are thorough ripe, and have been gathered some time, I think may be safely eaten at any time, and in pretty large quantities, especially apples; which never did any body hurt, that I have heard, after October."

Nonetheless, Locke's tolerance only extended so far. He closes his discussion of this "difficult" topic with advice that Rousseau would certainly not have agreed with:

> Fruits also dried without sugar, I think very wholesome. But sweet-meats of all kinds are to be avoided; which whether they do more harm to the maker or eater, is not easy to tell. This I am sure, it is one of the most inconvenient ways of expense that vanity hath yet found out; and so I leave them to the ladies.

Some Health Properties of Strawberries
(If you need the excuse...)

Over the centuries, strawberries have been used for curing a whole range of ailments, from kidney stones to gout and rheumatism. In 1653, *Culpeper's Herbal and English Physician* waxes lyrical on their benefits:

STRAWBERRIES. These are so well known through this land, that they need no description. They flower in May, and the fruit is ripe shortly after. Venus owns the herb. The berries are excellent to cool the liver, the blood, and the spleen or a hot choleric stomach; to relieve and comfort the fainting spirits, and to quench thirst....

The water of the berries, carefully distilled, is a sovereign remedy and cordial in the pacification of the heart; and is good for the yellow-jaundice. The juice dropped into foul ulcers, or the decoction of the herb and root, doth wonderfully cleanse and help to cure them.... The juice, or water, is good for hot and red inflamed eyes: it is also of excellent property for all puflies, wheals, and other breaking forth of hot and sharp humours, in the face and hands, or other parts of the body, to bathe them therewith; and to take away any redness in the face, or spots or other deformities in the skin, and to make it clear and smooth.

Culpeper's offers a neat idea for a healthy, fermented strawberry juice drink: take as many strawberries "as you shall think fitting," stuff them into a glass jar, put the lot into a bed of horse dung for twelve or fourteen days, "and afterwards distill it carefully, and keep it for your use." However, for some reason, the drink never really caught on.

Chapter 12

Philosophers Still Arguing
over the Veggies

A vigorously pro-veggie philosophical argument, linking eating meat with waging wars, can be found, written all those thousands of years ago, in Plato's *Republic*. In fact, *everything* can be found in Plato's *Republic*. Anyway, it is here that Plato describes a world in which we will all feast upon barley meal and wheat flour, making "noble cakes," and nibbling olives, and cheese, "for relish." All of this served on a mat of reeds. For dessert, he recommends some roasted myrtle berries or acorns, perhaps boiled figs and roots. These are, for true philosophers, the foods of peace and good health. Plato was clearly following the teaching of the great Pythagoras here.

It turns out, when you look at the history of philosophy, that there are plenty of reasons to see Pythagoras's fingerprints everywhere. But very early on, his rivals did their best to overturn his views—including even his dietary recommendations! So, Plato downplays the link.

In any case, some people think that Zarathustra, perhaps better known as Nietzsche's unlikely mouthpiece, was Socrates's and Plato's inspiration. (Remarkably, some people think that Zarathustra, and in particular his idea of societal "food cultures," was also Robert Atkins's inspiration for his well-known diet.) The details of Zarathustra's life are unknown but it is thought he lived sometime around the early sixth century BCE. He established a radical community in ancient Iran based on horticulture. These were the original "gardens of paradise," full of fruits and vegetables (much of them newly introduced from China), with the rearing and caring for animals a solemn duty, the only exception permitted being their occasional use for transport. Zarathustra's philosophy was that the fundamental dualism—Good and Evil—is all about the difference between giving Life or condemning other beings to Non-Life.

So why did plates of vegetables not become the fashionable meal? Ah, but such stuff was not favored by Plato's pupil, Aristotle, a great fan of roast ox and so on, who deduced (from both observation and first principles) that animals—and he includes women in this category!—exist solely to be useful to men. Because Aristotle's thinking in many matters fits in better with that of the Bible and the Koran, his philosophy has always been the one most of us have been, shall we say, "fed."

Pythagoras's Myrtle Berry Jam (and Crumble)

In Roman times, myrtle berries were considered an aphrodisiac and were used to make a sauce eaten with wild boar. Originally the Mediterranean people used the myrtle berry to flavor wine, but the more common use now is in liqueurs and desserts.

Time to make it: A sunny afternoon

Time to cook it: 30 minutes

Time to eat it: Lunchtime

About 1 quart myrtle berries

lemon juice

2 cups sugar

For crumble topping:

2 cup flour

1 cup sugar Erst kommt das Fressen, dann kommt die Moral

1 cup cold butter, diced

Find a tree covered in myrtle berries. Wash and dry a good bowlful of them. Soak berries for 12 hours in the lemon juice and sugar. Cook the mixture gently for at least one hour or until it reaches a slightly thickened consistency. To make the crumble, mix together the flour, sugar, and butter. Place the prepared berries in a greased baking dish, spread the topping over the berries, and bake at 350°F for 30 minutes or until the topping is golden brown. To make jam, pour the berry mixture into jars, put lids on the jars, and let cool. Store in the refrigerator. If you prefer thicker jam, add pectin.

Part III
Food Myths and Legends

Chapter 13

Sugar is Good

Nibble on a Cookie, Enjoy an Ice Cream or Have a Soft Drink before your main meal.

These three unusual, but perfectly serious, diet tips came in the form of newspaper and magazine advertisements from Sugar Information, Inc., which even won an award* for "advertising in the public interest"!

> Are you getting enough sugar to keep your weight down? Sugar can be the will-power you need to under-eat.

Of course, these days, the talk is all about reducing sugar intake, but back in the 1950s, when Americans were already worrying about being overweight, it really seemed as if sugar could be the secret weapon for dieters who were having trouble reining in their appetite! The story of how it all happened has profound implications for both how knowledge is created and defined and how it is disseminated.

Here's how the "sugar is good" idea works: before a meal have a sugary drink—for example, a coffee with a teaspoon of sugar or maybe a fruit juice—and because sugar is almost instantly converted by the body into energy, it will immediately reduce your appetite. (Detail, evidently, doesn't matter here. You eat less, and hey *presto*, you get slim!) Plus, the helpful advice continued, sugary drinks contain fewer calories than you might think, since sugar has only 18 calories per teaspoon, so they're not themselves fattening.

By now you may be a little skeptical—which is exactly what philosophy warns us to be about all advice, and not only that regularly trotted out as "facts about food." This counsel came not, as naive folk might imagine, courtesy of some well-meaning public body but rather via an industry front run by the big sugar manufacturers. "Sugar Information," set up in 1943 and "dedicated to the scientific study of sugar's role in food," was the PR arm of the sugar industry and producers.

And, in the years following the end of the Second World War, the sugar industry proved very good at getting its "research findings" not only into the public eye but also into the official views of government agencies—like the reports of the all-powerful Food and Drug Administration. Here, it was ultimately all about politics. The FDA had already chosen its preferred target—dietary fat—and to consider sugar as an alternative cause of things like heart disease and obesity would undermine that message.

Back then, as they still do today, a handful of influential academics decided public policy—like Frederick Stare, founder and chairman of the Department of Nutrition at the Harvard School of Public Health. Professor Stare and his department had long enjoyed support from the sugar industry, which provided funding for some thirty papers produced by Stare and his colleagues from 1952 through 1956. In 1960, the department broke ground on a new $5 million building funded largely by private donations, including a $1-million gift from General Foods (which is now called Kraft General Foods), the maker of sugar-loaded treats like Jell-O and Minute Tapioca, Kool-Aid, and Tang.

> ## Note to Mothers
>
> Here's a sprinkling of the thoughtful dietary advice offered by the sugar industry's experts: "Exhaustion may be dangerous—especially to children who haven't learned to avoid it by pacing themselves. Exhaustion opens the door a little wider to the bugs and ailments that are always lying in wait. Sugar puts back energy fast—offsets exhaustion. Synthetic sweeteners put nothing back. Energy is the first requirement of life. Play safe with your young ones—make sure they get sugar every day."

Frederick Stare didn't call himself a philosopher, of course. Rather he was an expert—in the new science of nutrition. But, in advocating a broad, sweeping theory about how the world worked, he was acting in a tradition that would have been entirely familiar to ancient philosophers from Aristotle to Zeno. And just like them, his theories rested on certain assumptions that have only very, very slowly been unpicked and exposed as flawed.

In fact, for more than two decades, right up to the early 1970s, Professor Stare was one of the food industry's star advocates, regularly testifying in Congress from that all-important objective observer position about the wholesomeness of sugar—even as his department gobbled up funding from sugar producers and food and beverage giants such as Carnation, Coca-Cola, and Kellogg's.

Now you may think that public health messages should not be outsourced to food businesses, but, well, they always have been and today they still are. In 2015, for example, the White House–backed Partnership for a Healthier America was still unashamedly mixing academic research with data provided by the big food corporations. Because, as its website explains: "In order to solve the childhood obesity crisis, we must harness the resources, expertise and most importantly the free-market creativity that drives this nation." No suggestion there that an unmanaged free market might actually be part of the problem. Or concern that, as recently as 1995 the American Heart Association was recommending "healthy" snacks of "low-fat cookies, low-fat crackers…hard candy, gum drops, sugar, syrup, honey" and other carbohydrate-laden foods.

But maybe we *wanted* to hear this kind of sugary advice. Although the conventional map of human taste buds on the tongue has a big zone for bitter, the sides "grab the sour and salty"—and only a relatively modest spot on the tip of the tongue for detecting sugar and sweet, as the food writer Michael Moss points out that the tongue map was the creation of a German graduate student back in 1901 and in truth "the entire mouth goes crazy for sugar." In fact, "There are special receptors for sweetness in every one of the mouth's 10,000 taste buds, and they are all hooked up, one way or another, to the parts of the brain known as the pleasure zones," says Moss. Put short, sugar makes food irresistible.

In his aptly entitled book *Salt Sugar Fat: How the Food Giants Hooked Us* (2013), Moss explains that over the years the reliable strategy of the food industry in trying to keep up with new discoveries about potential hazards from their core products, discoveries, and controversies that have variously seen all its "core pillars" of salt, sugar, or fat fall out of societal favor, is to simply swap from pillar to pillar depending on which one is currently the focus of public attention. After all, it is elementary human psychology that people tend to only be able to worry about *one* thing at a time!

Aristotle taught that the world was the center of the universe, that it sat in place unmoving while the heavens whirled around it—and because of his stature people accepted the theory for nearly two thousand years! Thank goodness that modern-day hypotheses come under fiercer scrutiny. As far as those about diet and nutrition go, the key takeaway here is that over the years, the food industry has not changed its spots, and its advice has not grown any less cynical. Its incredible ingenuity in finding new ways to make money has to be set against public health issues like tooth decay, diabetes, and obesity, which have all increased in incidence. Only philosophy can make it honest—and keep us thin!

Fat: An Economist's View

Statistics can give a surprisingly different view on things. For example, as a group, Americans now weigh three million tons more than they would have if they had remained as slim as they were in the 1960s. This excess weight requires the burning of two billion more gallons of fuel—just to move it around!

In his book HEAVY! The Surprising Reasons America Is the Land of the Free and the Home of the Fat, Richard McKenzie discusses the economic causes and consequences of America's dramatic weight gain over the past half-century. Relating weight gain to the growth in world trade freedom, the downfall of communism, the spread of free-market economics, and so on reveals some key statistical links between time spent preparing meals and body weight, and how lower food prices relate to higher food consumption.

McKenzie concludes that fast food has become cheaper, in part because of mechanization and in part because the workers producing it are, in relative terms, paid less and less. At the same time, the economic forces propelling 1960s housewives away from the kitchen and into jobs also propel families toward eating processed foodstuffs and dining out, or just snacking.

Fat: An Economist's View (cont.)

But what's the solution? Alas, McKenzie doesn't say specifically, other than utilizing the free market to ensure that the broader social costs of the obesity epidemic are passed on to the people causing it. Farmers, food processors, and restaurants should meet their own full costs, otherwise "foods will be underpriced, encouraging excess eating." Governments should cease to subsidize the research and production of fattening foods. Secondly, McKenzie sees a role for public education on nutrition— and a place for policing more tightly the industry's nutritional claims. But he's firmly against the usual "policy fixes" preferred by today's governments—such as taxing sugary or fatty foods, because the tax, of course, affects healthy people as much as the unhealthy.

Food Myth:

Drink More Water

The ancient thinker Thales is often called "the first philosopher" but also has some claim to being "the first scientist" because of his interest in examining practical evidence before finalizing his theories. And Thales's grand theory, inspired by finding the shapes of shells fossilized in rocks, was that everything—ultimately—is made of water. The evidence was weak and the theory was wrong, but the approach has echoed down the centuries. And in food matters, water plays a central role. But that role is not quite the one water is often given.

Consider an article recently published in the (at least fairly serious) *British Medical Journal*. In it, Rachel Vreeman and Aaron Carroll (while denying any special knowledge) take apart some of the food myths that they say are regularly "propagated" by newspaper hacks and trained doctors alike in the name of science and health.

Their first example concerns the old reliable advice that people need to drink more water or, to be precise, to drink "at least eight glasses of water a day." That Vreeman and Carroll are onto a very real health issue is underlined by the fact that the opening years of the third millennium saw public campaigns in the U.S. that even included the First Lady, Michelle Obama, whose "Drink Up" initiative combined a philosophical belief in the primacy of water with worries about a new generation getting fat.

Michelle Obama took the watery message to a dozen TV shows, including *Today*, *Good Morning America*, *Live! With Kelly and Michael*, *The Tonight Show*, *The Late Show*, and *The*

Doctors. All featured positive "Drink up" recommendations, but the last show, because it offered "practical health and wellness information five days a week" (you can be unhealthy on weekends), went a little negative and told viewers unambiguously to *stop* drinking sugary, fizzy drinks. Nonetheless, the hosts (ER physician Travis Stork, plastic and reconstructive surgeon Andrew Ordon, gynecologist Jennifer Ashton, and family practitioner and sexologist Rachael Ross) all agreed enthusiastically with the First Lady's core insight.

> "We all know you are what you drink," Michelle Obama told the doctors via VideoLink. "And when you drink water, you're at your best!"

The backers of the campaign, producers of bottled water like Evian and of water-filtration systems like Brita, helpfully made available 500 million bottles of water emblazoned with the "Drink Up!" logo. Extra scientific details were provided by Sam Kass, a White House nutritional policy adviser, who explained that "40 percent of Americans drink less than half of the recommended amount of water daily."

Diogenes's Homemade Wine

Put a jug of water in the fridge.

Wait one hour.

Add ice cubes.

Pour into glasses and serve.

It's delicious! Not much of a recipe? Well, true, but the fact is that drinking a little extra water is the easiest and least expensive way to both lose weight and help your body cleanse itself of impurities.

Now certainly it's awful to think that in today's America, half the population is (water) malnourished. One study even found a quarter of American children drinking no water at all! Not even the expensive bottled kind! And yet, paus worldwide levels of hydration. Studies showed that osmolality ranged widely, from just under 400 mOsm/kg in Kenya to a well-lubricated 964 in Sweden.

Skeptical types should worry that the first drink-more-water study was funded by Nestlé Waters (producers of Perrier, Vittel, Acqua Panna, et cetera) and the second by Nestec, a Nestlé subsidiary that provides "research services" to...er...Nestlé. In short, it's a profit-guided trail that led in due course to the White House's recent initiative.

But back to Rachel Vreeman and Aaron Carroll, whose interest was originally prompted by noticing how seldom dieticians and health experts pause to examine the beliefs that they already hold as true. Their conclusions are highly relevant:

> Even physicians sometimes believe medical myths contradicted by scientific evidence [and] the prevalence and endorsement of simple medical myths point to the need to continue to question what other falsehoods physicians endorse.

Meanwhile, pending a greater role for philosophical doubt on food policy, sales of bottled water continue to increase. That said, if there's no obvious case for drinking more water, from the point of view of watching your weight, there's nothing better than eating more water. What do I mean?

Well, recall that ancient theory, put forward by Thales, that ultimately everything is made of water. In food terms, this actually provides many insights.

In fact, the key to eating as much as you like and not getting too fat is actually to eat water. You don't need to be a food genius to work that out! Nor indeed to twig that salads are mainly water. A green salad (lettuce leaves plus cucumber) is 95 percent water by weight, but what about other foods? Here are some revealing facts and figures.

Food	Water content
Fresh fruit	Typically between 75 and 95%
Watermelon	99%
Cantaloupe Melon	90%
Strawberries	92%
Apples	84%
Oranges	87%
Grapes	81%
Courgettes (Zucchini)	95%
Red, yellow, and green bell peppers	92%
Broccoli	91%
Potatoes	75 - 80%

Even dried fruit, like raisins, are still one-third water. However, the entry that caught my eye in this League Table of Food Water Content is that for potatoes. The fact that it turns out that potatoes are a bit less watery, coming in at around 75 to 80 percent, helps explain why chips are fattening. *Detail matters!*

But back to fruit—and fruit juice is often perceived as healthy, because it comes from fruit, right? Well, yes and no. All too often, fruit juice is actually just fruit-flavored sugar water. It may contain only water, sugar, and some chemicals that taste like fruit. Even if you can get your hands on real, 100-percent fruit juice, you still may be getting the kind of sugar content associated with artificial ingredient–stuffed beverages like Fanta and Coca-Cola. Because the problem with fruit juice is that, yes, it is made of fruit but, no, not all of it. Taken whole, the sugar in fruit is bound within fibrous cell walls, which slows down the release of the sugar into the bloodstream. However, since most people don't like drinking fibers, most fruit juice contains no fiber, and there is nothing to stop you from swallowing in a matter of seconds a huge helping of sugar that otherwise sensible folk would run a mile from. That is, of course, unless it's been labeled an "energy drink," in which case the sugar almost miraculously become an asset—particularly if the sugar was created in a laboratory and cloaked in one of its many *noms de plume*, such as maltose, dextrose, sucrose, or (the manufacturer's favorite) high-fructose corn syrup.

Tomato sauces are 90 percent water—which makes sense given that tomatoes are technically a fruit. But what if your tomatoey stew is served with rice? No worries, as the water content of cooked rice is pretty high at about 65 to 70 percent.

Meat and poultry are about three-quarters water but when cooked can dry out to less than 60 percent. Fish is 70 percent water. Raw beef is 73 percent water, while cooked beef (e.g., a hamburger patty) is 62 percent water, about the same as cooked chicken. Even processed meats (like salami) contain around 60 percent water. As meat is generally cooked for a long time (necessarily, in order to remove dangerous bacteria), it is not unusual for a beef roast to lose one-third of its original size and weight when cooked at a high temperature, meaning its water content drops dramatically, and its fattening quality shoots up. In general, the higher the cooking temperature, the more moisture will be lost in cooking. On the other hand, these days, supermarket meat and fish may contain deliberately added water—which you pay for, of course. Strange to say, businesses have not publicized this fact, despite its potential appeal as a slimming aid!

Surprisingly perhaps, jams and preserves are quite "dry" at 30 percent water—making them even more fattening, of course. And there's really no escaping the consequence of tucking into cookies and crackers, which are almost completely bereft of any water, rated at a mere 6 percent. The driest food of all is peanut butter, which is only 2 percent water. It is usually eaten with bread—how watery is that? Well, the dough is about 40 percent water, but once baked reduces to about 35 percent. Wheat flour itself is dry too—just 11 percent water.

However, smoothies, one of the things that you might imagine were a good, watery way to fill your tummy without getting too fat, turn out to often be quite the opposite.

Chapter 14

In Praise of Not Eating

What happens to your body if you spend a few days fasting? (Well, semi-fasting anyway?)

For countless thousands of years people had a rhythm of eating slightly too much interspersed with periods of eating far too little. In consequence, the human body, as is the case with the bodies of all animals that live in regions where they must prepare for winter, prefers to have periods of little or no food, and periods of bingeing (to put a few extra pounds on for later). It is only modern life that has created the possibility of a stream of constant food on demand.

Now here's the magical thing about going without food for a bit. It seems that after just half a day (twelve hours, because the important element is the level of glycogen—sugar—in the liver, which drops after twelve hours of fasting) without new nutrients being poured into the blood stream, the body starts to look for alternative sources of nourishment in the form of its own diseased or damaged cells. This is the process called *autophagy*: a word which comes from the Greek words *auto*, meaning self, and *phagy*, meaning eating.

This insight came only recently, in the 1990s, when a medical researcher, Valter Longo at the University of Southern California, found that if yeast cells (which are, as he stressed to me by email, microscopic living organisms) were starved of sugar and fed only water, instead of dying or becoming weaker, they actually grew healthier and stronger. The finding intrigued Longo enough that (despite general skepticism from medical journals and colleagues) he investigated further. The hunch began to pay off when he discovered that if mice were deprived of food for three days, which is a very long time for mice, their bone marrow started to produce stem cells. Now stem cells are the holy grail of medical treatments as they have the ability to become any other kind of cell—smoothly replacing damaged ones like an efficient mechanic restoring a veteran car engine.

Exploring the phenomenon further, Valter found that several short fasts over a six-month period apparently left the mice with completely rejuvenated immune systems. That, at least, was the claim, and to subsequent magazine reporters it mattered not the least that mice are in fact completely different in their metabolisms from human beings.

However, since fasting is a relatively innocuous intervention (compared to injections with cocktails of powerful drugs), approval for actual human trials was easily obtained, and here too it seemed that fasting really did have some kind of rejuvenating effect. The journal *Cell* reported:

> Interestingly, self-digestion by autophagy—a process that is potently triggered by fasting—is now emerging as a central biological pathway that functions to promote health and longevity. One of the most evolutionarily conserved cellular responses to organismal fasting is… a process in which the cell self-digests its own components. This self-digestion not only provides nutrients to maintain vital cellular functions during fasting but also can rid the cell of superfluous or damaged organelles, misfolded proteins, and invading microorganisms.

The first day of going without food is the hardest, as the body only slowly switches over to burning the alternative stock of energy known as fat. In fact, the body first of all raids other, easier sources of energy—including the muscles and liver!

For once, people who are overweight have the edge over their thin cousins, as their bodies are relatively quick to offer up the surplus stored energy. This is also why, if paradoxically, fit and healthy people die of exposure quicker than their overweight companions.

Many religions have a tradition of fasting in some form: Christians have Lent and Muslims have Ramadan (which usually involves a twelve-hour, dawn-to-dusk fast), for example, but even if it's been done for millennia, depriving the body of all nutrients is not without risks. For one thing, it can create problems with the liver and kidneys; for another it can cause people to feel dizzy and even faint. Professor Longo's recommendation is something called the Fast Mimicking Diet, which comes in at about 750 calories a day and allows people to eat real food, albeit in the form of bars, soups, and shakes.

Alternatively, consider trying a day or two just eating fruit (avocadoes are fruit, incidentally)—which I'd call "semi-fasting." While you're still resetting your body's cravings, semi-fasting is difficult enough! However, if you're tempted to try fasting, then this variation, eating lots of different fruits for two days, can be—should be—fun. Because healthy eating is not about punishing your body; it is about treating it with more care.

Thales's Refreshing Smoothie

Thales is often (wrongly) called the first philosopher, and rather tragically is reported to have died of thirst one hot day while watching an athletic contest, so the least we can do is honor him with this drink made of ingredients his followers are known to have used as staples.

Pour a cup of milk into a blender; add some ice cubes. Add a cup of seedless raisins, a handful of cilantro leaves (fresh coriander), a cup of a mixture of chopped mallow (leaves, flowers, or fruits) and purslane seeds, a cup of grated cheddar cheese, a cup of cream, and wild honey to taste. A word about mallow. It is a much-maligned weed to gardeners— but the whole plant is actually edible. Indeed, it is exceptionally rich in vitamins A, B, and C, along with calcium, magnesium, and potassium. Speaking of marshmallows, the confection eaten today was originally made from the sap of the roots of mallow grown in marshes. Hence the name.

Anyway, back to the recipe. Purée until smooth. Chill before serving.

Pre-Socratic alternative

The easy version, again not to be sniffed at: buy a ready-made fruit smoothie. Yes, it's full of sugar (and maybe other things too) but still better than a Coke. That's the benchmark!

Sadly, although fruit smoothies sound healthy, in fact, today's food industry's versions contain huge amounts of sugar. If children's unhealthy orange fruit punch has perhaps 8g of sugar per serving, it's positively low-cal compared to the typical smoothie, which contains almost double that!

Chapter 15

Eat Dirty

Socrates says, in Plato's little play known as the *Phaedrus*, that people make themselves appear ridiculous when they are trying to know obscure things before they truly know themselves. But there's something even more ridiculous about some of the new scientific insights into what we really are. Consider the new idea that human beings are a kind of mobile home for countless millions of different bacteria. Actually, the possibility doesn't only seem ridiculous—it's positively *repugnant*.

We don't have anything like the same resistance to being reduced to mere chemical reactions, the way nutritionists and biochemists routinely do. But bacteria—microorganisms— are built into our psyches as not only "not us" but indeed "the enemy."

So phobic are we about germs that when it comes to food matters, unpasteurized milk is all but illegal, and cheeses made in the traditional way (with traditional tastes and flavors) have been forced off many supermarket shelves in favor of synthetic kinds. The only bacteria we allow are those carefully raised in laboratories and inserted into "live yogurt."

Yet nowadays it is acknowledged that microscopic organisms are the hidden puppet masters of human health. Even as the mechanization of food production has made them the enemy, our bodies continue to rely on many millions of "good bacteria" for our basic functioning. Researchers recently identified an ancient virus that cunningly inserted its DNA into our ancient ancestors, and I don't mean a few thousand years ago but millions of years ago into creatures that bear no resemblance to us except that they had four limbs. That snippet of genetic code is part of the nervous system of modern humans and plays a key role in human consciousness, facilitating nerve communication, the storage of memories and higher-order thinking itself. We celebrate the discovery of antiseptics and antibiotics that fight and destroy the "bad bacteria" that cause things like plague, meningitis, and pneumonia, even as research shows that they play more subtle roles in the body than we formerly imagined. In ever more ways, it turns out that microorganisms are able to affect the way our brains work, potentially even directing us toward certain eating habits that are not in our interest—but are in theirs!

As to that last possibility, Dr. Carlo Maley, formerly of the University of New Mexico, where he led one of the studies, says that microbes in the gut may control our eating behavior in a number of ways, including production of toxins that alter mood, changes in taste, and the hijacking of nerves between the gut and the brain. Dr. Anna Zakrisson, who has analyzed the evidence for the journal *Acta Physiologica*, thinks that carbohydrate cravings may really be the result of our system being hijacked by gut microbiota—in a sense, that is, the result of "microbes controlling the mind."

Many ancient cultures used molds, soil, and plants to treat bacterial infections. In ancient Serbia, China, and Greece, old, moldy bread was pressed against wounds to prevent infection. In Egypt, crusts of moldy wheat bread were applied to scalp infections, and "medicinal earth" was dispensed for its curative properties. At a time when microscopic life forms were unknown, the remedies were explained in terms of possibly influencing the spirits or gods responsible for illness and suffering.

Unappetizing or not, one of the most important medical breakthroughs in history came in the sixteenth century when Paracelsus surreptitiously fed villages tiny amounts of their own excrement in the form of an additive to bread—protecting them from contracting the plague, and thereby demonstrating a way in which germs could not only cause illnesses but protect people from them too. The story illustrates the key principle of vaccinations, which typically are made from weakened or dead forms of microbes.

Whisper it, but as well as being the enemy, *E. Coli* is good for you. It sounds paradoxical, but that's the price you have to pay for appreciating the fantastic complexity of the human body's relationship with food. There's an illuminating story from the last century about this that features not only germs but Hitler's personal physician. Back in the 1930s, a little-respected and undistinguished doctor named Theodor Morell, then early in his political career, assured the new German Führer that he had miracle drugs that could cure Hitler's health problems. First, he prescribed little black tablets called Dr. Küster's Anti-Gas pills, to be taken sixteen a day. They provided only temporary relief—and at a cost, as the active ingredient was the deadly poison strychnine. More interesting is that Dr. Morell next prescribed a pill called Mutaflor, which seemed to further stabilize the Führer's bowel problems. Indeed Hitler was so pleased with the doctor's work that he invited him to join the inner circle of Nazi elite.

Mutaflor's active ingredient was not a poison but a bacterium, in particular a type of hydrolyzed *E. coli* derived from human feces. Which pill would you prefer to have after dinner? Perhaps surprisingly, this pill actually worked, and for the first time in many years Hitler's stomach settled down.

E. coli (Escherichia coli) is the name of a germ, or bacterium, that lives in the digestive tracts of humans and animals. There are many types of *E. coli*, and most of them are harmless. But some can cause stomach upsets, some can cause urinary tract infections, and some may even cause severe anemia or kidney failure, which can lead to death. The best source for *E. coli*, Dr. Morell understood, is the feces, or stool, of humans or animals.

Mentioning this brings me to an interesting and revealing story about Hitler and the Nazi approach to food.

Like the philosopher Nietzsche, whom Hitler greatly admired (albeit not for their shared health problems), the Führer suffered from ill health, including stomach cramps, bowel problems, and chronic flatulence. The most likely reason Hitler originally had stomach trouble was because he boiled all his vegetables—killing the good bacteria. A bizarre ritual at Nazi meals was that the Führer left the table after each meal in order to expel vast quantities of wind.

Hitler, as every meat-eater seems to know when faced with a vegetarian, was firmly against eating animals. Less well known is that he generally had strong views on food. He had creepy opinions about meat, the eating of which he said reminded him of eating a human corpse. So instead, he ate large quantities of watery vegetables, mashed to a pulp.

Dr. Morell's remedy for restoring stomach harmony undoubtedly seems rather disagreeable, especially considering that (unlike Paracelsus' pioneering work with plague victims) the feces were not even Hitler's own but were supposed to have been obtained from German soldiers (who I suppose were "following orders" as it were). Nonetheless, in biological terms, another person's bacteria are just as good as our own. Indeed, we don't really have "our own" bacteria, any more than microorganisms are fussy about their host. But back to Hitler: the unfortunate fact was that the cure was so complete and so remarkable that it gave him the energy to start World War II.

If it is ironic that a positive thing—a doctor treating a patient—should have terrible consequences, then it is also ironic that despite this personal experience of the advantages of bacteria, the Nazis were obsessed with hygiene (including, as they called it, "racial hygiene") and infections. The obsession was there right from the start, in Hitler's rambling and odious autobiography, *Mein Kampf*. Nonetheless, the story underlines the key point that a healthy stomach is not one fed carefully hygienic food.

Another of Hitler's doctor's ideas was less successful. With Hitler's help, Dr. Morell created a pharmaceutical empire out of businesses confiscated by the Nazis—often by putting the previous owners in concentration camps. The plan for Morell was to become rich, but for Hitler the appeal was to generate an army of Supermen powered by vitamin supplements. Thus, the Nazis built up a vitamin industry as they destroyed Europe and killed millions of people. Physical excellence was always part of the Nazi ideology, and a good Nazi was supposed to be fit and strong and slim.

Fortunately for the world, the approach of injecting vitamins to create supermen does not work. Again, we can learn from this the foolishness of relying on artificially prepared supplements. Morell even injected Hitler with glucose every morning—a completely pointless way to achieve roughly the same result as drinking a glass of fruit juice or eating a piece of toast and jam. At night, Hitler's doctor injected him with barbiturates to help him sleep. Morell's influence went wider too; between April and July of 1940, more than 35 million tablets of methamphetamine—speed, in street parlance—were shipped to the German army and air force, undoubtedly reducing any limited sense of self-control and moral responsibility. (Similar drugs were used by soldiers in the Gulf War of 1990 to 1991.)

As the tide of war turned against Hitler, Morell stepped up the Führer's injections to include a range of bizarre drugs, including testosterone from bulls and methadone. Hitler was in constant pain, his mind became addled, his movements were uncontrollable, and his body became a kind of broken shell that the official propaganda films struggled to present convincingly. In one clip, as his right hand pats a member of the Hitler Youth approvingly, his left hand, clasped firmly behind his back shakes uncontrollably—a giveaway sign of the brain damage caused by the dangerous cocktails.

But back to ordinary life, as it were. Our daily concern is with the bacteria that often migrate from human or animal intestines into things like water sources—which is why drinking stream or lake water can give you an upset stomach. Another frequently contaminated food is meat, which is why meat needs to be cooked to high temperatures. Meat contamination is the most common way people in the United States become infected with *E. coli*. What a lot of people don't realize is that any food that has been in contact with raw meat—for example, by being sliced on the same cutting board before the cutting board has been thoroughly cleaned—can in turn become home to the same bacteria. Those microorganisms will then flourish in foods that aren't given the heat treatment (for example, in raw vegetables used in a salad!).

Speaking of foods that aren't cooked, it is often said these days that unpasteurized milk and cheese are full of *E. coli*, and that is why we should accept factory-made simulacra instead. It's a position that certainly suits the usual players in the food industry, interested in mass production and long shelf lives, and it is their preferences that have influenced government food policies in countries like the UK and the United States— if rather less so in countries like France. Here, unpasteurized cheese is part of a cherished *patrimoine*, or cultural heritage, and partaking of it is considered almost a fundamental human right! But in fact, there is very little evidence for the prohibition of dairy products, and it could be argued instead that the cases of food poisoning incidents stem from modern food processing techniques—for example, keeping cows (and chickens) in factory farms and even feeding them meat and excrement.

In any case, if fear of germs leads you to drop unpasteurized milk products, maybe to be consistent you should also stop eating fast food, cut out restaurants, and certainly never eat beef—as public health statistics invariably show these are where people are most likely to pick up a dangerous strain of *E. coli*. But I'm not really saying that, any more than I think you should drop raw fruits and vegetables such as lettuce, alfalfa sprouts, or unpasteurized fruit juices. Nor, of course, you should avoid other people and lakes, pools, and water supplies, generally all of which are known risk factors for *E. coli*, meaning that to really avoid the germ you would have to refuse to touch or be touched by anyone else, or indeed anything that they have been near. The point is, *E. coli* is *everywhere*, including in our intestines, where it helps the body break down food, produce vitamin K, and absorb nutrients. Alas, the modern notion that a germ-free world is healthy has allowed the over-prescription of antibiotics that can upset this digestive balance, as a diet of excessively sterile foods can do too. Thus, this ubiquitous bacterium underlines all three food principles: *Detail matters*, *Everything connects*, and (above all) *Don't mess with the crystal vase*.

Chapter 16

Eat Something While It Is Still Alive

One of the great philosophical disputes of science was about this question: does life spring from chemicals—say, a patch of wet mud (although it might equally well be a piece of quiche left in the fridge too long)—or does it actually depend on tiny, invisible "seeds," what we now call bacteria? For thousands of years, the great Aristotle's teachings held that indeed, life could spring from mud, if not at the drop of a hat, certainly without the need for the click of God's fingers. It was only after a long experimental and intellectual battle in the nineteenth century between Louis Pasteur, himself a committed Catholic, and the scientific establishment that Pasteur was able prove that life *cannot* spontaneously generate from simple chemical reactions.*

Even today, when evolutionary biologists maintain that life (including bacteria, of course) did indeed arise, over the course of millions of years, from chemical reactions between inorganic molecules, the process is so complex that they often resort to the fortuitous arrival of simple organic compounds to early Earth on meteorites.

Ever since then, the story of modern food has been the story of bacteria. As food production became industrialized, bacteria became a big problem. Refrigerators play a supporting role in spreading the "bacteria are bad" mind-set too.

As indicated in chapter 15, "Eat Dirty," humans have a rather conflicted attitude toward bacteria. For a start, we don't really accept that our bodies are (more or less) convenient vehicles for these ancient life forms, and that while they can do quite well without us, we would soon die without them. And we are conflicted too about what bacteria say about the very origins of life, which seems to reduce us to being merely the product of randomness.

The end result is that today, about the only way people will knowingly "eat" bacteria is in the form of yogurt. It is precisely because of its bacteria that yogurt is considered to be a healthy food...and so it is, in principle. Unfortunately, most modern-day yogurt—the kind you buy in many supermarkets—is little containers of denatured, sugary milk in which only the fruity bits are a treat. Add to which, most yogurts these days, being carefully pasteurized, have no bacteria left, although some brands make a feature of having added them back in.

By contrast, the special thing about "real" yogurts is precisely the micro-organisms in it. Amazingly, once swallowed, they tuck into everything else you eat and help keep you slim. Or rather, they would do that if given the chance. Even well-intentioned yogurt makers may struggle to produce healthy yogurt as farmers have for decades. This is because cattle are routinely given antibiotics in order to make them put on weight. A similar fattening effect may have been unwittingly passed on to human customers. Certainly, as Professor Martin Blaser of New York University puts it, "It is possible that early exposure to antibiotics primes children for obesity later in life." He noted, back in 2012, that the rise of obesity around the world coincided with increased antibiotic use, and that laboratory studies (those poor mice again!) have demonstrated a possible linkage.

Diet Tips: Know Your Yogurt

• Most commercial yogurts are fattening junk foods.

• Low-fat yogurts often contain things like high fructose corn syrup instead—which is much worse than dairy fat.

• Greek yogurt made from whole milk is a tasty and healthy alternative to other commercial yogurts. The Greeks make yogurt by straining it to remove much of the sugar, lactose (another sugar that milk naturally contains), and whey—which is the liquid remaining after the milk is curdled—all of which makes it not only thicker and more creamy but doubles the amount of protein in it compared to regular yogurt.

• And if most yogurts are made from cow's milk, don't forget there are specialty yogurts made from sheep and goat's milk too. These are rich, creamy milks that are also easier to digest.

But there's a potentially more direct fattening effect from yogurt too. Most of the stuff found in stores is the low-fat variety…which may be highly fattening. Sounds paradoxical? That's food science! When manufacturers remove the fat from foods, it makes them taste awful, so they add a whole bunch of other stuff to compensate. Things like high-fructose corn syrup (HFCS). Consider yourself lucky if you find a yogurt with just added sugar! One variety that otherwise sounds healthy, for example, is Tillamook's Oregon Strawberry low-fat yogurt—and each 6-ounce pot contains an amazing 30 grams of sugar! (At least this particular brand doesn't contain HFCS.) By contrast, conventional, unsweetened, full-fat Greek yogurt contains no added sugar, but only whole milk and bacterial cultures.

There is no evidence that eating dairy fat makes people fat. In fact, some studies have found the opposite! Since it is generally accepted nowadays that saturated fat is actually harmless, low-fat yogurt, like low-fat or skim milk, is something from which the good stuff has been removed, often to be replaced with something that is much worse. And fattening.

You Are Your Bacteria

It was Louis Pasteur who proved that lurking in the most unexpected places were tiny seeds of life—bacteria. Pasteur is rightly considered one of the great names of science for showing how such seeds could cause illness and how to destroy them. Yet if pasteurization—the process whereby foods, especially dairy, are robbed of their living bacteria—opened the way to safe and efficient dairy products, canned food, and the like, it also had the unintended consequence of upsetting the natural balance of our bodies.

Mere hippy talk? Consider this: cell for cell, the human body contains more bacterial life than it does human! Justin Sonnenburg, a microbiologist at Stanford University, has even suggested that we would do well to begin regarding the human body as "an elaborate vessel optimized for the growth and spread of our microbial inhabitants." The old saying "no man is an island" should remind us that each human being is actually an archipelago of life—many thousands of different organisms, most of them bacterial—coexisting. Amazingly, the human body contains about 90percent bacterial cells! At least, that is, by number. These bacteria are essential for processes like digestion, growth, and fighting disease, and they also seem to have subtler effects like changing one's mood from negative to positive. Sound impossible? Bacteria directly regulate our nerve transmission system.

Few things illustrate the importance of respecting our invisible inhabitants more than the issue of breast milk. Until recently mothers' milk was supposed to be bacteria free—it is of course nothing of the kind. This explains why babies reared on carefully sterilized artificial preparations enter life with inadequate protection from disease and digestive problems. Radically opposed views of the health advantages of mothers' milk over formula came to a head in the late 1970s over the issue of what was considered excessively aggressive marketing of the latter to women in developing countries, particularly in Africa, by the Swiss-based Nestlé corporation. A boycott was launched in Europe in the mid-1970s against the multinational company, and soon expanded to the U.S. One British campaign group, War on Want, even dubbed the company "The Baby Killer" in a 1974 report that accused multinational companies of causing infant illness and death in poor communities by promoting bottle feeding and discouraging breastfeeding. So great became public concern (not to say outrage) that the matter was debated by the UN World Health Assembly (the governing body of the World Health Organization) and in 1981 it recommended the adoption of an international code of conduct to govern the promotion and sale of breast milk substitutes. Thus a battle over baby milk formula became a key factor in a new recognition that there needed to be global regulation of the global food industry.

But back to weight control: researchers have found that, exactly as one might expect, a healthy bacterial community living in the gut is associated with a healthy weight—and obesity is marked by deficiencies in gut bacteria. This is not to say that one causes the other (but the correlation is there and indisputable. Maybe it is because people who eat lots of whole grains and fresh vegetables have many more bacteria in their digestive systems. Because, as food writer Michael Pollan has put it in an article called "Some of My Best Friends are Germs", *:

> The less a food is processed, the more of it that
> gets safely through the gastrointestinal tract and
> into the eager clutches of the microbiota. Al dente
> pasta, for example, feeds the bugs better than
> soft pasta does; steel-cut oats better than rolled;
> raw or lightly cooked vegetables offer the bugs

more to chomp on than overcooked, etc. This is at once a very old and a very new way of thinking about food: it suggests that all calories are not created equal and that the structure of a food and how it is prepared may matter as much as its nutrient composition.

Part IV
The Economics of Eating

Chapter 17

The Marxist Theory of Snacks

The truth about snacks is that, yes, we do get peckish, but that's not really why we snack. It is the promise of something more that makes the bag of chips or the square of chocolate grow immeasurably in importance.

The revolutionary leader of yesterday, Karl Marx, gives a possible insight into this snacking tendency. He once said (or rather, laboriously explained in one of his long, rambling philosophical treatises) that any commodity serves not merely a particular need but also the promise of "something more," something unfathomable, indeed fantastical.

In this sense, it is the inadequacy of the snack that defines it: a three-course meal can never be as tempting as a sneaky snack or an illicit nibble. The idea extends to the concept of the dessert too—again often, and paradoxically, more enticing than the main course.

Marx knew all about this kind of deception, of course. For Marxists, all capitalism is a fraud on the public—and the food industry is one of the worst offenders. It manipulates our desires in order to rob us of our pennies—and it is heartless enough not to care if in the process it ruins our health. Capitalism "dispels all fixity and security in the situation of the laborer... it constantly threatens ...to snatch from his hands his means of subsistence, and ...make him superfluous," Marx wrote of his imaginary working man.

And for strict Marxists, the logic of the "food industry" is that it must forever provide worse-quality food to more and more customers. As it is put in the Economic Manuscripts (1894):

> There are not too many necessities of life
> produced, in proportion to the existing population.
> Quite the reverse. Too little is produced to
> decently and humanely satisfy the wants of the
> great mass. There are not too many means of
> production produced to employ the able-bodied
> portion of the population. Quite the reverse....

Yet, time seems to have shown that he was wrong about capitalism "eating itself," as it were. Instead it seems to create enough wealth to avoid this desperate remedy. But in another way, food does seem to fulfill one of Marx and Engels' predictions: the rapacious demands of the market have torn down geographical and cultural distinctions and barriers. An otherwise politically reactionary blue-collar laborer will quite happily grab Chinese takeout, a Turkish kebab, or even a French baguette on the way home from the ballgame. For that, I suppose, liberals should be grateful.

Marx's dietary advice is to be aware of the capitalist forces compelling you to snack—and pre-empt them by packing your own healthy alternative in the morning. And although his writings largely pass over food matters, his personal life provides several valuable insights.

Karl Heinrich Marx was born in Trier, which was, and for that matter still is, a very bourgeois market town in Germany. His parents were impeccably bourgeois and ate very well. But although Marx himself benefited from not one but two substantial inheritances, he frittered away much of the money— partly on buying guns for revolutionary movements, partly on paying for a comfortable house near Hampstead Heath in a posh bit of London, and partly on sending the three of his children to the South Hampstead College for Ladies. Alas, the money eventually ran out, and Marx, still protesting furiously, wrote, "I will not allow bourgeois society to turn me into a money-making machine." But he had to redouble his money-making efforts, which consisted of writing letters to his revolutionary collaborator and friend, the factory owner Friedrich Engels.

When money was short, Marx fed the family solely on bread and potatoes, a diet many would worry about less for being fattening than for lacking certain essential nutrients. But in fact, potatoes, contrary to popular belief, actually contain a good supply of minerals and vitamins. They are a very good source of vitamin B6, potassium, copper, vitamin C, manganese, phosphorus, niacin, dietary fiber, and pantothenic acid. Plus, they contain important health-promoting plant compounds like carotenoids, flavonoids, and caffeic acid, as well as unique tuber storage proteins, such as patatin—all of which regulate the activity of free radicals (of the bodily tissue, not revolutionary, variety). It's the cheap oils they are often cooked in that are suspect. This all illustrates a very important and slightly Marxist point: the health properties of meals are often skewed in people's perceptions by considerations of how "posh" the foods are, with cheap foods often wrongly downgraded.

Marxists Living Off Water Get Too Thin

Potatoes are not, as you might imagine, full of fat. In fact, Russet potatoes, the kind we usually eat baked, mashed, fried, or as chips, contain a mere 0.1 percent fat by weight! The bulk of a potato is mostly water, which doesn't tell you much since most foods are full of water. But the next most significant component is carbohydrate, which does tell you something. It underlines the point that potatoes contain a kind of sugar, and that is why, assuming that you are not burning off the energy they provide, eating them can be fattening.

Marx himself suffered from perpetual ill health: carbuncles and boils and hemorrhoids. After one nasty incident Marx was prescribed three to four glasses of port and half a bottle of claret daily, and four times his normal food intake in order to restore the strength he'd lost. The fate of Karl and his wife, Jenny's, seven children was not to be envied either: malnutrition took the lives of four of them in infancy. By a strange contrast, one of his daughters suffered from anorexia.

But back to happier times. The word about Marx's drinking skills first got around in his days as a student. In 1835 he had a promising start at the University of Bonn to study law, of all things, but he soon became increasingly distracted from his studies, as he was the co-president of his tavern club. Marx even got imprisoned for a day for "disturbing the peace with drunken noise." His period of "wild rampaging," as his father Heinrich Marx called it, lasted only a year, because his father transferred his errant progeny to the University of Berlin, where Marx was instead encouraged to imbibe a heady brew of philosophical ideas. Even this didn't stop him from consuming large amounts of beer, though, followed by the occasional drunken donkey ride through neighboring villages.

Marx may be a terrible example to follow in many ways, but curiously there are surprising health benefits of a regular pub crawl, all of which may go to justify the long-established link between Marxism and beer-drinking on nutritional grounds.

The hops in beer have a very useful anti-inflammatory effect.

The bitter acids in beer improve digestion.

Two types of bitter acid in beer, lupulone and xanthohumol, are claimed (based on those unreliable studies on defenseless rats) to have cancer-fighting effects at relatively low doses—equivalent to what people might get from drinking beer. Xanthohumol has also been said to boost neurons in the brain by protecting against stress-induced cell damage.

Beer is a great source of silicon, which is important for building and maintaining healthy bones, and it combats bacteria that can lead to tooth decay.

Beer, like other alcoholic beverages, is rich in polyphenols that are thought to play a role in combating heart disease.

Last but not least, a study of 200,000 patients published in 2013 found that drinking beer reduced the risk of kidney stone formation by 60 percent.

Chapter 18

The Ethics of the Dinner Plate

There's a delicate dance performed at many meals between utility and ethics. For example, what should you do if it turns out your special celebration dinner consists of horse meat? Or if asked at a barbecue to eat dog burgers? And what about those fried grasshoppers?

Because, well, you know, someone may have gone to a lot of trouble to make those meals. Better not cause offense! Indeed, for many people, from German playwright Bertolt Brecht, who had philosophical pretensions, to U.S. president Barack Obama, the general principle to follow is "Erst kommt das Fressen, dann kommt die Moral" ("First comes the food, then comes the moralizing")—a line from Brecht's 1928 play *The Threepenny Opera*.

This is a very common approach. Dieters often defer to this way of thinking when faced with social occasions in which the only way to accommodate their dietary needs would be to eat nothing, which would surely be rather ungracious. But the former U.S. president Barack Obama takes the eating prerogative a step further in his autobiography, *Dreams from My Father* when he drops broad hints to his readers that he believes there are no moral limits on what can be eaten. Where others might have been worried about frightening away "floating voters," he freely admits a very unusual range of culinary experiences:

> With Lolo, I learned how to eat small green chilli peppers raw with dinner (plenty of rice), and, away from the dinner table, I was introduced

to dog meat (tough), snake meat (tougher), and roasted grasshopper (crunchy).

Yet even a president can only resist public opinion so far. During the 2012 election he had to counterargue that even if he ate dog as a child, his opponent, Mitt Romney, had once gone on holiday with his dog in a crate strapped to the roof rack of his car. Which is worse? To those of us in the West with a great love for our pet animals, horses, dogs, or whatever, eating our furry friends is just a no-no. But few animals exist that are not considered delicacies in some region of the world. Strongly held convictions can exist side-by-side, so (for example) snails and horse meat are considered rather grand ingredients for many dishes in France—but just 20 kilometers away, in England, companies risk prosecution for sneaking such things into their premade meals.

Perhaps surprisingly, archaeological evidence of human snail eating goes back thousands of years and the Romans are known to have been harvesting them and treating them as an elite food 2,000 years ago. However, eating horse meat in France is a socially engineered and relatively recent phenomenon. Indeed, in the Christian world, *hippophagy* (to give it its grand title) was strictly taboo, particularly ever since an eighth-century pope described it as an "abomination." Likely his concern had more to do with criticizing the pagans of northern Europe, who sacrificed and ate horses, than any carefully thought- out ethical principles or concern for animal welfare. Nonetheless, throughout Christendom, horse meat was considered a food to be resorted to only by those in the direst straits, such as the French peasantry during the food shortages of the Revolution, or the armies of Napoleon on campaign in the depths of the Russian winter, and right up until the mid-nineteenth century the French were as disapproving about it as anybody else in Europe.

The implausibly named Piu Marie Eatwell, a British writer who lives in France, has written a book, *They Eat Horses, Don't They?: The Truth about the French* (2014), about the forces that changed Gallic menus. She explains:

> In fact, it wasn't until the 1860s or even later that the French really got into horsemeat, largely due to the efforts of a zoologist named Étienne Geoffroy Saint-Hilaire, and a fanatical military veterinarian, Émile Decroix. Decroix was obsessed with proving (to a skeptical public) that horsemeat was edible, and to this end he chomped his way through several hundred dead horses suffering from every conceivable disease, and even a mad dog by way of comparison—the purpose of the rabid canine *amusebouche* being presumably to prove that, if you could survive eating a mad dog, you could survive eating a horse.

To promote the idea, a number of "horse meat banquets" were thrown, including a particularly famous one in 1865 at the Grand Hôtel in Paris. At this, according to the respected dining authority the *Larousse Gastronomique*, the menu was as follows:

A Horsemeat Menu
- *Horse-Broth Vermicelli*
- *Horse Sausage and Charcuterie Boiled Horse*
- *Horse à la Mode*
- *Horse Stew*
- *Fillet of Horse with Mushrooms*
- *Potatoes Sautéed in Horse Fat*
- *Salad Dressed in Horse Oil*
- *Rum Gâteau with Horse Bone Marrow*
- *Wine: Château Cheval-Blanc*

The horse meat banquets in Paris inspired similar events in Britain, such as one in Ramsgate at which the choice dishes were grandly and euphemistically described as "chevaline delicacies." However, neither in Britain nor in France did the taboo really weaken. What changed things across the Channel was the Siege of Paris during the Franco–Prussian War of 1870–71. At this time, Parisians found themselves cut off from their customary food supplies and in desperation started to eat not only horses but cats, dogs, and rats. As the siege dragged on, the diners even tucked into the exotic animals in the Paris zoo! As Eatwell recounts, camels, kangaroos, and finally the zoo's famous elephants Castor and Pollux—all were auctioned off to Paris butchers, who made a special dish out of slices of the elephant's trunks (culinarily speaking the most prized part of an elephant's anatomy) for wealthy Parisians.

How could eating elephant trunks have ever been chic? Yet with food, anything is possible. Continuing the theme of *haute cuisine,* one unusual food that you might refuse to eat in disgust at a BBQ is deep fried crickets—yet at the British Mexican restaurant, Wahaca, chili-fried grasshoppers is a pulling point, while in Thailand many people regularly enjoy them as a snack taken with a glass of beer. The fact is, the criteria for deciding which creatures we are prepared to eat are very confused. Insects, for example, are, according to the United Nations, an "overlooked protein supply"—and overlooked I'm sure they are.

The UN Food and Agriculture Organization argues that insects are a sustainable source of good-quality protein with a smaller environmental footprint than conventional meats. It points out, for example, that crickets need only one-eighth of the food input that cattle do to yield the same amount of edible protein. And even if you think that eating insects is just one step too far in the name of ecological awareness, hold on, because insect protein is more ubiquitous than you might imagine. Few of us have avoided inadvertently eating (or drinking) some small portion of ground-up insects. Indeed, it is claimed that 80 percent of the world already eats bugs. In Germany and other countries, people fry crickets and moths, and many more people consume the same bugs in ground-up form. Aketta cricket flour is admired by gourmets for its "earthy and nutty taste," and is used to make things like muffins and chocolate brownies. Yummy! Germans also have a taste for bee larvae, while in France and Belgium diners enjoy caterpillars. In South Africa, locusts, caterpillars, and mopane worms are the thing.

Restaurants alone won't change the world's eating habits, but farming might and, yes, a new insect farm near Los Angeles has started farming what it describes as "micro-livestock." These are crickets and meal worms. Now, meal worms sound promising, if you ignore the worm bit—but they are in reality black beetles at the particularly yucky larval stage. They've long been used for baiting fish hooks and as food for fish that live in aquariums. (If you're tempted to try them, bear in mind that commercial suppliers use hormones to affect the development of the worms, a practice that is far from established to be without side effects for humans.)

But back to President Obama. It might seem strange to bring a former president into a philosophy book, but Obama illustrates very well the link between eating and public policy. As mentioned above, in his perceptive autobiography, *Dreams from My Father: A Story of Race and Inheritance*, eating rituals are granted deep significance and in his second book, *The Audacity of Hope*, (Crown/Three Rivers Press, 2006) there is a very revealing food-related anecdote. In this, Obama describes how one time, when he was very young, the family returned home to find a man whose job it was to help with their luggage standing outside waiting for them, with a hen tucked under one arm and a long knife in the other. He recalls the man saying something, to which his mother replied, "Don't you think he's a little young?" Here, in a simple story, is something of the ambivalence we have toward eating animals.

Indeed, it seems that the killing of the bird did have a profound effect on the young Obama— but it wasn't what his mother expected! Instead, Obama recalls, he enjoyed seeing it so much that he couldn't help replaying it over and over again in his head that night as he was going to sleep.

The point is that eating is unavoidably a philosophical matter. All meals come with an ethical overlay, whether the meal is low-cal, vegetarian, halal, or one prepared to accommodate the guest who won't count as a meal anything that is not meat. All of these diets reflect in their own way deeply held beliefs. Brecht had it the wrong way around: *first* comes the morals, *then* comes the eating.

Grilled Eggplant and Tomatoes

So, what do you say if you're invited to a barbecue at which celebs like Barack Obama are eating dog meat (tough), snake meat (tougher), and roasted grasshopper (crunchy)? Happily, there are alternatives for free thinkers prepared to look for them.

1 large eggplant, sliced into rounds about ½-inch thick

3 to 4 medium ripe tomatoes, sliced

2 to 3 spring onions or scallions, white parts and a little of the green, sliced

Extra virgin olive oil and white wine vinegar to taste

1 to 2 cloves garlic, crushed (or more to taste)

3 to 4 ounces goat cheese

Fresh basil leaves, chopped

Grilled Eggplant and Tomatoes (cont.)

Place the sliced veggies in a dish and pour a little olive oil and white wine vinegar over them. Add crushed garlic to taste. Allow to marinate for 10 to 30 minutes. Remove eggplant slices from the marinade and grill until soft and slightly brown. Arrange the eggplant in a shallow serving dish. Next, grill the tomatoes and spring onions until soft and slightly charred. (A grill basket may come in handy for grilling these smaller items.) Arrange on top of the eggplant, crumble the goat cheese over the veggies, sprinkle with basil, and finish with a little more olive oil. Serve in barbecued Wittgenstein Bread or with Muffins of the Gods.

Chapter 19

The Economics of Obesity

Marxists would have no trouble seeing that fat is both a very political personal matter and also a global economic issue. And these days most conventional economists would agree with them. It is now estimated that obesity costs the global economy around $2 trillion, or around 3 percent of GDP. For a medium-sized economy like that of the UK, economists conjure with a cost to society of around $70 billion a year. This is because around 20 percent of healthcare spending is attributed to obesity, which is recognized as contributing to conditions like cardiovascular disease, type 2 diabetes, and some cancers. Much of the rest of the cost is counted in lost working days and increased benefit payments.

Whatever the exact reason, these are staggering sums. Little less amazing is how little attention economists, much less politicians, give to the "epidemic." Partly this is because the causes are complex, spanning the social sciences to biology and technology. Consider, for example, the shift toward urbanization and car transport. By reducing many people's daily physical activity, these are estimated together to reduce an individual's need for food by 300 calories a day. Explanations like these seem to make sense, yet, hold on: just how much less food would a car driver need to forego to compensate? About one or two cookies less per day—a trivial change that only goes to illustrate that few of us really understand the energy needs of our bodies.

In market terms, the idea is that to make rational choices people need to know how much energy they expend and how much they are getting, yet neither of these factors is known. In fact, as anyone who has ever tried to lose weight knows, in these matters talk is cheap and advice is unreliable. At various times sugars, protein, fat, starch, fast-foods, home cooking, and snacks have all been held responsible for the obesity epidemic. Even fruit juices!

Back in the 1950s, the dominant theory was that eating fat was responsible for making you fat—and by sating one's appetite, sugar could help prevent weight gain. As described in chapter 13, the sugar industry promoted an ostensibly virtuous public health message that sugar was actually a smart way to curb appetite. One ad (highlighted in that chapter) even said, "Nibble on a Cookie, Enjoy an Ice Cream or Have a Soft Drink before your main meal."

The campaign suited the U.S. Food and Drug Administration, which already had a preferred target—dietary fat. Identifying sugar as an alternative cause of conditions like heart disease and obesity undermined their message. And, as mentioned in the Food Myth "Drink More Water," even if you think that public health messages should not be outsourced to food businesses, well, they always have been and today they still are, as Michelle Obama's 2013 "Drink Up" campaign exemplified.

Today, food companies have a commercial interest to deflect rhetoric about poor diet being the primary cause of obesity; instead, they promote messages focused on exercise and other factors—a phenomenon termed "leanwashing."

Today, too, food companies have accepted that the political spotlight is now on sugar, with "environmental" changes proposed to reduce the appeal of sugary foods—such as warning labels and nutritional information labels. There's serious talk of taxing sugary foods, in the way that tobacco has been taxed. None of this is supported by any real evidence (it's pretty obvious, after all, that there are plenty of thin children who enjoy sugary foods, and plenty of fat people whose tastes lie elsewhere), but new taxes are always popular with governments.

Professor Kevin Fenton, of Public Health England, says there are "practical solutions." By these he means a sneaky and totally obligatory de-sugaring of foods like cakes, cookies, and pastries. But such foods aren't sugary by accident; they're sugary because that's what we like about them. It's like salted chips without the salt (yes, the health industry has pushed that one too). However, really making the overweight pay for their errors would present many ethical problems. Should obese people be charged more for health insurance? For air flights?

Another argument made for government intervention is that overeating results not from free-market choice—but from market failure. So it is the solemn duty of governments to intervene to redirect individual decisions. Nora Volkow, head of the U.S. National Institute on Drug Abuse, has even argued that food can be as addictive as drugs. In tune with this logic, in June 2013, the American Medical Association declared obesity a disease. If it is a disease, it is somewhat harder to hold individuals personally responsible for the consequences of their choices, a necessary condition for rational decision-making in properly functioning markets.

Seeing the issue very differently is the American economist Richard McKenzie, who links the rise of obesity precisely to free-market economics. He points out, for example, that fast food has become cheaper, in part because of mechanization and in part because the workers producing it are paid less and less relative to the budgets available to customers. At the same time, the economic forces propelling 1960s housewives away from the kitchen and into jobs also propel families toward processed foodstuffs and eating out… or to snacking in place of eating meals. *Everything connects.*

Perhaps the most paradoxical thing about obesity is that it is supposed to be a rich-world disease, and yet within the rich world it is generally the poorer people who are obese. We've all been brought up on images of poverty being linked to malnutrition and skinny, rake-like children. In cartoons and paintings, the rich are always portrayed as plump and greedy. Such stereotypes are hard to shake off. Yet the reality is that today, it is quite the other way around. Today, poverty and obesity go hand in hand.

The tragedy is that obesity is usually treated as a problem and responsibility of individuals or families—not as a social problem like, say, low-educational achievement or delinquency. And so the solutions are pitched at that individual or family level. However, the statistic points remorselessly toward obesity being a symptom with an underlying social cause.

In the United States, for example, the most "obese" state, Arkansas, is also the fourth poorest state of the Union, whereas the poorest, Mississippi, is also the third most overweight. But the picture in the second poorest state, New Mexico, is complicated by another factor: ethnicity.

Nonetheless, even if New Mexico has "only" the 33rd highest adult obesity rate in the nation, the correlation of wealth and health still leaves its unmistakable fingerprint. Here, the adult obesity rate is 34.4 percent among black adults, 31.3 percent among Latino adults, and a comparatively sprightly 23.9 percent among white adults, this again reflecting wealth distribution. Meanwhile, color correlates to poor health and reduced life expectancy.

At least there isn't a large health difference between New Mexican men and women, with 26.7 percent of men and 27.6 percent of women obese. But then, men and women form the same social units: families.

Recent studies in England reveal the link between obesity and income even more clearly. Of the ten worst areas in England, in terms of overweight or obese children, half are also in the worst ten for child poverty. England's most obese council, Brent, is also its ninth poorest, whereas England's wealthiest council, Richmond, despite being, in geographical terms, a neighboring council in London, is one of the least overweight, coming in toward the other end of the scale, at number 214. England's poorest council, Newham, is also the eighth most affected by childhood obesity.

In its way, the obesity epidemic is as disgraceful an indictment of social priorities and inequality as the nineteenth-century health epidemics of rickets or typhoid—and the solutions needed are every bit as collective rather than individual.

A good illustration of confused public priorities is that substantial amounts of public funds, billions of dollars in the U.S. alone, go toward subsidizing junk foods, through farm subsidies for producing their junky ingredients—corn oil, soybeans, and high-fructose corn syrup. (One study cites more than a $1.3 billion in the U.S. in just the year 2011.)

That said, it still remains the case, as Mark Bittman put it in an article "Is Junk Food Really Cheaper?" for the *New York Times*, that, in general, highly processed supermarket food is more expensive than food prepared and cooked at home. However, it suits Big Ag for people to think healthy eating is expensive—because it corrals them into the supermarkets as passive consumers.

Ironically, the free market shows its hand most clearly in the activities of the food companies accused of selling energy-dense food that leads to obesity. These same companies have seamlessly moved into making money from the obesity crisis by selling weight-loss products and programs! In the words of the American economists George Akerlof and Robert Shiller:

Free markets, as bountiful as they may be, will not only provide us with what we want, as long as we can pay for it; they will also tempt us into buying things that are bad for us, whatever the costs.

One of those revealing national polls conducted in the United States, this one from 2012, surveyed more than 1,000 women about their habits and feelings vis-à-vis healthy eating. Among the practical issues they raised were:

- *Number 1. Healthy food is too expensive.*
- *Number 2. Healthy eating takes up too much time.*

Of course, people are often poor judges of what is really motivating them. Reasons like number 1 here are often chosen because people feel they make sense—even though, of course, our behavior is based more on feelings than logic. This response shows a disconnection from reality, because, for example, although governments have poured money into junk food—through the agricultural subsides mentioned above—in general, hyperprocessed food remains more expensive than food cooked at home.

No, the real challenge is that most of us are too busy to cook. "People really are stressed out with all that they have to do, and they don't want to cook," says Julie Guthman, associate professor of community studies at the University of California, Santa Cruz, and author of a book that focuses on what she calls "food justice" called *Weighing In: Obesity, Food Justice, and the Limits of Capitalism* (UC Press, 2011).

Americans are so short of time that, as another of those peculiarly revealing studies found, those between the ages of 18 and 50 now consume one-fifth of their daily food while driving! No wonder research indicates that most of the excess intake of calories comes in the form of snacks, not in actual sit-down meals.

This is terrible on so many levels. We can feel sorry for folks who eat like that. But wait: if people like Michael Pollan are to be believed, the typical, modern sit-down meal, the one *we* eat (when we do have time), in reality is a mix of soybeans and corn oil. *That* doesn't sound very appetizing or healthy—and it isn't. What's more, it is, of course, fattening. So why are we eating this junk; why are we doing this to our bodies? But corn syrup and soy oil are hidden in the most unexpected places—even in things like low-fat milk! These two junky ingredients are inserted surreptitiously into many modern foods in one form or another. Indeed, it's estimated that three-quarters of the vegetable oils in the average American's daily diet come from soy, representing about one-fifth of their daily quota of calories. Add to that the fact that half of the sweeteners consumed each day, the ones put into food to replace supposedly evil natural sugars, come from corn, and it brings the contribution of both crops to one-third of the day's calories! Yet you wouldn't even think you had had any. It really is "force-feeding," and if that seems unethical, the industry's response is "too bad." Because soy and corn are the two cheapest and most profitable crops for agriculture—and therefore are profitable for food manufacturers. So, if you consume any processed foods at all, you're going to eat them whether they are good for you or not.

Soy is so profitable for the world's largest multinational agribusinesses (companies like Cargill, Archer Daniels Midland, and Solae) that collectively these companies are sometimes referred to as "Big Soy." And the food industry long ago fell head over heels in love with Big Soy (as well as his inseparable mate, GM corn), which as well as being cheap is incredibly versatile. With soy, no fragment of the plant is discarded. Soy milk isn't really a "milk" at all (meaning it doesn't come from dairy animals) but merely the liquid left over when soybeans are cooked in water, maybe along with added flavorings and sweeteners. During the manufacture of soy oil, the bean produces a substance called *lecithin* that is used to bind oil and water in many processed foods (it is an emulsifier). And the husk of the bean can be added to breads and breakfast cereals as a source of fiber.

Processed and refined, soy appears on ingredient labels as everything from "soy protein isolate" to "textured vegetable protein" to "plant sterols." Worldwide, soy oil is the food industry's most widely used plant oil. It is often listed as "vegetable oil" on packaging, and can be found in margarines, spreads, and salad dressings. Soy turns up in premade meals, sausages, soups, takeout food, chips, pet food, and agricultural feed.

All of which explains why, in the U.S. alone, the retail soy-foods industry is worth more than $5 billion a year. And it helps explain why one of the food industry's best-kept secrets is that, *sssh*...soybeans are actually an *anti food*—eat them and they wreck your digestion. Industrial soy is made in a way that denatures proteins and increases levels of carcinogens. *Don't mess with the crystal vase.* Once it gets into your stomach it quickly gets to work blocking the body's absorption of essential vitamins and minerals—things like calcium, iron, and zinc—and inhibiting the digestion of protein, thus making you fat—as if being poisoned and getting cancer wasn't enough! Last but not least, soy *isoflavones* imitate the female hormone estrogen, with unpredictable consequences for the development of certain cancers and menopause.

You've probably heard soy's supporters claim numerous health benefits for the plant, but most likely not that studies have linked it to thyroid problems and impaired endocrine function as well as harmful effects on reproductive development. In the UK, parents are formally advised not to feed infants soy formula before they are six months old. Because, as Retha Newbold, co-author of a U.S. National Institute of Environmental Health Sciences study, says: "Giving an infant or child estrogen is never a good thing."

But hang on, you may say, hasn't soy been eaten in China for thousands of years? Well, yes and no. The U.S. nutritionist Kaayla T. Daniel, who admittedly enjoys controversy but equally has made a special study of the history of soy consumption, dismisses such comparisons, pointing out that the soy eaten in China and Japan, such as tofu and miso, is very different from the industrially processed variety used in today's Western food. These long-established soy foods, including soy sauce, tamari, miso, tempeh, tofu, and soy milk, were developed using traditional fermentation or precipitation methods that neutralize the toxins in soybeans. Many of these foods use the whole bean and are healthier than foods based on soy protein isolates, which are extracts from the beans.

Bottom line is that soy, like many foods, has both supporters and detractors. At which point, people, like my nine-year-old, who loves soy milk, tend to say, well, if soy really was that bad, wouldn't governments do something? But governments are doing plenty—only it's got more to do with money than health. Sorry, kids! All over the developed world, governments that lecture people about not eating sweets and getting more exercise have, over the last fifty years, been busy pouring public cash into farming in such a way that the price of soy and corn have dropped by about a third while the price of real foods like vegetables and fruit have increased by 40 percent.

In this way, whatever the facts about the health effects of soy beans, government policy for years has been pushing people toward buying snacks, instant meals, and the like that happen to contain cheap soy and corn products and away from expensive real foods! One way or another, modern cash crops are contributing to a public health crisis.

All of which only goes to show that home cooking is, as the Slow-Food Movement puts it, a very political act, all about returning to traditional foods, quality ingredients, and leisurely meals in family-owned restaurants. For more about the Slow-Fooders, check out part V on "Futurist Eating"!

Slim Rascal

Dieters run a mile from cakes and other desserts because they're sugary and, well, fattening. Scones at least are not sugary but then, they're not as tasty either. Which is where the traditional "Fat Rascal," made famous by Bettys Tearooms in Yorkshire in England comes in. Basically a large scone, it is made temptingly delicious by the addition of dried fruit, almonds, and cherries. (It's worth investing in a good food scale; for baked goods, measuring dry ingredients by weight instead of by volume—the traditional American way—is much more precise.)

250g of white self-raising flour

1½ teaspoons baking powder

Pinch of salt

1 teaspoon nutmeg

½ teaspoon cinnamon

100g butter, softened

75g currants

50–75g mixed candied citrus peel,* minced fine

75g superfine sugar

2 eggs

½ cup milk

Glacé cherry halves and blanched almonds
(for decoration)

*Available in better grocery stores.

Slim Rascal (cont.)

Preheat the oven to 425°F and grease two baking trays.

In a mixing bowl, blend the flour, baking powder, salt, nutmeg, and cinnamon. Add the butter, blending with your hands. Mix in the currants, candied citrus peel, and sugar. Beat one of the eggs with the milk and add to the mix. Add more milk as necessary to form a dough.

Form several dough balls, each about 3 to 4 inches in diameter. Decorate each dough ball with candied cherry halves for eyes and blanched almonds for teeth. Arrange the dough balls close together on the prepared baking sheets (when the dough softens in the oven, the cherries and almonds will spread quite a bit). Beat the second egg, and brush over the scones for a glaze. Bake for 15 to 20 minutes, until golden brown. Check on them after 15 minutes, as an overcooked "rascal" is not good to anybody.

Serve warm, sliced in half, with butter.

Chapter 20

Eat All Your Meals Out and Only Nibble Snacks at Home

That's the deeply politically incorrect advice of the French existentialist philosophers. The glittering star in this firmament of imposing-sounding philosophy is Jean-Paul Sartre, author of heavyweight tomes like the 600-page-plus *Being and Nothingness* (1943). One of the characteristic themes of the existentialists is that what people say they are doing, speaking not only to others but to themselves, is often not what they are doing at all. Sartre calls this kind of hypocrisy "bad faith" and, of course, we are all particularly prone to it in food matters.

Despite, or perhaps because of having a privileged, impeccably bourgeois background, and being brought up enjoying rich, heavy meals always washed down with plenty of red wine, Sartre harshly attacks fat, seeing the "involuntary movements" of the extra layer as a "deformity" and emblematic of a loss of control, both because (most) people do not wish to be overweight, and because fat cannot be controlled in the same way as muscle can. He even wrote of his own deep dread of one day becoming "a bald little fatty."

In a book he called his *War Diaries*, Sartre says that the "horror of growing fat came upon me quite late," and he had only realized with a shock that overindulgence had left him "a real little Buddha."

At first he and his friends just joked about it, but later he admits he developed "a horror of fat people." He realized that this stemmed from a kind of fear, the fear that he had a tendency to gain weight if he didn't watch himself. Yet this watching oneself (and this is the existentialist theory coming in) was precisely the difficulty, precisely "the problem."

Dieters Making Their Excuses?

Because there's often a gap between what we do and what we think we should be doing, polls can mislead more than they inform. A nationwide survey in the United States in 2012 by *ShopSmart* magazine asked more than 1,000 women about their eating habits and feelings vis-à-vis healthy eating and found that the very understandable reason for snacking on junk was that "healthy food is too expensive." Other "real life factors" often cited by nutritionists were well down or even not included in the list. These are things like:

- A "dysfunctional family situation," such as divorce, single parenting, or foster care.

- A busy schedule with large amounts of time spent traveling.

- Feeling a need to save money by buying the cheapest foods.

- Depression or other emotional extremes.

- Lack of knowledge about what is healthy to eat.

Anyway, the end result was that Sartre became an on–off dieter, starting strict diets and torturing himself while anxiously checking for results in the bathroom mirror, and then, having achieved some small reduction and reassuring himself that his weight was back under control, becoming a lapsed dieter the next month.

> I go back to living as I please, I no longer watch myself, I grow fat, until the day I begin looking

anxiously at my belly again and reflecting on what measures must be taken to deflate it.

The problem is, Sartre observes, that a dieting resolution is not quite like any other self-imposed rule—say, to give up smoking a pipe or wearing a hat. Because it is very easy to just accidentally break your diet: to find yourself at the local bar enjoying a glass of red wine and the rolls French waiters always bring, even though in theory these have been banned.

Add to which the dieter, Sartre ruefully acknowledges, is always able to find exceptions to his or her rules. "Yes. I did decide that I'd eat nothing in the evenings, but that was on the assumption that I'd get a proper meal at midday." Or there was the "reasonable trade-off," to have not eaten bread at lunch, so a little now could be allowed. The end result was that Sartre would find himself quaffing red wine and eating bread in the bar while despising himself.

When he was not on a weight-loss regimen, though, Sartre's favorite light meal was saveloy, a spicy red pork sausage, with sauerkraut, all washed down by beer. Sausages fit in with his theory of food, a philosophy which led him to consider that processing food was good—by making it more truly a man-made product, which for him meant therefore better. This led him to prefer canned fruits and vegetables to the fresh ones, which he disliked as being "too natural."

Mainstream philosophy only really remembers Sartre. But Jean-Paul was just the showier half of a famous philosophical couple, formed in the 1930s at one of France's elite universities; his long-time partner was the writer and feminist Simone de Beauvoir.

Actually, Simone, of more modest origins, seems to have been cleverer than Sartre and also, their correspondence reveals, responsible for most of the big ideas in Sartre's later books— such as the importance of the gaze of the "other." De Beauvoir (nicknamed "the Beaver" by Sartre) used the concept of "the gaze of the Other" in detail in her books, including in passages describing what it was like to wander through an empty theatre (the stage, the walls, the chairs unable to come alive until there is an audience), or in her description of a woman in a restaurant who ignores the fact that her male companion has begun stroking her arm: "it lay there, forgotten, ignored, the man's hand was stroking a piece of flesh that no longer belonged to anyone." As well as this one:

> "It's almost impossible to believe that other people are conscious beings, aware of their own inward feelings, as we ourselves are aware of our own," said Francoise. "To me, it's terrifying when we grasp that. We get the impression of no longer being anything but a figment of someone else's mind."

In this passage, from She Comes to Stay (1943) Francoise expresses concerns that are no doubt similar to those of many dieters who are concerned with their appearance. Some have shifted directions and taken a deliberate stance against such worries. One such, Taryn Brumfitt, a former bodybuilder, has founded what she calls the Body Image Movement and campaigns against dieting in general and idealized body types in particular.

But back to the existentialists. Of the two, it seems that de Beauvoir was not only the better philosopher; she was the better cook. Or at least, as Sartre put it, he was "a worse cook than her." In keeping with the couple's famously unconventional relationship ("travel, polygamy, transparency"), if not fitting quite so well their avowedly progressive political views, they preferred to have all their meals in cafés and restaurants.

Unfortunately, the Second World War complicated their charmed existence along with their eating habits. De Beauvoir recalls how, during the winter of 1941–42, the period of the war when food was most scarce, and without the money to eat out, she had to interest herself in the minutiae of food for the first time. "I had little natural liking for domestic chores" she told one biographer, Carole Seymour-Jones, but now "the alchemy of cooking" became an obsession. And for three years, until the end of the war, she would serve up to Sartre meals like "turnip sauerkraut" made of turnips and beetroot, over which she poured a tin of soup. As others queued for their rations, the existentialists, being well-connected, received regular packages of rabbit meat from friends living in the country, albeit by the time the meat arrived it might be rotting and even covered in maggots. The next winter was even worse, and an already slim de Beauvoir lost 7 kilos (16 pounds) on a forced diet of bread and water. After the war, de Beauvoir never cooked again, and if she had to prepare a meal it was cold meats, cheese, and salads that she bought readymade. From the point of view of losing weight, a definite plus for both Sartre and de Beauvoir is that they also seem to have regularly engaged in vigorous cardio exercise—in the form of sex, and usually not with each other, but with rather younger third parties.

In her biography of Sartre, which allows only a supporting role for de Beauvoir, Annie Cohen-Solal reveals how his life was more or less equally divided between intense socializing—trips, rich meals, heavy drinking, drugs, and tobacco—and the monastic austerity of a rigid work schedule:

> Work till noon at Rue Bonaparte. Twelve-thirty: one hour of appointments, scheduled by his secretary. One-thirty: back at Rue Bonaparte, with Beauvoir, Michelle, or some other woman .... Two hours over a heavy meal, washed down with a quart of red wine.

Sartre had a sweet tooth and finished every meal with a dessert, and he liked chocolates with his coffee. But eventually, even French lunchtimes have to come to an end. Away from the table, Sartre tried to stimulate himself with more coffee, tea, wine, and a whole host of drugs, which he crunched through like candies:

> Punctually, at three-thirty, he would stop in mid-sentence, push away the table, get up, and run back to his desk at Rue Bonaparte.... When he felt really sick, and the doctor prescribed rest, he would opt for a compromise: less tobacco and fewer drugs for a week .... His diet, over a period of twenty-four hours included two packs of cigarettes and several pipes stuffed with black tobacco, more than a quart of alcohol—wine, beer, vodka, whisky, and so on—two hundred milligrams of amphetamines, fifteen grams of aspirin, several grams of barbiturates, plus coffee, tea, rich meals.

And now we have all the essential ingredients of the Existentialist Diet:

- Leisurely lunches and suppers with meat and wine and coffee
- Cigarettes and prescription drugs during the day (to help you through the gaps between meals)

Does it work? Well, no—not for weight loss or for overall health. But it is less fattening than you might imagine. The Existentialist Diet shares some key attributes with certain binge-eating diets, which hinge on eating one big meal a day. One recent (if small-scale) research study even found supporting evidence for it—but only if overall you under-eat. As long as you do this, since snacking generally helps the body to use the limited foods more efficiently, quite likely bingeing with a small number of big meals is actually a strategy for weight loss. When the newsmagazine *Nouvel Observateur* published a picture (taken in 1950) of de Beauvoir at age 42, nude in her bathroom (from behind), she was in fine form. The same cannot be said of Sartre, who (being short) even as a youth appeared a bit stout. Indeed, he seemed fated to rapidly become after all "a bald little fatty." Ah, the existential angst!

Indeed, in later life Sartre was put on a diet for health reasons. Or should we say he "chose" to go on a diet? The new diet, in any case, was still very much to his choice: steak *au poivre* (served with a generous amount of coarsely ground black pepper) and green beans.

Chapter 21

"Mindful" Eating

Being something of a snacker, or "grazer" as I prefer to put it, I've sometimes been accused of "mindless eating.' To be sure, this is said rather unkindly—but it's still a good reason to ask, "What is 'mindful eating'?" The good news is that there is, in fact, a proper answer to this, indeed a whole philosophy, dating back broadly to the work of various American hippies in the 1970s. Philosophically speaking, mindful eating approaches are rooted in Zen and other forms of Buddhism, with links to yoga. It is about experimenting with different facets of life, with eating being just one. The aim in all aspects is the same: to rediscover a lost harmony guided by ancient wisdom.

Practically speaking, mindful eating starts by learning to pay attention. Instead of eating, well, mindlessly—putting food into your mouth almost unconsciously, without really tasting it—you focus on food-related thoughts, feelings, and sensations. You learn to pay attention to:

- *Why* you feel like eating.
- *What* the food looks, smells, and tastes like.
- *How* you feel: both as you eat the food and later on as you digest it.

And you think about *where* the food came from: who might have grown it, how much it might have suffered before it was killed, whether it was grown organically, whether or not it is healthful.

That's quite a lot to think about! So no wonder lots of people seek some expert advice. One mindful food guru is Ram Dass, an American spiritual teacher and author of the book *Be Here*

Now, which describes his travels to India and his relationship with a Hindu guru called Neem Karoli Baba.

Ram Dass was actually born plain old Richard Alpert, on April 6, 1931, and for a while he worked at Harvard University conducting research on psychedelic drugs—until he was rather abruptly dismissed for, ahem, "breaking university rules." Let's not go into that. Anyway, it was shortly after this that he went to India, met another American spiritual seeker called Kermit Michael Riggs (I'm not making this up) and renamed himself Ram Dass, which means "servant of God."

Another highly respected mindful eater that people follow is Leo Babauta. He's a Zen-practicing vegan who lives in Davis, California, with his wife and six kids. Leo has described the benefits of the approach as follows:

- You learn to eat when you're hungry and stop when you're full.

- You learn to really taste food, and to distinguish the healthy from the less good stuff.

- And you start to appreciate that the unhealthy food isn't as tasty as you thought, nor does it make you feel very good.

Leo promises that as a result of these insights, overweight people can regain control of their eating, and everyone starts on a longer but important process of beginning to sort through the emotional issues we all have around food and eating. This takes a bit longer but is even more important.

But baby steps first: where do we start? One appropriately named "Mindfulness Diet" suggests finding a small piece of food, such as a raisin or nut, or (for the less radical, like me) a small chocolate, and to eat this morsel very slowly. Start by taking a close look at the food. Look at its texture. Look at its color. Next, close your eyes, and explore the food with your sense of touch. Is it hard or soft? Sticky or dry? And explore the food with your sense of smell. Take your first bite with your eyes closed, feeding yourself with your non-dominant hand. And sit at a table and formalize the occasion.

The initial aim is to become aware of different aspects of the food, using one sense at a time. This is what it means to eat mindfully. Now, begin eating. No matter how little the food is, take at least two bites to finish it. Chew very slowly, while paying close attention to the actual sensory experience of eating: the sensations and movements of chewing, the flavor of the food as it changes, and the sensations of swallowing.

As the mindfulness author and psychotherapist Christopher Willard recalled recently:

> I can still remember the raisin from that first mindfulness class I took in a family friend's basement office, almost twenty years ago. I myself was only 20 years old and from that first awe-inspiring taste of that raisin onward, I was hooked on exploring mindfulness. I walked out of the basement promising myself I would eat every meal like I ate that raisin.

Ah, memories! But this one is important for him, as mindful eating helped him to distinguish between emotional and physical hunger and became a powerful tool to regain control of his eating. However, all this focus on the food is only the preceding stage of a longer journey. "The liberating power of mindfulness takes deeper effect when you begin to pay mindful attention to your thoughts, emotions, and bodily sensations, all of which lead us to eat," or so advises the website mindfulnessdiet.com. It is this kind of awareness that is really the route out of stress eating and the guide to changing your whole relationship with food.

So we see that mindful eating has its roots in hippy philosophies. Some adherents go a little too far for me. What is presented as "an advanced meditation," revealing the Buddhist roots of the approach, is called simply "Emptiness." The idea is that in taking a piece of food, you learn to see that the food is "not self." *Er, what?* We need Ram Dass again:

> There is no one there, just food. Next, you see that the hand holding the fruit is not you either, it is just a part of body. After looking at the mind that is thinking about the hand, you will recognize that the mind is not you either.

The bottom line? "Eating is like putting nothing into nothing." Oh dear. Because it turns out that serious, "mindful eating" is not really compatible with enjoying food. Or as the American Buddhist monk Jack Kornfield says:

> The body is simply a vehicle to be cared for, and not to be pampered. Food is simply a means of sustaining life to continue your spiritual practice. *You are not eating because you enjoy eating*, but you are eating as a way to sustain your energy to continue your practice on the spiritual path. [Emphasis added.]

That's why another meditation on the "Repulsiveness of Food" is recommended for mindful eaters. This one promises that in rebalancing our eating habits we will come to contemplate the true nature of food.

Now learning to find food repulsive is surely a route to becoming thinner, but is it really a wise one? For myself, I'd settle instead for a milder form of mindful eating. Something more like the approach described by the Vietnamese Buddhist monk Thich Nhat Hanh, who says, "Drink your tea slowly and reverently, as if it is the axis on which the world earth revolves."

As wise people have long recognized, in the bottom of your tea cup lies true wisdom.

Food Myth: Eat More Fiber

Fiber is good, right? And because the body does not digest it, it's definitely non-fattening. But now "stealth fiber" is being added to processed foods. Too much can cause gastrointestinal "discomfort" and, of course, people have no way of knowing if they are consuming too much. It may lurk in everyday chocolate bars, drinks, and snacks. The fiber is called inulin (not to be confused with insulin, of course). There are two kinds of explanations for its increasing use. Joanne Slavin, a registered dietitian in the Department of Food Science and Nutrition at the University of Minnesota at St. Paul, offered Reuters Health this one:

> Food manufacturers, faced with demands to
> reduce calories, fat, and sodium while increasing
> fiber and flavor, are increasingly turning to
> products like inulin. They have discovered
> they can chemically manipulate the chemical
> structure of inulin to mimic tastes and textures
> consumers want in food. It's like a food
> manufacturer's nirvana.

Another reason is that inulin is cheap and reliable and makes products more profitable. But there's that problem. As Joanne Slavin says: "Normal fiber foods like wheat bran and legumes are self-limiting, it's hard to over eat them." But not inulin... it's very easy to overdo eating it and never know you're doing so, a situation made worse by the fact that the label may not say inulin, but rather oligosaccharide, oligofructose, or even the very natural-sounding chicory root extract. Certainly, if I had the choice, I would rather eat "chicory root" than any chemical-sounding things that I can't even pronounce! Which just goes to show how easily terms and associations can confuse in food matters, as in fact, even oligosaccharides and oligofructose are natural compounds found in plants.

Chicory (also known as "coffeeweed") is a common and sometimes misunderstood plant. It belongs to the sunflower and daisy family—close cousins to lettuce and dandelions. Couldn't get friendlier sounding than that. It was introduced by Europeans only relatively recently to the Americas, but it now grows so prolifically there that it's a common sight along roadside ditches and in meadows, recognizable by its soft blue flower. There are broad- and curly-leafed versions, sometimes known as endive and escarole. Chicory's outer leaves are green and a little bitter, while its lighter green inner leaves are milder.

The plant has long been used in Europe in salads, along with radicchio, a red-leafed variety. The leaves are low in calories and a good source of fiber, potassium, and vitamins C and B9. Chicory is blessed with small amounts of nearly every essential vitamin. It contains relatively high levels of the two minerals selenium and manganese, the first of which helps regulate the thyroid and the immune system, while the second supports the formation of healthy bones and other tissues and regulates the body's hormone levels. Then there's potassium, which aids kidney function, and phosphorus, which metabolizes proteins, sugar, and calcium. Among the vitamins it contains are vitamin B6, which helps regulate blood sugar levels and supports the nervous system, and vitamin C, which has many benefits including helping the body resist infection. Herbalists have long valued chicory as a treatment for a variety of ills, including as a liver tonic, to relieve upset stomachs, detoxify, to "calm the nerves," regulate the heartbeat, and treat osteoarthritis, gout, and diabetes.

And yes, chicory roots, as opposed to the leaves that some people use to enhance salads, contain inulin. This fiber is what biochemists call a prebiotic, a kind of fertilizer that stimulates the growth and activity of probiotics, which in turn regulate imbalances in the bacteria in the stomach and bowels. Chicory root contains oligosaccharides, which are present otherwise in only a few sources, including onions, leeks, garlic, legumes, and bananas.

Chicory and Walnut Salad

½ cup coarsely chopped walnuts

1–2 tablespoons sherry vinegar

3 tablespoons extra virgin olive oil

½ teaspoon Dijon mustard

Salt and freshly ground black pepper

4 cups (or so) tender chicory leaves, shredded

2 cups (or so) green leaf lettuce, shredded

1 head radicchio, chopped

½ cup dried cranberries

¼ cup shaved Parmesan

In a dry skillet, toast the nuts over medium-high heat until fragrant, about 2 minutes. Set aside to cool. In a small bowl, whisk together the vinegar, oil, mustard, and salt and pepper to taste. In a large bowl, toss the chicory, green leaf lettuce, radicchio, and dried cranberries with the dressing. Arrange on serving plates, and top with the toasted walnuts and the shaved parmesan cheese.

These days, inulin is extracted from natural sources and concentrated for industrial use. Unlike more familiar carbohydrates, which are broken down in the small intestines and turned into fuel for the body, inulin passes through the small intestines to the colon, where it stimulates the growth of "good bacteria." However, particularly in concentrated, extract form, it can also upset some stomachs. The first sign of protest is an unpleasant sensation of flatulence. Next is the full range of disturbance to the bowels as the body protests at this strange and indigestible intruder. In this way, inulin is a kind of unwanted symbol of a "brave new world" of artificially processed and manufactured food.

Part V
Futurist Eating

Chapter 22

Inventing a New Cuisine

It all started with the Futurist Manifesto, addressed to "all the living men on earth" and unveiled via the front page of the French newspaper *Le Figaro* on February 20, 1909. Written both to shock and to inspire, it promised nothing less than the "re-fashioning of the universe."

In practice, most of it concerned art, rather than politics—let alone food. The ideas on cooking only really came to fruition later with Filippo Tomasso Marinetti and Luigi Colombo's *Manifesto of Futurist Cooking* (1930) and Marinetti's even more outrageous *Futurist Cookbook* (1932). In both, Futurist food was proposed not merely to meet individual needs but to create a country of light, fit, quick men, ready to step into the new airplanes and throw grenades on villagers.

But whether the subject was art or cooking or warfare, the themes were always the same: danger, speed, and action—with plenty of glorified violence. War (as the ancient philosophers had promised) was again to be "the sole cleanser of the world," militarism was "beautiful," and science and technology were the new gods.

Futurism was the brainchild of Marinetti, a wealthy Italian playboy and poet. Even if relatively few people recognize the name, he was, in his way, a very influential political philosopher—because he was one of the key intellectuals behind the sparkly new doctrine of Fascism.

Fascism claimed sometimes to represent old traditions, but for Futurism, it was always out, out with the old and on, on to the new. Away with those traditional great artists and their dreary "old pictures," paintings that he described as so many graves lined up in a cemetery. And of course, "good riddance" to museums and libraries with their associated "gangrene" of professors and archaeologists. Futurism was all about, and only about, the new, the powerful, the modern.

As for food, Marinetti's big idea was that "what we think or dream or do is determined by what we eat and what we drink." It followed that meals should convey political and social messages. Indeed, of course, they inevitably do: anyone who eats a Big Mac with fries is celebrating the American Way, anyone who tucks into roast beef and potatoes is probably attempting to make themselves a rural English gentleman (or lady), and those who nibble avocado salad with pine nuts are likely aligning themselves with northern European social values, not to mention environmentalism and health.

Marinetti himself swept nutritional factors briskly aside by asserting that such matters could more efficiently be dealt with through routine doses of government-provided nutritional pills or powders. (The Nazis actually applied this approach on a huge scale, as explained in chapter 15.) He even confidently looked forward to a future when knives and forks (but maybe not spoons) could be dispensed with: "The really miraculous idea, which may even have escaped Marconi, is the possibility of broadcasting nutritious radio waves."

Sending a Message with Food

One of the core notions of Filippo Marinetti and the Futurists was that life and art should be considered inseparable. Food for them, was an excellent vehicle for promoting this message. Culinary devices allowed the Futurist cooks to comment on traditional Western art practices and values, and to subvert the hierarchy of senses that elevates sight and sound over taste and smell. Also in their sights was the philosophical yearning for permanence over transcience (the idea that art objects were better the more resistant they were to decay and change) and yes, the idea that high art could never actually be useful. For the Futurists, food, in these many ways, challenged all that.

Less comfortable were some of the overtly Fascistic messages of the Futurist recipes. These included chauvenistic celebrations of Italian power and might, and sectarian criticisms of 'bourgeois' cooking!

Of course, Futurism's influence on the evening meals, and quite possibly the military strategies, of the twentieth century's Fascist dictators is much less well known than its influence as an artistic movement. Long before Hitler's *Panza* spread the darkest aspects of the Futurist vision, hundreds of artists peacefully invaded the less dangerous space of the world's art galleries. The movement's themes were speed and technology, epitomized by its favorite objects: the motorcar, the aeroplane, and the modern city.

However, alongside the artists, sprouting from those same forgotten philosophical roots was the Futurist food movement, which bizarre as it seems, is still generally counted as the forerunner of *nouvelle cuisine*. This is the ultra-stylish culinary trend that took off in France in the 1960s, with an emphasis on small servings, lighter ingredients, playing with colors and flavors, and elaborate, decorative presentation. Futurist meals had all this but were also renowned for their deliberately bizarre combinations and provocative names. For example, "Excited Pig" consisted of a cooked and peeled whole salami, placed vertically on the plate with coffee sauce mixed with eau de cologne—the Futurists' favorite perfume. "Drum Roll of Colonial Fish" consisted of poached mullet marinated in a sauce of milk, liqueur, capers, and red pepper and stuffed with date jam, banana, and pineapple. The "drum" bit was that it had to be eaten to the sound of drumbeats. (And you thought restaurant *muzak* could be irritating.)

Futurist Cocktails

Futurist banquets require Futurist drinks. And these, too, followed the movement's style of clashing contrasts and fearsome names. One cocktail, called Fire In the Mouth, created by the Italian Futurist engineer Barosi, consisted of whisky with liqueur cherries, which had been carefully rolled in spicy cayenne pepper. On top of this was a layer of honey, forming an impermeable barrier, and then vermouth and the liqueurs Strega and Alchermes.

Alchermes is an Italian liqueur prepared by infusing neutral spirits with sugar, cinnamon, cloves, nutmeg, vanilla, and various other herbs. Supposedly it was invented by nuns, who are scarcely role models for the manly Futurists, but likely Marinetti was attracted to the original source of its color: crushed insects—kermes— whose carcasses made it a bright, bloody red.

Other recipes seem actually inedible. "Chicken Fiat" was flavored with a stuffing of ball bearings, roasted and served with whipped cream. However, the trick with most Futurist meals was that the names of dishes sounded more alarming than they actually were. "Diabolical Roses," for example, consisted only of red roses cooked in batter and thus was perfectly safe. "Green Rice" was merely rice served with a pea sauce, and "Divorced Eggs" was boring old eggs in which the yolks and whites had been separated.

Futurist Favorites

In her popular 1974 account of Latin cooking, *Italian Food*, the food writer Elizabeth David rather misleadingly (because the bulk of Futurist cooking was concerned with presentation and style, rather than boring old ingredients) includes a selection of Marinetti's more digestible recipes, including:

- Fish and apple—cutlets of fish cooked between slices of apple, soaked in rum and then set alight

- Pheasant, bathed in "heavy white Sicilian wine and milk"

- Rice and coffee, mixed with eggs and lemon peel, orange-flower water, and milk

---

Food sculptures were another hallmark of Futurist cooking. In the *Manifesto*, Marinetti describes "Equator + North Pole," a work composed of "an equatorial sea of poached egg yolks seasoned like oysters with pepper, salt and lemon. In the centre emerges a cone of firmly whipped egg white full of orange segments looking like juicy sections of the sun. The peak of the cone is strewn with pieces of black truffle cut in the form of black aeroplanes conquering the zenith."

But back to "Green Rice," a dish that embodies to Marinetti's most radical culinary idea a shocking one (shocking for Italians anyway) of giving up eating pasta. What?! No more spaghetti, tortellini, even ravioli?

*Wonderfully obscure though it is, the story of the Italian's 'war on pasta' has already been retold in a fascinating article by Philip McCouat in the Journal of Art in Society (2014). See notes.

Pasta. For true Futurists there could be no relenting against something they saw as the embodiment of everything that was wrong with the old Italy. Marinetti described pasta as "an absurd Italian gastronomic religion," that "tied up Italian men, with its tangled threads to Penelope's slow looms and to somnolent old sailing-ships in search of wind." So eloquent, yet so misguided.

Anyway, the *Manifesto of Futurist Cooking* explained that pasta would leave anyone who was foolish enough to eat it heavy and shapeless, and that it induced "lassitude, pessimism, nostalgic inactivity and neutralism." It was unmanly, "anti-virile" and "no food for fighters." In sum, real men did not eat pasta. But how to convert Italians from their favorite food?

Marinetti suggested that restaurants should tell customers that "we have come to this decision" (to ban pasta) because:

> Pasta is made of long silent archeological worms
> which, like their brothers living in the dungeons
> of history, weigh down the stomach making it ill
> and rendering it useless. You mustn't introduce
> these white worms into the body unless you
> want to make it as closed, dark and immobile as
> a museum.

One of his fellow Futurists, Marco Ramperti, summed up the visceral Futurist dislike of the dish saying that "swallowed down the way it is, spaghetti poisons us," twisting throughout itself, round and round, mixed up and tangled "like the vermicelli we have taken in."

If this all seems rather silly, there was in fact a practical side. Under Italy's new Fascist leader, Benito Mussolini, with war in the political program, becoming self-sufficient in food was a priority, and the key ingredient for pasta (regardless of what the BBC told viewers in 1957 in a spoof April Fools Day report, which showed Italian farmers growing pasta on trees), of course, is wheat. Unfortunately, Italy had rather limited abilities to produce wheat, and so the Fascists vigorously promoted the consumption of other things that Italy could produce, notably rice, grapes, and oranges.

As part of the so-called Battle for Grain, Mussolini tried to encourage the switch to the consumption of rice, particularly by claiming that it was much more *manly*. A second propaganda theme was to switch from white to brown bread, because the latter requires less wheat for its production. (You can make whole-wheat pasta too, but it is nasty stuff. Not even a Futurist would contemplate it!) In his cookbook, Marinetti made specific mention that his own anti-pasta views harmonized with Mussolini's policy and reminded his readers that getting rid of pasta would help "free Italy from expensive foreign grains and promote the Italian rice industry."

But enough of politics. The real issue for us today is: does pasta really make you heavy and shapeless? And the real answer is no. In fact, pasta is not bad for you at all. It is made from semolina flour (which comes from a high-protein variety of wheat known as durum wheat) and breaks down relatively slowly in the body, thus delivering energy in a steady, measured way that makes it less likely to end up as fat. The chemistry of pasta is that of a starch, which means it is a complex carbohydrate—whereas sugar is a simple carbohydrate. All carbohydrates eventually get broken down into glucose in the body—the fuel that circulates in the blood to power the cells. For the body, the important thing is how easily food can be turned into glucose. Sugars rapidly raise blood glucose levels, but starches are digested more slowly.

Although they also consist of starches rather than sugars, foods like white bread and white rice are often made from grains that have been stripped of their dietary fiber; thus, depending on the exact product, they may act more like sugar in the body, easy to digest and rapidly ending up as sugar in the bloodstream. (See the sidebar on the Glycemic Index on page 187.) Too much of these refined grains can cause insulin spikes, potentially contributing to liver disease and other health problems. A similar problem arises with potatoes, which, although starch, happen to be very digestible and so behave like a sugar. The most popular kind of potato, Russet, depending on how it's prepared, is actually quicker to turn into glucose than pure sugar itself! This (along with the salty flavor) is why potato chips are so successful and tempting a snack.

As recently as 2015, the "does pasta make you fat?" question was sufficiently hot that a new study into the issue was considered mainstream news. Researchers found that lovely white pasta actually has a very resistant starch structure that makes the flour in it break down slowly in the gut, just like healthy (but less immediately palatable) foods like buckwheat or brown rice. Thus, it seems that as long as you eat it al dente, white pasta provides a steady release of energy that reduces the desire to eat and is, in that sense at least, positively thin-making. Just fancy that!

Spinach Tortellini

Tortellini are little packets of pasta stuffed with a filling. If you don't fancy spinach, then choose mushroom or ricotta or something else. Purchase a good-quality premade tortellini, and boil for three minutes in salted water. You don't need to add a sauce, which can make the meal too heavy and drown out the flavor of the pasta pouches. Once the pasta is cooked to al dente, drain, add a bit more salt, a twist of ground black pepper, and butter.

If you live near a genuine Italian grocer, you may be able to obtain the freshly made variety, which tastes completely different and much better. But even dried tortellini, with an expiration date of virtually forever, is worth keeping in your pantry. It's both convenient and filling!

Spaghetti al Tonno

For another very convenient Italian dish, chop an onion and a clove of garlic, and sauté in some olive oil with a bit of fresh, chopped thyme and basil. Once the vegetables are softened, add a can of dolphin-friendly tuna and a moderate amount of freshly cut tomatoes and black olives (optional). In a pinch, you can use canned tomatoes, but be prepared to sacrifice taste. In either case, add a generous squeeze of tomato paste. Simmer the sauce over low heat for at least 15 minutes. Add salt and pepper to taste. Serve over freshly cooked spaghetti.

Chapter 23

Back to the Future with the Slow-Food Movement

Immanuel Kant had a great fear of the side-effects of coffee, which he thought contained dangerous oils. Only in his last year of life did he relax his rule and allow himself a cup of freshly brewed coffee. One biographer recalls how when he was told that his coffee would be brought in a moment, he replied: "Will be? Will be? There's the rub that it only will be."

Trivial anecdote? The point is that in rushing things like brewing his beloved coffee, Kant betrayed his lifelong pattern of doing everything very slowly. And this deviation matters as Kant is considered one of the greatest of the great philosophers mainly on account of his steely conviction of the importance of following rules. Philosophers particularly admire the rule he called the "Categorical Imperative," which is basically all about treating people as you would like to be treated yourself. In his writings, Kant put the Imperative at the top of all other rules, the "master rule" we might say, but in practice (always a very different matter in ethics) he clearly considered it to be second in importance only to the one concerning coffee. I say this because nowhere did he apply his rules with more zeal than on dietary matters.

The "Chinaman of Königsburg," as Nietzsche dubbed him obscurely but probably unkindly, awoke at 5:00 a.m. each morning, not a minute earlier, and certainly not a minute later, and started the day with a cup of tea. The tea had to be very, very weak. He would then, without pausing for breakfast—no, not even a little pastry!—begin writing. He wrote not merely on philosophy but on a whole range of topics, from science to healthy eating. Few people remember this, but Kant's first love was in fact science. (His doctorate, completed in 1755, was not on philosophy as such but rather "About Fire"). It was only in his late forties that Kant was able to specialize in philosophy; before this he was but an hourly paid lecturer for whom it made sense to be an expert on as many subjects as possible.

By skipping breakfast, Kant followed the Continental habit, and his lunchtime, too, was in the local style. It was a grand occasion, conducted leisurely with a number of shrewdly chosen intellectual, but non-academic, friends. There always had to be at least three (corresponding to the number of the ancient goddesses known as the Graces) and never more than nine (the number of the ancient Muses). The lively conversation at Kant's table spanned a broad range of topics, and Kant himself was always keenly interested in the latest political, economic, and scientific developments. With his memory for detail, he could describe at length foreign towns and places, although, having no desire to ever leave his hometown of Königsburg, he had never visited any of them. Another of his little categorical imperatives (unbreakable rules) concerned his favored beverage. Since he considered the oil of coffee beans to be unhealthy, lunch did not finish with coffee but always over a cup of weak tea. If the meal was grand and took up valuable time, it was Kant's only meal of the day.

Kant's grandest discovery, the one he called "a Copernican revolution" in philosophy, is offered in his book Critique of Pure Reason. Here he explains that the world takes on the form it does only due to our looking at it. Does his insight apply to food too? Certainly, in terms of grander philosophical concerns about the physical universe, the answer is bound to be yes, although all this is a pretty old philosophical story, demonstrated earlier and much more elegantly by Ancients like Zeno—the one who "proved" that a tortoise could win a race with a rabbit. Kant, however, sees himself as having no predecessors, and describes his breakthrough in terms that would make Wittgenstein or perhaps, if we want a more recent figure, President Trump, look modest (well, less immodest), writing: "I venture to say that there is not a single metaphysical problem that has not been solved, or for the solution for which the key at least has not been supplied."

Be Skeptical of Supplements

According to the *Readers Digest*, in any given week, "nearly a third of adult Britons take some sort of supplement in the hope that they will feel healthier." Or indeed, actually *be* healthier. Either way, as the authors of the guide explain, they are likely deluding themselves. In fact, not only are supplements often ineffectual; some are actually harmful. For instance, vitamins A and D cannot be easily excreted from the body when taken in excess as supplements and are actually dangerous. Too much vitamin A is harmful for the liver and the bones; an excess of vitamin D can cause calcium to accumulate in the tissues of the heart and in the kidneys, causing irreversible damage.

Weight loss supplements seem to be particularly dodgy. Research by Pieter Cohen (no relation) in the U.S. has identified popular supplements that contain things like anti-depressants, laxatives, and thyroid hormones.

But what of his culinary discoveries and dietary advice? Kant himself, after all, was short and pot-bellied, suffered from poor digestion, and scarcely seems a convincing health guru. He was surely wrong about coffee, just as he was wrong about many practical things—such as his idea that all the planets in the solar system had life on them, with the intelligence of that life increasing the farther out from the sun they were. He was also off-beam with some of his core ethical notions, for example that it is always wrong to lie. Always. Perhaps the most useful bit of his food-related advice is the recommendation—no matter how busy you are!—to have a proper lunch, ideally in company, and to eat it very slowly.

So how are we doing today when it comes to this suggestion? Alas, the situation is not so good. At least according to one of those rather dodgy surveys, most Britons only spend six minutes on breakfast, eight on lunch, and a shocking nine minutes at dinner, making a total of just 23 minutes for all three meals. The low figures also represent a lot of meals being skipped—for lack of time! In the U.S., people are even more determined, and even faster ways to eat have been developed.

America long ago took the sandwich concept into a new dimension with the famous burger in the bun, stuffed with lettuce and tomato, maybe cheese, a pickle, mustard, and ketchup. McDonald's set itself the challenge of getting a burger and shake and fries cooked and served to customers, on foot or in a vehicle, in just one minute.

John Nihoff, a professor of gastronomy at the Culinary Institute of America, has estimated that about one in five American meals are now consumed in cars, ranging from the classic three-course meal of burger, fries, and a shake to one-course sugar fixes like a bag of doughnuts. Americans, it seems, like to eat while moving, either walking or driving.

"We're grazers. We're snackers," Nihoff said. "We don't have time to sit down and eat a big meal."

But fast food is not very healthy; it's highly processed, and thus more likely to lack nutritional value and be high in sugar and fat.

"It's snack foods that very often replace meals…so nutritionally [people are] not really getting what they need," said a spokeswoman for the American Dietetic Association.

For this reason, their advice to dashboard diners is to bring along healthy foods that can be eaten safely in the car, like a peanut butter and jelly sandwich on whole grain bread. (That, I think, is what they call a compromise solution.)

In a way, American fast food was a kind of revolution. But every revolution has its counter-revolution, and sure enough, on December 10, 1986, the slow-food movement arrived. It had been born in Italy a few years earlier but was christened via a manifesto released in Paris. The trigger was the sight of a McDonald's opening in the beloved Piazza di Spagna of Rome. A company that puts salad in a cup and a slice of cheese on beef, landing right in the cultural heart of Rome! Enough was enough! Basta! "Against the universal madness of the Fast Life," the Slow Food Manifesto declared:

> ... we need to choose the defence of tranquil material pleasure. Against those, and there are many of them, who confuse efficiency with frenzy, we propose the vaccine of a sufficient portion of assured sensual pleasure, to be practiced in slow and prolonged enjoyment ...

Behind the manifesto was one Carlo Petrini. Behind the idea of a manifesto, though, was the example of the Futurist one (see chapter 22), published at the start of the century, whose theme was also speed and modernity. But that which the Futurists worshipped, the slow-food movement was dead set against. If Futurism was all about looking ahead and moving fast, Petrini's new movement was determinedly backward looking and, of course, in no rush to get anywhere. Not for them was a world in which pizzas were being microwaved, where yogurts and soups were put in tubes "with smaller solid bits" for easier sipping as you walked (or maybe drove) to work. Such things had to be stopped!

Futurism went on to become Fascism and encircle the earth in wars and chaos, but Slow Food has had rather less influence. Not none, mind you, but definitely less. On the other hand, it's still in the early days and, well, as I say, you can't rush such things.

One achievement the movement can claim is a substantial improvement in the quality of "budget" Italian wine—this following the shaming of quick, cheap, and nasty wines via the first-ever comprehensive guidebook to the wines of Italy. The campaign was aided by the scandal of a distributor that adulterated bottles with methanol to ever so slightly increase profits. In 1986, nineteen people died, hundreds of others were poisoned, and exports of Italian wine were decimated— by which I mean, of course, not reduced by one-tenth, but "greatly reduced."*

The wine scandal allowed Petrini and his colleagues to transform their movement from the hobbyhorse of a few friends into something much more ambitious and politically resonant. It also highlighted that salvaging the good name of Italian food and wine was for many Italians not merely a matter of sentiment or nostalgia, but of commercial necessity. For members of the slow-food movement, the purest act is to sit for hours in tiny trattorias (Italian cafés which serve food, but are less grand than restaurants) and eat food produced "in-house" and from local ingredients. This was the movement's authentic form of "direct action." (You can try it too by going to a real Italian restaurant or pizzeria.) Not for them to press for new laws or write impassioned opinion pieces; instead the important thing was that the links between consumers and farmers be restored. Fast food locates the producers far way, usually rendering them invisible, with only the brand—McDonald's, Starbucks, etc.—mattering. This is why another tactic of the slow-food movement is to produce catalogues and courses that improve information about "foods of excellence" from all over the world. Media interest in the launch of the second edition of the catalogue, from a former Fiat factory on the outskirts of Turin in 1998, showed that the movement now had global reach. The underlying philosophy is that of the famous Noah's Ark, into which animals went two by two. Into this ark, though, go (one by one) gourmet cheeses; unusual apples and oranges; and unusual varieties of bread. Whether the flood waters of mass-production and consumerism will actually ever go down seems unlikely, however.

Exports of Italian wine dropped by more than one-third, from 17 to 11 million hectoliters.

The Glycemic Index: An Almost Futuristic Way to Look at Food

The glycemic index* was first proposed, researched, and developed in the 1980s by the Canadian researcher David Jenkins, but since then the idea has been greatly expanded by others, including the Australian nutrition professor Jennie Brand-Miller, who has written several books utilizing the concept, such as the *Low GI Diet Shopper's Guide 2015*.

The glycemic index is all about speed—to be precise, about the rate at which food is converted into sugar (glucose) in the bloodstream. The index compares various foods to pure glucose for the rate at which they turn into sugar in the blood, with pure glucose counted as 100.

Consuming foods that rapidly increase blood sugar levels can be a particular problem for people trying to control their weight. The insulin produced by the body to lower blood glucose can overshoot the mark, causing a "sugar dip" and a rapid return to feeling hungry. A food that is slow to turn to blood sugar, on the other hand, may be good for those watching their weight.

Starting the day with a bit of baguette may be problematic for people trying to watching their blood sugar levels, as baguettes, with a GI of 95, have among the highest ratings. (This finding infuriates French food experts like Jennie Brand-Miller, who has toiled to lower her beloved bread's rating. But even on her most optimistic assessment—perhaps by using better flour—the stick still comes in at a relatively high 75.) It is fortunate that baguettes are light, because by weight, they are nearly equivalent to eating pure sugar. Cornflakes are little better; a good muesli would come in at a much lower value.

The Glycemic Index: An Almost Futuristic Way to Look at Food *(cont.)*

Perhaps surprisingly, peanuts and hummus (whose values are a mere 7 and 6, respectively) are very hard for the body to turn into blood sugar despite being quite snackable. And because they are rich in wholesome fats, they can usefully delay the return of hunger. Green vegetables generally have almost no effect on blood sugar and so are both "unfattening" and useless for energy.

Some revealing entries at the "high" end of the glycemic index are:

- French baguettes 95
- Cornflakes 93
- White rice 89 (Sorry, Futurists!)
- French fries 75
- White bread 71

The following foods fall into the "low" zone of the glycemic spectrum:

- Oatmeal 55
- Pasta: generally 50 (46 for spaghetti and 32 for fettuccine, which can come in different flavors)
- Apples 39
- Carrots 35
- Skim milk 32
- Black beans and lentils 30
- Grapefruit 25

* To be precise, as the researchers at the University of Sydney put it on their special Glycemic Index webpage, the index is "a relative ranking of carbohydrate in foods according to how they affect blood glucose levels."

Chapter 24

Counter-Revolutionary Eating

The majority of European and American farmland is dominated by industrial agriculture—the system of chemically intensive food production developed in the decades after World War II, featuring enormous single-crop farms and animal production facilities. This is truly Big Ag.

Big Ag is a handful of huge corporations that decide what everyone eats. Yes, even you (and even me). And it is Big Ag's love of monoculture that is the greatest threat to our food supply. The food activist Dena Rash Guzman explains why:

> Monoculture produces almost everything we eat, and is practically all you can buy at big supermarkets like Costco or Safeway. But monoculture isn't farming. It's strip mining. It's violent. The meat we eat is produced in factory farms, and most cow milk comes from these farms. Fruits and vegetables are grown on giant tracts of land, with no regard for damage to the environment.

> Monoculture farming relies heavily on chemicals, such as synthetic fertilizers and pesticides.

> Farmers grow the same food, often commodity crops but also strawberries and wine grapes, year after year, mile after mile after mile. Native plants are viewed as weeds and exterminated. Pests are sprayed with chemicals that often take down beneficial insects as well. Fungus, an important part of a healthy ecosystem, is annihilated. Monoculture farming methods take from the earth but do not give back.

The fertilizers are needed because growing the same plant (and nothing else) in the same place year after year quickly depletes the nutrients that the plant relies on, and these nutrients have to be replenished somehow. The pesticides are needed because monoculture fields are highly attractive to certain weeds and insect pests. Another effect of monoculture is that bee populations decline. A third of the food that we eat every day depends on bees and other insect pollinators.

Similarly, the industrial system of meat production means that meat animals are "finished"—prepared for slaughter—at large-scale facilities called CAFOs (Concentrated Animal Feeding Operations), where their mobility is restricted and they are fed a high-calorie, grain-based diet, often supplemented with antibiotics and hormones, to maximize their weight gain.

Guzman sees herself as a crusader, engaged in a war on Big Ag and bad food. Guiding this, she has her own radical philosophy:

> For me, the battle starts at home when I make my grocery list. Every product I drop into my grocery basket and every seed I plant could potentially lead to a healthier world, but only if I sense the landmines soon enough. I take my small budget and try to spend it like a warrior. It's hard to feel I am making a difference with the little money I have to spend, but I have to do something. That something takes research, awareness, and patience.

Recent scares, like the European mad cow crisis, which resulted in hundreds of thousands of cattle being killed and burned in medieval funeral pyres by military troops, illustrates the inherent problems of the approach. (Mad cow disease is a fatal brain disorder that is spread when cattle are fed the ground-up corpses of other infected animals. By June 2014 it had killed 177 people in the United Kingdom alone.)

But it is the Irish Potato Famine, the worst famine to occur in Europe in the nineteenth century, that is the best (worst) example of what happens when monoculture goes wrong. Between 1845 and 1852, the population of Ireland fell nearly 25 percent. The proximate cause was disease and starvation, along with mass emigration. But the cause of all these was potato blight. Potatoes, a staple food of the Irish since the plant's first arrival from the Americas, had caught a rather nasty virus, and since all the plants were of the same variety, there was no stopping the disease.

The natural solution is to grow a range of crops and rotate them regularly. Equally naturally, this is not what happens. Instead, farming is ever more focused on just a few plants, which are protected from disease with chemicals and sometimes via genetic engineering. The result is that every so often diseases spread across countries, wiping out whole crops. *Don't mess with the crystal vase.*

In 2010, for example, citrus-greening disease spread to top orange-producing countries, including the United States. Citrus greening sours oranges and leaves them half green. The 8,000 Florida growers who sell most of the nation's oranges for juice had to fight citrus greening for years. To slow the disease's spread, they cut down and burned hundreds of thousands of infected trees and sprayed a variety of pesticides. To no avail. They then searched around the world for a naturally immune tree that could be used to establish new crops. They found none. The only solution left for the farms? To pay for a genetically modified orange. In this fiendish way, Big Ag destroys the old citrus varieties and then charges farmers new fees to access the patented disease-resistant ones.

How did Big Ag come to dominate the food scene? It happened during what, in almost Orwellian language, is called the "Green Revolution."

The Green Revolution

The Green Revolution started, like so many others, in the 1960s. It sounds modern and positive (as it was intended to), but to its critics it soon became an agribusiness plot which gained speed in the 1960s, displacing not just seed varieties but entire crops in the Third World. And, for better or for worse, it really was a global revolution affecting nearly everybody.

Just as the sixties generally were the heyday of "out with the old and in with the new," during the Green Revolution, seeds deemed "primitive" or "inferior" were replaced with high yielding super-seeds. In India, traditional crops like *ragi* (millet) and *jowar* (sorghum), which contain high levels of protein and minerals, were replaced by mainstays like wheat and rice, despite these grains being inferior in nutritional value. Why? Because the new crops were much more profitable. The traditional crops became "weeds" and were destroyed with poisons, as food activist Vandana Shiva explains in her book *Monocultures of the Mind: Perspectives on Biodiversity and Biotechnology* (1993).

Shiva campaigns instead for *polycultures* that use ecologically balanced farming methods, incorporating crop rotation, inclusion of multiple plant species, and "companion planting." These practices make plots less attractive to pests and help maintain soil fertility. Multiple layers of vegetation offer diversity within the farm environment, which is beneficial to plants, animals, and insects alike. In a sense, campaigns like this along with the move toward organic farming in general, are the farming *counter-revolution.*

Food Myth: There is a Pill for That

The Futurists put a great emphasis on being slim. For one thing, the new-fangled flying machines simply wouldn't work if people weighed too much. For another, as mentioned already, there actually wasn't much real food in Futurist dishes—rather lots of petals and maybe ball bearings. But Futurism went out of favor sometime in the twentieth century, and with it the veneration of dainty portions.

Obesity is a problem. You can see that if you look around you. Indeed, for many of us, you can see that if you look at yourself! More precisely, some two-thirds of people in industrialized countries like the United States are now either overweight or obese. In England, the government says that nearly 61.9 percent are eating the wrong foods and not only ceasing to be "beach ready," as an irritating London Tube advert recently put it, but risking diabetes, heart disease, and certain cancers. Compounding the problem, carrying too much weight makes it more difficult for people to find and keep work, and it affects self-esteem. One (rather unkind) U.S. research study even calculated that the excess pounds of all the overweight and obese Americans require approximately one billion gallons of additional fuel annually as they travel around the highways, at a cost of $2.7 billion a year.

Everyone agrees that it is a problem—but equally, everyone disagrees on what to do about it. As most of us know, simply cutting back a bit on the carbs, swapping to low-fat milk, or walking up the stairs instead of taking the elevator doesn't seem to work.

Serious, published scientific research has linked obesity to any and all of the following:

- excessive consumption of protein, or of sugar, or of fat
- eating big meals or eating snacks
- using fast-food, or visiting full-service restaurants, or even eating at home

Different countries seem to favor different solutions. The French often favor surgery and physical interventions. The UK favors pricing people away from supposedly unhealthy choices—by taxing "bad" foods (e.g., as the recently imposed levy on sugar).

It seems that the only thing that is agreed upon in diet research is that no one agrees. Which leads some desperate dieters to entertain radical solutions—like diet pills. In recent years, many have come to market, each heralded with enthusiasm by much of the media. But if you're tempted to try them, let me say straightaway, from what I've read, I think diet pills could be the biggest mistake you'll ever make.

First of all, evidence for their efficacy is very, er, slim. At the same time, the risks seem to be very high. Yet because diet pills are not necessarily "medicines," important decisions— life threatening decisions—about their safety are made much less carefully.

The U.S. government in particular seems to authorize drugs for tackling weight issues, just as they authorize them for solving educational problems (indeed, the active ingredients in the two kinds of medicines are often the same!)—and to reflect on the effects later. Take two of the new drugs on the market. (I say "new," although many diet pills are, in fact, old drugs that used to be employed for different illnesses but have been repurposed.) One, called Belviq, claims to ever so slightly reduce weight but has been associated with valvular heart disease and congestive heart failure. Another, Qsymia, is designed to increase resting heart rate and is known to risk severe birth defects if taken by pregnant moms, who make up a good number of the people attracted to taking diet pills.

A weight-loss supplement called Xcel even contained Prozac, the antidepressant famous for its dangerous side effects such as anxiety, diarrhea, drowsiness, dyspepsia, insomnia, nausea, tremor, headache, anorexia, decreased libido, xerostomia, and bulimia nervosa—to mention just a few! That last side effect is an obsessive desire to lose weight, in which bouts of extreme overeating are followed by fasting or self-induced vomiting or purging.

Incredibly, the FDA allows the sale of diet pills it knows are potentially fatal, relying instead on printed warnings as its opt-out for responsibility. As I say, the agency even seems to think it is a reasonable strategy to approve products and then, after a few years, evaluate how much harm or not the pills have done and maybe reconsider. Is that the right way around? But then while they're waiting for the FDA's final verdict, Americans spend about $2 billion a year on weight-loss dietary supplements in pill form, so there's as ever a financial impetus to the policy. Governments like to protect geese that lay golden eggs, and the diet industry, whose pills need to be taken for long periods—almost permanently—certainly does.

Some pills that were originally licensed in the U.S. as dietary aids have become quite notorious. Dinitrophenol, DNP for short, has been banned for human consumption but is still available to those who are fanatical enough in their quest for thinness to ignore all the warnings. It belongs to a group of drugs that encourage the body to burn fat even if you're sitting on the sofa watching TV. Sounds great, doesn't it? Only it isn't.

DNP was first manufactured as an herbicide and fungicide and is chemically similar to the stuff that explosives used to be made of. It is perfectly legal, and quite easy, to obtain for various non-food industrial uses. British newspapers reported in the spring of 2015 that a 25-year-old woman from Worthing, West Sussex, took the substance and was dead a few weeks later. Her inquest was told she may as well have been "taking rat poison."

Another tragic victim, 26 years old, was found dead in a cold bath, after trying desperately to reduce her body temperature.

DNP works by speeding up the metabolic rate so the body burns more fat. But it can easily cause the body to overheat, literally burning users up from the inside! In the UK alone, it has officially been recorded as the cause of death for sixteen people—and many more deaths are likely to have occurred without the cause being accurately recorded.

Yet despite the high stakes from adverse reactions, as Tam Fry, from the UK's National Obesity Forum, has put it, "People are taking drugs that put their lives at risk in order to look their best at a party."

Mind you, the example set by the scientists and governmental bodies that authorize diet pills is not a good one. Safety concerns are typically set aside following tests in which people taking the pills seem to have lost fractionally more weight than people taking a placebo. Warnings and dose limits are relied on to make pills safer even though people in the real world tend to ignore both. Enthusiastic dieters or bodybuilders may visit several doctors to obtain multiple prescriptions for fat-burning pills, which they are then free to guzzle in one fell swoop.

From the research professional's point of view, findings that certain pills produce small reductions in weight are statistically "significant," even if the effects are only equivalent to tiny lifestyle changes. Governments cheerfully extrapolate such small improvements to justify funneling large sums of public money via various health insurance plans toward Big Pharma. Few seem worried that there's no limit on how many trials drug companies can carry out in seeking evidence for their pills, or that trials might be cherry-picked to achieve a small but positive finding of effectiveness.

How Diet Pills Work

"Fat burning" pills trigger chemical reactions in cells, converting sugar to energy that dissipates as heat in the body. Side effects include death! People who take diet pills are really using a hammer to adjust their Swiss watch or polish their crystal vase.

Variants, usually involving caffeine, merely aim to speed up the metabolic rate. This sounds like a healthy idea, but the approach can still cause side effects. One study by the U.S. Mayo Clinic found that a pill made up of a mixture of caffeine and bitter orange extract led to increased blood pressure and strokes. Other fat-burning pills have been accused of causing a buildup of lactic acid and then kidney failure.

"Fat blockers" interfere with the digestion of food and produce an effect similar to having a permanently upset stomach. Apart from the obvious, short-term downsides (e.g., nausea and diarrhea), the pills can prevent the body from absorbing fat from food, which creates problems for normal functioning—including that of the nerve cells and brain.

Chapter 25

Living in an Obesogenic Environment

Two of the great strengths of the philosophical approach (when it works at its best) are, first, the desire to look at the whole picture, and, second, the open-mindedness to follow ideas and arguments wherever they may go. A good example of the power of this is the research of Boyd Swinburn, a social scientist who started investigating a narrow health question and ended up discovering an entirely new—and scary—perspective on health in modern society. He maintains that obesity is just a symptom of a wider social and economic malaise of over-consumption driven by corporate interests.

That's a highly political statement. Initially, Boyd Swinburn was only trying to find out why the Pima Indians, living on a Native American reservation outside Phoenix, Arizona, had in recent years started to develop so many cases of diabetes. He soon realized that the *real* question was why so many of the Pima were obese. "I came to the conclusion that obviously the driver of diabetes was obesity and that obesity was just a normal physiological response to an abnormal environment," he wrote later. This is what he later dubbed the obesogenic environment. Today the word *obesogens* is an umbrella term given to a range of chemicals that interfere with the body's natural mechanisms. Or, to be more precise, interfere with the endocrine system: the collection of glands that produce hormones, which are released into the bloodstream to regulate the body's growth, metabolism, and sexual development and function. Just one known effect of messing with this delicate system is diabetes—while others are that the body starts to stock fat—and heart disease.

So where were the Pima coming into contact with these chemicals? One of the key problems was that the Indians were consuming too much plastic. By which I don't mean failing to reuse plastic shopping bags. They were *eating* too much of it. And the mechanisms for this dangerous overconsumption of chemicals are far from unique to Native American tribes. The problem for everyone is that today plastic is hiding in the most unexpected places. Even in that healthy-looking fruit bowl piled high with apples, pears, and grapes. And if mass-produced fruits are the worst, more exotic fruits like peaches, nectarines, and cherries are dodgy too. Only thick-skinned fruits like oranges, grapefruit, kiwi, bananas, pineapple, mango, and watermelon seem to cope well with their dose of chemicals— under their protective and indigestible coverings.

Plasticizers also lurk in your fridge ready to be consumed in the form of peppers, celery, strawberries, kale, lettuce, and carrots. And in your cupboards in the linings of cans of tuna, soup, beans, and tomatoes. They're even in canned versions of energy drinks and baby formula. Plasticizers include chemicals that the human body was never designed to consume. It's been calculated that three billion kilos of the plasticizer bisphenol A (BPA) enter the food chain every year in the U.S. alone, with the result (according to the National Institute of Health Sciences) that it's now detectable in 93 percent of the U.S. population. Now here's the fascinating bit: *BPA interferes with the hormones that tell your body when it's full.*

Phthalates, chemicals used to soften plastic, are, by comparison, detectable in a mere three-quarters of the U.S. population. (Don't ask me why it's less.) Phthalates mimic estrogen, and a recognized side-effect of estrogen supplements is, again, weight gain. About half a billion kilos of phthalates are made each year worldwide, and they make their way easily into our bodies.

In addition to this invisible swirl of plasticizing chemicals that we're surrounded by at the turn of the millennium, a study in the *International Journal of Obesity* by researchers at ten different universities, including Yale University School of Medicine and Johns Hopkins University, found that the use of steroid hormones in meat production and on conventional dairy farms could be a possible contributor to the obesity epidemic.

Consumption of meat from cattle treated with hormones inevitably means you are consuming a dose of them too. Naturally occurring ones, such as estrogen, progesterone, and testosterone, are given in high doses to cattle. In addition, a substance called trenbolone acetate (TBA) is given to, er, "beef them up." TBA is an anabolic steroid that's eight to ten times as potent as testosterone. That means if your beef cow consumed it, your meat has it, and you will get a dose too. For bodybuilders hoping to bulk up, this might sound like a good shortcut. (It isn't.) TBA suppresses natural testosterone and natural estrogen—both of which (contrary to popular belief) men and women produce, albeit in different amounts—resulting in night sweats, aggressiveness, and increased appetite. Basically, it messes you up.

While we're talking about messing around with nature's subtle mechanisms, let's not forget that antibiotics are often fed to chickens and farmed fish to promote growth and keep them from getting sick, as they are often housed in crowded pens. Antibiotics are another kind of obesogen. In particular, they interfere with lipid metabolism (the process that breaks down and stores fats for energy), which can lead to obesity.

Last but not least, mass-produced, highly subsidized soy is stuffed into chickens, cows, and fish to save farmers money (and thus it is stuffed into us too). Since the 1950s, antibiotic feed supplementation has been commonplace, to the extent that several of the large pharmaceutical companies went into the feed supplement business and have ever since been hard-pressed to keep up with demand.

The bottom line is that many modern foodstuffs contain chemicals that upset our hormones. The line under the bottom line is that among the many undesirable effects of this practice is a tendency of tampered-with food to make the body put on fat. But avoiding the problematic chemical compounds is hard because most of us aren't even aware that we've been eating plastic at all. In fact, Boyd Swinburn's research upturns diet and nutritional certainties.

If for years people have been cutting down on breads and cakes to reduce calories, have included extra fish in the diet, and have eaten lots more fruits and vegetables, now things are more complicated. Otherwise healthy fruit and vegetables are likely to have been treated with a cocktail of poisons and other nasties. The fish we eat is usually farmed, and that means it has been fed hormones and antibiotics, and maybe canned too, which means sitting in a plastic-lined can soaking up chemicals. And don't forget the plastics in wild fish. Plastic products end up in the ocean and get consumed by fish, who end up with it in their flesh, which we, in turn, eat. Meat from land animals comes with its own complement of drugs and poisons. In sum: foods that were healthy for countless thousands of years are not any more.

Skeptical? Consider salmon, perhaps the finest symbol of the great outdoors and the best of nature. Today, however, many people eat farmed salmon, which are fed a completely artificial mix of soy and fish meal, a diet so unnatural their flesh becomes white, not pink. (The pink flesh of wild salmon is created by their diet of tiny crustaceans known as krill.) To create that natural pink salmon color, farmers use pellets that come loaded with pink dye. They select the desired shade of the fishes' flesh by consulting a "Salmo-fan" or "Salmo-ruler," similar to a paint fan. And, again, because they are farmed in enclosed pens, the salmon are fed antibiotics (an obesogen).

"Okay! I'm really worried now! But what can I do? I've given up eating nearly everything (except chocolates) already!" you may well ask. Fortunately, there are ways that you can cut down on your plastic intake.

- Buy organic. Yes, I know it's a bit of a rip-off, but real organic food tastes a whole lot better, so there's a value in that.

- Buy fresh fish, or fish in date-stamped pouches—not in cans.

And don't forget, even if it all seems a bit grim, there is this bit of good news. Several research studies suggest that switching to "real" foods and avoiding the most contaminated ones can rapidly reduce your body's load of obesogens and boot out the disrupting chemicals.

Not-So-Organic Food

Today, the organic food industry is a victim of its own success. Sales of organic food in the United States increased from approximately $11 billion in 2004 to an estimated $27 billion in 2012, according to the *Nutrition Business Journal*—far faster than food sales generally.

Industry experts forecast that the organic food market in the United States will grow at about 14 percent during the period from 2014 to 2018. However, as demand increases, organic farms start to look more and more like their conventional cousins. As a result, many organic ingredients such as almonds, corn, soybeans, and coconuts come from monoculture environments. And the use of pesticides is in fact allowed in organic farming, although there are rules about what's allowed. However, it seems pretty likely they won't originally have been lovingly mixed in an old copper pot on a family farm with cows and apple trees and a fishpond either.

Chapter 26

The Future of Food Is Vegetables

Ironically, even as they planned to look ahead to the new, twentieth century, the Italian Futurists echoed a very ancient piece of dietary advice: vegetarianism. Even though the rallying cry of Futurist cookery was "Pasta is dead. Long live sculpted meat!" Marinetti repeatedly warns against eating too much meat, and reminds people that vegetables, too, are tasty—especially if you don't rob them of their flavors and their goodness by boiling or overcooking. This reminder could have been taken straight out of the ancient philosopher Pythagoras's mouth and indeed is a timeless tip.

One trademark eating experience that even vegans would happily sample was called *Aerofood*, featuring a very Pythagorean salad of fennel, olives, and candied fruit accompanied by a small rectangle containing various textured materials. While eating the foods, the diner "delicately passes the tips of the index and middle fingers of his left hand over … a swatch of red damask, a little square of black velvet and a tiny piece of sandpaper." Sound and a heightened level of scent are introduced into the experience too: "From some carefully hidden melodious source comes the sound of part of a Wagnerian opera, and, simultaneously, the nimblest and most graceful of the waiters sprays the air with perfume." At other times, the diner is blasted with a giant fan (ideally an airplane propeller) while "nimble waiters spray him with the scent of carnation." And you thought being asked if "everything was all right" was annoying!

Another non-meat dish, the food sculpture of poached egg yolks entitled "Equator + North Pole," described in chapter 22, recalled Marinetti's vegetarian (or more strictly, his naturist) side. The recipe given in the *Futurist Cookbook* specified that to enhance the eating experience, music and perfumes be selected for maximum impact.

> Marinetti claims "astonishing results" on the diners at the one and only Futurist restaurant, an angular, aluminum-plated bar in Turin called the "Tavern of the Holy Palate" (this with a sneer at the Pope).

However, in practice, the centerpiece of most Futurist banquets was the very opposite of vegetarian. "Sculpted Meat" is a tower of veal stuffed with vegetables, with honey dripping down the side, onto a base of sausages and "three golden spheres of chicken meat." The painter Fillìa (the name adopted by Luigi Colombo) claimed this to be a "symbolic representation of all the varied landscapes of Italy," and Marinetti refers to the recipe more often than any other, making it truly the cornerstone of Futurist cooking.

A Fine Mediterranean Stew

One of the many understandable reasons people overeat or eat unhealthily is a lack of anything to cook at home. This is where Mediterranean cuisine comes in handy. At its simplest, Mediterranean food requires a medium onion, some cloves of garlic, and some tomatoes, fresh, canned or jarred, or whatever. Together, these ingredients form the basis of a good stew, and each of them can be stockpiled in the kitchen for months on end.

Chop a medium onion. In a large saucepan, heat a couple of tablespoons of olive oil until shimmering. Sauté the onion with some chopped garlic, herbs, salt, and pepper to taste. Cook until golden—or even dark brown and burned. (Burned onion actually tastes better than the "just cooked" stuff.)

Add whatever appealing ingredients you have on hand: diced zucchini, diced carrot, cashews, almonds, pine nuts, or a can of tuna. The choices are endless! Stir in a spoonful of honey and a splash of wine for a little extra je ne sais quoi.

Simmer the stew on very low heat for about an hour. Serve with rice or pasta or pita bread or a baked potato, whatever comes to mind. (And don't (per Mussolini) worry about the national economy.)

Food Myth: Sugar is Bad, Chemicals are Good!

The rise, fall, and rise again of artificial diet sweeteners.

These days, illustrating the philosopher Thomas Kuhn's point about the highly political and basically unstable nature of "scientific facts," Big Sugar is back again playing the role of the villain in diet matters, and everyone is looking for ways to cut down on it. This is why low-fat yogurts and such often contain artificial diet sweeteners. Helpful chemists have fine-tuned the uses of many strange-sounding sweeteners, some of which occur in nature and some of which exist only courtesy of laboratories.

Yet several large-scale studies have found a correlation between artificial sweetener consumption and weight gain. High-fructose corn syrup (HFCS), the mass-produced crop that is ingeniously inserted into almost every processed food you can buy (once triumphantly marketed as preferable to sugar), is now considered to be a key driver of the obesity epidemic. Writing in the *Huffington Post* in 2013, Mark Hyman, a food blogger, health campaigner, and practicing family physician (how does he fit it all in?), warned:

> … we are eating huge doses of sugar, especially high-fructose corn syrup. It is sweeter and cheaper than regular sugar and is in every processed food and sugar-sweetened drink. Purging it from your diet is the single best thing you can do for your health!

Dr. Hyman even suspects the already-awful HFCS of containing significant amounts of dangerous chemicals—like mercury. Okay, but what to do? Maybe shake some of those little pills of artificial sweeteners over your food after all?

For dieticians, sweeteners come in two kinds: nutritive and non- nutritive. The first provides the body with energy— measured in calories—and the second does not. Somehow, we've become brainwashed into thinking that food that is non-nutritive is good.

Nutritive sweeteners, chemically speaking, are carbo-hydrates, and they provide calories. Carbohydrates (which come in the form of sugars, starches, and cellulose) are organic compounds created by living things, especially plants. They contain carbon, hydrogen, and oxygen in a form that the body can easily break down to release energy. Honey is the most natural form of this kind of sugar, usable in exactly the state that it is to be found. Nutritive sweeteners are identified as "sugars" or "added sugar" in the ingredient lists of packaged food, and sometimes as glucose, fructose, sucrose, or maltose. Maybe with the healthy sounding word *syrup* added.

Okay, that's the first kind of sweetener—the nutritive. But what about the non-nutritive? These are mostly laboratory chemicals. For example, one whole group is called polyols (think "many alcohols") and includes unfamiliar names like erythritol, isomalt, maltitol, mannitol, sorbitol, and xylitol. Polyols contain fewer calories and have less of an effect on blood glucose levels than sucrose (which comes from cane sugar or beet sugar). That may sound good, but when the blood sugar levels stay low, as the defenders of sugar like to say, you eat more.

Food for Thought

At the turn of the millennium, worldwide, the prevalence of diabetes amongst all age groups was estimated to be just a shade under 3 percent but was said to be on course to rise to 4.4 percent by 2030. If even that does not sound like much, in terms of the total number of people with diabetes, it represents almost a 50 percent increase—from 171 million sufferers to 366 million in just 30 years.

Typical of the kind of findings fanning the public's fear of sugar, researchers at Cambridge University in the UK claimed in 2016 that cutting out just one sugary drink a day, such as orange squash or a can of fizzy lemon, could reduce the risk of developing diabetes by 25 percent.

But is all this scientific fact or scientific fad? After all, diabetes is associated with all kinds of foods, especially in excess, and as the sugar industry likes to remind us, apples and oranges also contain a good helping of sugar. We should remain skeptical.

The case of sugar is instructive because it's complicated: big sugar producers and food companies whose products rely on added sugar had an interest in downplaying health risks—and equally powerful corporations stood to benefit from the replacement of natural sugars with artificial sweeteners.

To make sense of it all, climb into the time machine, if you will, and travel back to the 1960s, when weight-conscious Americans were already switching in droves to diet sodas—particularly Diet Rite and Tab—sweetened with cyclamate and saccharin. From 1963 through 1968, diet soda's share of the soft-drink market shot from 4 percent to 15 percent. For soft-drink manufacturers, as Independent Social Research Foundation vice president and research director John Hickson warned in an internal review, "A dollar's worth of sugar could be replaced with a dime's worth" of sugar alternatives.

In fact, the traditional sugar industry spent more than $4 million, at today's prices, in a bid to find harmful effects for harmless-sounding sweeteners, like Sugar Twin and Sucaryl. And sure enough, some studies soon linked them. Now, these sorts of studies involve massive doses in animals with completely different metabolisms from humans and mean essentially nothing. Nonetheless, that is how "safety testing" is done, and so, in 1969, the FDA banned cyclamates in the United States. In 1977, saccharin, too, was linked to cancer, but in this case, the sweetener avoided being formally banned. Foods containing it just had to add this: "Use of this product may be hazardous to your health. This product contains saccharin, which has been determined to cause cancer in laboratory animals."

Only in 2000 was saccharin released from the labeling rule, when further research demonstrated that it was physically impossible for the effect on rats to be repeated in humans. Of course, that did not prove that saccharin does not cause cancer, but no one seems to mind that. On the other hand, the holy aura that artificial sweeteners had at first never returned.

Take the case of aspartame, also known as NutraSweet and Equal. It was approved by the FDA in the early 1980s after passing the usual "will this give animals cancer?" tests. However, the only way to really know what new chemicals will do to people is to get people to take them, and sure enough, unfortunately for the manufacturers, a new report came along in 1996 highlighting a rise in the number of Americans with (untested for) brain tumors that went in lockstep with the introduction and use of this sweetener.

Correlation is not causation, and there were reasons why this statistical link might have been coincidental, so the authorities in America decided that aspartame could continue to be used as long as a not-entirely-reassuring message was added stating that there was no clear link known *yet* between its consumption and the development of brain tumors.

More research was conducted in 2005, this time involving feeding rats the equivalent volume of aspartame as would be contained in up to 2,000 cans of diet soda daily. It found an increased risk of lymphomas and leukemias. Yet actual human data from half a million retired Americans found no link between consumption of aspartame-containing beverages and the development of lymphoma, leukemia, or brain cancer. Academics who had criticized the sugar industry's attempts to undermine its rivals by citing bad outcomes in animal experiments welcomed these "all clear" results, even though, methodologically, they were just as suspect.

The point is that the research clearing chemical sweeteners is far from conclusive, and personally I would say somewhat suspect—and anyway, I'm still very much a fan of natural sweeteners, quintessentially those beautiful jars of wild honey from small, local producers.

Part VI
Secrets of the Chocolate Tree

Chapter 27

A Believer's History of Chocolate

Chocolate. The word itself comes with so many connotations. As a food, it is the perfect example of something which comes not only with myriad social and cultural associations but also with surprising biological and chemical properties. And for many dieters, chocolate comes to the rescue of those whose enthusiasm and ardor for being vigilant about what they eat begin to flag. Chocolate, "the food of the gods," is as healthy as it is mysterious, as it is misunderstood.

Everyone knows that the ancients worshipped chocolate (I use "everyone" rather loosely, indeed I use "worshipped" and "chocolate" that way too). But few people know that for many years the main chocolate manufacturers—George Cadbury of Birmingham, Elizabeth Fry of Bristol, and Joseph Rowntree and Terry's of York—were not only all English but more significantly all founded by Quaker families. Quakers, you see, are highly philosophical people whose sense of the divine led them away from things like holy texts and official creeds and instead toward a personal ethic built around shared humanist values. Harmless though this may sound today, in the seventeenth and eighteenth centuries they were often persecuted, leading some to flee to the New World.

There, however, things were no better. Indeed, somewhat worse. In Massachusetts, anyone suspected of being a Quaker was stripped, searched for witch marks, and then whipped. The ears of the men were cut off, and women were tied to a cart's tail, branded on the left shoulder, and whipped through every town until they had reached the borders of the colony.

But back to England. So spiritually minded were these early chocolate makers that their companies allowed time in the working day for religious readings and even breaks for hymns to be sung. The Quaker owners insisted on fair wages and good conditions for the workers, built them houses, and employed doctors and dentists—this at a time when other companies in Britain, indeed their rivals, still used child labor. These ethical practices contributed to a public impression that Quaker confectioners were trustworthy, an image that particularly mattered during a period when contamination of sweets was a big issue. Red lead, for example, was a common coloring for sweets, despite being poisonous, and a mixture of odd things,

The Quakers

The Society of Friends, to use the formal title of the Quakers, was founded in England in the 1650s by George Fox. It was a gentle and pacifist religious group that followed no particular rules but said instead that all people share a divine spark and that there's something of God in everyone. As Quakers are wary of alcohol, and even coffee, hot chocolate seemed to them a very good substitute. There are competing accounts of how the Quakers got their nickname. One is that their founder told a magistrate to tremble—quake—at God's name, another that it comes from their shaking during religious experiences.

Quakers are a very small group: in 1851 they only accounted for 0.1 percent of the 21 million souls of England, Scotland, and Wales, which makes their near monopoly of the world's chocolate industry at the time so remarkable. Today there are only about 17,000 Quakers in Britain and 210,000 worldwide. Several of the big names in chocolate are still European—Cadbury, Droste, van Houten, Suchard—although the names are really all that is left of the original ideals.

like brick dust, might be added to the expensive cocoa powder to make it go further.

The issue of using cheap ingredients in place of expensive cocoa and cocoa butter continues to be a live one, just as food manufacturing generally revolves around ever more ingenious substitutions of traditional ingredients (like cream) for cheaper ones (like vegetable oil). Indeed, there has been a thirty-year war between Britain and the European Union that still rumbles on over whether UK chocolate manufacturers should be able to sell as chocolate the sugary mix containing lots of vegetable fat and hardly any cocoa. Their Continental competitors claim the substance should be branded "vegelate" or "chocolate substitute."

But back in the nineteenth century, the Quaker families put plenty of cocoa in their chocolate and put ethics before profit, so customers were reassured. And yet, somehow, despite their firm moral beliefs, as late as 1907 the companies were still using slave labor on their West Indian sugar plantations. Funny how stuff happens. Or maybe not so funny, as it was all "under conditions of great cruelty," as an official report into Cadbury put it. Quaker values bent to provide the chocolate makers with the all-important chocolate beans at a low price. Ultimately, the Quaker chocolate bosses remained people of their own era, forcing women to leave work once they married and employing slaves, even as they helped kick-start Britain's campaign against the slave trade in the early nineteenth century.

At the close of World War I, George Cadbury, the top chocolate maker, earned the nickname "the Chocolate Uncle" by sending three tons of the brown gold to "Viennese waifs" to help them recover from the stress of wartime. Later on, in the U.S., Milton Hershey acquired the nickname "the Chocolate Man" along with the rights to sell a particularly milky, sugary version of Cadbury's chocolate. Hershey was also a committed philanthropist, building workers' houses to standards that were so high for the time that one worker, Monroe Stover, wrote later of his new home:

> It was a small house for the nine of us but it was our first modern home and I'll never forget it.
> Moving to Hershey was like moving to paradise...

And, of course, Stover recalled, "Everybody kept chocolate in their cupboards."

Happy days! Alas, back in Europe, Cadbury was being bought by rivals. First it was Fry's, which in 2010 was purchased by the world's second-biggest food company, the Swiss corporation Kraft for the princely sum of £11.5 billion (about $16 billion). Just two years later, Kraft itself was gobbled up by Mondelez International—all of which goes to show how almost everything in the food world can be traced back to a handful—or is it a mouthful?—of giant multinationals. One of the changes Cadburys' new owners insisted on, apart from shrinking the chocolate bars, was stopping the traditional Christmas hamper given to retired former workers, a small economy they explained as necessary. The company sent a note to the affected pensioners explaining that the decision was to plug "a pensions black hole." They enclosed a gift voucher for £15, adding: "The voucher is enclosed with this letter to spend as you wish. The voucher replacement is just for one year and will not be repeated."

The Quaker habit of frugality evidently lived on! Or maybe not. Irene Rosenfeld, the Kraft chief executive who authorized this kind gesture, at the same time allocated $10 million extra for herself as a pay raise—taking her annual remuneration to $21 million. Merry Christmas!

The Chocolate Song

In an essay on happiness, Sebastian Purcell, an assistant professor of philosophy at SUNY Cortland in New York, recalls a strange work of poetic philosophy entitled "My friends, stand up!," written by Nezahualcoyotl, the polymath and ruler of the ancient city-state of Texcoco, in what is today Mexico.

My friends, stand up!

The princes have become destitute,

I am Nezahualcoyotl,

I am a Singer, head of macaw.

Grasp your flowers and your fan.

With them go out to dance!

You are my child,

you are Yoyontzin [daffodil].

Take your chocolate,

flower of the cacao tree,

may you drink all of it!

Do the dance,

do the song!

Not here is our house,

not here do we live,

you also will have to go away.

Chapter 28

Chocolate Lovers

The founders of the great British confectionary company Cadbury studied their subject well, and so they will have known all about chocolate's mysterious powers and reputation. They may even have read a curious little booklet published in 1741, *Om Chokladdrycken*, by one Carl von Linné. The pamphlet examined the medicinal uses of chocolate and described it as an effective aphrodisiac or love potion. It's author, von Linné, aka Carl Linnaeus, was the great naturalist who developed the organizing system for plants and animals that we continue to use today.

Linnaeus didn't try to explain why chocolate held these properties, but nowadays we know that chocolate contains an amphetamine-like substance called phenylethylamine. This is said to control "the euphoric feelings" associated with being in love, as the *Oxford Companion to Food* puts it delicately.

It was almost inevitable that one of the most intense chocolate experiences offered by that venerable UK confectionary company eventually caused much embarrassment and controversy. The story starts when someone came up with the idea of making a tubular sweet comprising lots of strands of chocolate and coated in a final layer of chocolate. The company launched the Flake in 1920 under the straightforward slogan "Dairy Milk that Just Crumbles on your Tongue," and for years a candy was all it remained. But by the late 1960s, Cadbury's TV commercials had become rather more, er, exciting, portraying "beautiful, bohemian Flake Girls" slowly licking the chocolate bar. This, incidentally, illustrates a very important truth that all dieters should remember: what beautiful people do in ads has nothing to do with us being healthy and beautiful ourselves.

Anyway, one such commercial featured a model, naked apart from her mascara and lipstick, letting her bath overflow while eating a Flake, while another showed a young woman in a negligee sitting on a window sill on a hot evening. Both women were clearly losing themselves in their moment of indulgence. A third, featuring former Miss World Eva Rueber-Staier, went even further and had to be taken off the air after numerous complaints about the suggestive manner in which she enjoyed her chocolate.

Cadbury didn't seem to mind the controversy. There's really no such thing as bad publicity as long as you (*ahem*) get it every night, and so, sure enough, in 2001, a poster campaign featured another scantily clad woman sucking on the chocolate bar, along with the tagline, "How much would you like this woman's job?" But this time, it seemed the company had gone too far. Thirty people complained to the UK's Advertising Standards Authority that the campaign essentially showed a woman simulating oral sex, colloquially known as a blow job. Not that a fine Quaker chocolate maker would have known that.

Indeed, Cadbury said it was horrified at the very idea. It insisted that its ad was simply an invitation for people to consider how much they would like to be *paid* to eat a Flake— but to no avail. The company's explanations that the ads only showed women enjoying chocolate (ah, yes, but enjoying *what* about chocolate?) fell on deaf ears.

The fact remained, as the Advertising Standards Association clearly understood, that enjoying chocolate is quite risqué no matter the circumstances. As soon as it started making the stuff, Cadbury had strayed well into dangerous territory, long before it even considered making sexy TV ads. On the other hand, the advertisements showed that even if chocolate doesn't make you look gorgeous and sexy, it can help you to feel that way. This is surely a good reason to include it in any diet.

Recipe for Romance: Salmon with White Chocolate Sauce

1 tablespoon butter

1 tablespoon flour

1 cup milk, or more, adjust to get the right consistency

4 ounces white chocolate, broken into small
   chunks (not too sweet) Ghirardelli make a 4-oz
   white chocolate baking bar that is suitable

¼ cup olive oil (for cooking the salmon)

4 (4-oz.) filets of salmon

1 medium lemon, ½ cut into slices, ½ juiced

1 tablespoon chopped parsley (or other fresh herbs)

Salt and pepper to taste

Make the white sauce: in a medium saucepan, over low heat, melt the butter. Stir in the flour to form a paste. Add the milk, stirring constantly with the back of a wooden spoon, and cook, still stirring, until a pourable consistency is obtained. Stir the white chocolate into the sauce, cooking until it's melted. If needed, add a bit more milk to make the sauce a pourable consistency.

Meanwhile, in a separate skillet, heat the olive oil over moderately low heat; add the salmon, and cook, turning once, until the flesh is cooked through. Add slices of lemon and lemon juice; sprinkle with parsley, salt, and pepper. Go easy on the salt. Chocolate and salt do not go well together.

Serve the salmon with steamed rice, the sauce in a little jug alongside, and a green vegetable, such as steamed asparagus or broccoli.

Chapter 29

Chocolate for Stimulation
and Reassurance

Eating a bar of good-quality dark chocolate is like gobbling a handful of amphetamines (admittedly rather tiny ones). And whether it is the amphetamine-like substances or the cannabinoids it also contains, or just the taste, when chocolate was first brought to Europe, the "stimulating" effects were considered so great that the Church immediately banned it's consumption—at least, that is, during periods of religious fasting. Thomas Gage, a British-born Dominican friar who traveled to the Americas in the mid-seventeenth century, reflected the thinking of the time regarding the powers of chocolate, describing how the drink had caused conflict between the Creoles and the Spanish. One story tells how the Creole women were particularly fond of chocolate and how their church services were occasions for "drinking a few." However, given the drink's associations, the Spanish bishop tried to end this ritual, and when shortly afterward he was found dead, a story spread that the women had so hated the loss of their chocolate mornings that they had added poison, appropriately enough, to his chocolate. Whether true or merely foolish gossip, it led to an important sounding new saying:

Beware the chocolate of Chiapa.

Thomas Gage sided with the locals on the right to chocolate, if not on the bigger issue of killing bishops. And as for the stimulating properties of the food itself, he merely noted that it helped him to stay alert when staying up late writing. After several years of reflection, and in recognition of how much its ruling against chocolate bothered monks and priests, the Church reversed its position in a ruling with wide implications. In 1662, one Cardinal Brancaccio declared that henceforth *liquidum non frangit jejunum* would be the new Church policy. In plainer language: "liquids do not break a fast."

In this way, chocolate provided a general service to countless thousands of observant people. And even if, to be honest, chocolate didn't have the Cadbury Flake effect on everyone (see chapter 28, "Chocolate Lovers"), good-quality chocolate high in cocoa solids *does* seem to provide a bit of a boost. That could be because cocoa contains within it small amounts of powerful, mood-enhancing drugs. One of these, tryptophan, is an amino acid used by the body to make a key chemical messenger in the brain called serotonin, high levels of which are linked to feelings of elevated mood.

When two U.S. researchers, Emmanuelle di Tomaso and Daniele Piomelli, investigated the chemical components of chocolate, especially dark chocolate, they found three substances that "could act as cannabinoid mimics." (Cannabinoids are the substances found in cannabis, also known as marijuana, that produce and sustain the feeling of being high.)

If all this begins to make chocolate consumption sound rather like drug culture, well, that's because it is. Hippies at 1960s pop festivals sometimes smoked a concoction made of hashish (cool), sugar (be careful!), flour, butter, milk and (naughty!) chocolate. One of the cannabinoids a rich, dark chocolate contains—anandamide—affects exactly the same regions of the brain as its naughty cousin, cannabis. Admittedly, the quantities of anandamide contained are so small that you'd almost have to be a homeopath to expect much of an effect. Christian Felder at the U.S. National Institute of Mental Health has estimated that the average person would have to eat 25 pounds of chocolate at one time to get any significant effect. But the proof is in the trying.

Then there's the amphetamine-like substances found in chocolate. These have interesting properties as both stimulants and appetite suppressants. They work by triggering the nerves and brain into increasing the amount of certain chemicals in the body that, among other things, increase the heart rate, raise blood pressure, and decreases appetite. Chocolate does all that?!

Chemists long ago worked out that chocolate contains two chemical stimulants: the famous caffeine, albeit in modest amounts, and the less famous theobromine, in quite significant quantities. It is the latter that gives dark chocolate its characteristic bitter taste. Most commercial milk chocolate is too full of dairy or sugar for either the taste or the effects to be apparent, but a good cocoa powder can vary in the amount of theobromine, from 2 percent to more than 10 percent. The bottom line is that a cup of *real* hot chocolate at night is maybe not such a good idea. Or perhaps it is if your night is intended to include euphoric feelings. However, as a mid-morning pick-you-up it is invaluable—and surprisingly diet friendly.

Theobromine

Theobromine gets its name from the ancient Greek words *theo* meaning "god" and *broma* meaning "food," which is why chocolate is really "the food of the gods." In the human body it relaxes the nerves that govern blood flow, producing a mildly stimulating effect. (Theobromine has nothing to do with the poisonous chemical bromine, by the way.) In concentrated form, it is taken as a supplement by bodybuilders, who appreciate its potential to reduce levels of water in the body, giving them, they hope, that "ripped," or "walnut in a condom," look. Less drastically, indulging in a bit of dark chocolate can be part of a healthy weight-loss plan by, among other benefits, reducing the body's retention of water.

Pet owners should note that it is this chemical that is dangerous for their animals if they should happen on a bar of chocolate.

The early writers on chocolate often became lyrical when they wrote of its value as a food. In *The Natural History of Chocolate* (1730), the French writer known as D. de Quelus, excitedly explains that a single ounce of chocolate contains as much nourishment as a pound of beef, and that:

> Before chocolate was known in Europe, good old wine was called the milk of old men; but this title is now applied with greater reason to chocolate, since its use has become so common, that it has been perceived that chocolate is, with respect to them, what milk is to infants.

Another early European account by Antonio Colmenero de Ledesma praises chocolate, saying that it:

> ... vehemently incites to Venus, and causeth conception in women, hastens and facilitates their delivery; it is an excellent help to digestion, it cures consumptions, and the cough of the lungs, the New Disease, or plague of the guts, and other fluxes, the green sicknesse, jaundice, and all manner of inflammations and obstructions. It quite takes away the morpheus, cleaneth the teeth, and sweetneth the breath, provokes urine, cures the stone, and expels poison, and preserves from all infectious diseases.

Now this is all very well, but the big question is, *does chocolate make you fat?* Well, there's good news and not-so-good. The not-so-good is that the ancient authorities are unambiguous and their answer is yes. For hundreds of years three consistent medicine-related claims for the cacao bean were made. First, eating chocolate produced weight gain. This, I stress, was considered a good thing back then. Ancient, colonial, and early-modern physicians regularly recommended or prescribed chocolate with the specific purpose of adding or restoring "flesh" to emaciated patients. Francisco Hernández, for example, wrote a botanical text called "A History of Plants in the New Spain" in 1577, which concluded by identifying a beverage called *chocolatl* that had the properties of making the consumer, as he puts it, "extraordinarily fat" if used frequently. *Chocolatl* was, therefore, the ideal prescription for thin and weak patients. Antonio Colmenero de Ledesma also wrote in his own "curious treatise" on chocolate, *Curioso Tratado de la Naturaleza* (1631), that cacao made those who drank it "fat, corpulent, faire and amiable," which sounds pretty conclusive to me.

However, as so often, the context is important, and certainly in this case, it changes the sense. What these observers were describing was "good fat," not bad fat, as modern dieticians like to say. At a time when food was often scarce and illness a constant companion, the chocolate drink was considered very nutritious—more "fresh-squeezed orange juice" than Fanta.

That said, chocolate retains a bit of a bad health reputation because of its indubitable component of *saturated* fats, which we used to be told were a Very Bad Thing. Nowadays, though, the expert advice has changed, and indeed the kind of saturated fat that chocolate contains (stearic and oleic acid) are considered to be good fats. Specifically, they do not raise blood cholesterol levels.

Indeed, chocolate may *protect* the heart because it also contains *flavonoids*, such as epicatechin, which some researchers have claimed reduce the risk of heart disease by reducing blood pressure; and may even guard against cancer. Flavonoids are also present in tea and red wine, which is why similar claims are made for these beverages, but it is only in dark chocolate that the amount becomes large enough to imply a significant effect.

Unfortunately, a modern bar of chocolate contains quite a lot of sugar, even when it is sold as dark chocolate, while cheap chocolate is mainly sugar and industrially produced vegetable fat. This kind of candy simply makes you fat. But don't give up on the cocoa yet—there's surprising evidence that chocolate *snacks* make you thin. Skeptical? That's good!

But hard facts as well as vague theories support this assertion, including a research study in 2013 that found that eating chocolate cake helped a group of obese people to lose significant weight. The key thing was to have it early in the day—the researchers said breakfast, but to my mind that *is* going a bit too far—I'd rather get my caffeine fix via a cup of tea. Why not save the chocoholism until at least midmorning? Whatever your preferences, though, the morning is the time to set the metabolism burning at higher speed.

Anyway, an Israeli study led by Daniela Jakubowicz split two hundred or so clinically obese adults into two groups. Both were put on diets for nearly eight months (a commitment that would challenge most people's dietary zeal!) with the same daily total calories: 1600 calories per day for the men and 1400 for the women. Amounts, in other words, well under the usually accepted daily requirement. One group followed a low-carb diet that included a 300-calorie breakfast, and the other was given a balanced 600-calorie breakfast *that included chocolate cake*.

Now here's the curious thing: halfway through the 32-week study, both groups had lost 33 pounds (15 kilos) per person. But in the final months of the study, the "no chocolate cake" group put most of it back on, regaining on average a rather sad 22 pounds per person. Meanwhile, the happy cake eaters lost another 15 pounds each! For Professor Jakubowicz the explanation was that the treat early in the day decreased cravings during the rest of the day. Put in biochemical terms, the sweet start to the day regulated the body's production of ghrelin (the hormone that increases hunger pangs) and thus offset the dieter's paradox: that restrictive eating regimens which are initially effective often lead to failed dieters who eat even more unhealthily than they did before.

All of which goes to show that a diet must be *realistic* if it is to become a new lifestyle. Regulating food cravings is better than crude deprivation for long-term success.

The Chocolate Tree

Good things really do grow on trees! The chocolate tree, for example. You don't see them in vast European orchards, or indeed in North American plantations. This is because the tree only grows in South and Central America, in the area around the upper Orinoco River basin, in the Venezuelan Amazon, where it first originated several million years ago, as well as, nowadays, in Central Africa, where it was transplanted.

The original chocolate eaters were the indigenous peoples of the New World. Curiously, the word itself comes from the sound made during the processing of the seedpods into chocolate, which involved beating the pods in water. The cacao tree is just one member of a family of at least seventy trees of the genus Theobroma, many of which are believed to have special properties and are used in traditional medicine. The one we are interested in is Theobroma cacao, which produces the seeds that are made into chocolate. The pods grow directly out of the trunk. Intriguingly, this important variety is thought to be a mere 10 to 15 thousand years old and to have differentiated from its much older Theobroma cousins through association with humans.

Although there are no written records from so long ago, early evidence of chocolate cultivation has been found by archaeologists in Belize, on the eastern coast of Central America, from a staggering 3000 years ago, and an image of the plant has been found on 2500-year-old Peruvian pottery. The pods were fermented, dried, roasted, and winnowed—four separate steps. So why would the ancients have gone to so much trouble to prepare a bitter drink? The answer is due to its mind-altering properties. As Sophie and Michael Coe explain in their book *The True History of Chocolate*:

The Chocolate Tree *(cont.)*

The impetus for the spread of cacao cultivation in pre-Columbian Mesoamerica and northern South America might have been fascination with the seeds as a source of addictive, even hallucinogenic substances, of use in popular mystical and ritualistic ceremonies.

Curiously, though, when it's not being used as a stimulant and an aphrodisiac, chocolate has a reputation as a comfort food. These reassuring things, as the twentieth-century Swiss psychologist Clotaire Rapaille has observed, are nearly always drawn from childhood memories. "The influence goes way beyond developing preferences for certain dishes and includes a whole set of intrinsic values about convivial and affectionate family structures and cultural practices," he says.

Rapaille was once employed by the Swiss chocolate company Nestlé to persuade Japanese customers to start buying coffee. Nestlé is the global brand that made a not-so-good name for itself selling ethically-suspect baby milk formula to African women who didn't need it, an observation that is relevant to our discussion. Nestlé wanted Rapaille's expertise because they thought it might help them to sell instant coffee to the Japanese, who not only didn't need it but basically disliked the stuff. The $250-billion company wondered if Dr. Rapaille could help them change a nation's preferences. Indeed, he could! His highly successful advice was to give up trying to persuade the Japanese that coffee was a nice change from their beloved green tea, and instead to introduce a coffee-flavored dessert for children into the Japanese market. With this stealthy strategy, a few years later Nestlé was able to start selling coffee through other sweet products, always playing surreptitiously on its customers' childhood memories. "And when the children were teenagers, the company found that they now had a big market for coffee in Japan," finishes Rapaille proudly.

This is how, for a new generation of Japanese, coffee became a comfort food. The tale also illustrates that what we like has less to do with taste buds and more to do with brainwaves. That's social science though, and dietary matters continue to be dominated by nutritionists, who, not having much feeling for the subtler workings of the human brain, continue to explain our cravings for chocolate in terms of biochemistry. (What the body really craves, they say, is dark leafy greens, nuts, seeds, fish, beans, whole-grain, avocado, yogurt, and bananas— loftily ignoring the fact that, actually, we don't. The scientific reasoning, you see, is that all these foods, including chocolate, are rich sources of magnesium, the shiny metal that school chemistry teachers set fire to with grand effect.)

Food experts add knowledgably that 80 percent of the population is lacking magnesium in their daily diet. "Magnesium has a vital role in supporting the immune system by preventing inflammation, in balancing the nervous system and it also helps easing anxiety," says Shona Wilkinson, a nutritionist at NutriCentre. Eighty percent of people are anxious? But that makes the state of anxiety the norm, which seems paradoxical. On the other hand, it also seems to make having a supply of emergency chocolate even more important than before!

Chapter 30

Food Therapy

The School of Life is a philosophically minded organization, founded by the modern-day aristocrat, Alain de Botton, that has offices in several European cities. Each location comprises a classroom, a library of philosophical books, and a café-bar. Because, after all, philosophy runs better when lubricated and even better when sustained with good food.

In an article titled, characteristically, "Food as Therapy," the school presents some of its core ideas. First of all, food is not just "fuel" but "offers help with certain of our psychological needs." It has, in short "therapeutic potential." This is because every kind of food has not only a nutritional value but also a psychological value.

> The value emerges from its character. Every food hints at a personality, an orientation, a way of apprehending the world, who it would be if it was magically turned into a person. You could ascribe to it a gender, an outlook, a spirit, even a political dimension.

It is no coincidence that in many religions, particular foods play special roles. A Jewish tradition that lives on in observant families is to use unleavened bread and bitter horseradish during Passover to symbolize the courage the believers displayed on their flight from Egypt. However, to illustrate their point, the School of Life considers some fairly humble foods: the lemon, the hazelnut and ... "fish and chips."

Let's start with the lemon. It is, nutritionally-speaking, quite straightforward: each 100-gram serving contains 29 calories, 2.8 grams dietary fiber, and quite a lot of sugar. But, psychologically-speaking, it has particular "ingredients."

> It is a fruit that "speaks" (quietly but eloquently) of such things as: the south, the sun, the upstanding and the hopeful, the morning and the simple. It suggests calls to action, it wants us to brace ourselves to take on what matters and focus on what we know we have to do. It is against sentimentality: it is brutally honest, but kind.

I think there's some truth in the first few claims—but lemons are against sentimentality? It is the fruit that makes us cry! The symbolism is becoming subjective (but that's symbolism for you). How about the School's second example, the hazelnut? Again, it is easy to describe as a mixture of nutrients, but what is the therapeutic mix? For the School of Life it is:

> ... at the same time a receptacle of such things as: autumnal briskness, maturity, soberness, self-sufficiency and an almost childlike neatness (like a ten-year-old who keeps his drawers tidy...).

I don't know many ten-year-olds who do that—again the comparisons seem to disappear into something totally personal and subjective. The general claim, though, is that each food contains a particular philosophy of life, and this is where the connection with chocolate might be made:

> "We are ingesting physically, but also trying to take into our souls the psychological nutrients we intuit." We choose and use food to "bolster certain sides of our natures and compensate for certain weaknesses of spirit... we want to take on the avocado's confident serenity, the fig's ease with sensuality, the scallop's dignified privacy, the asparagus's resolute commitment to individuality."*

On this view, of food as therapy, each meal, indeed each nibble, is chosen to rebalance us in some way: whether from being too intellectual or too irritable—or too emotional. People who are stressed can munch bowls of muesli, people who are fatigued can snack on a bar of chocolate. The only important thing to appreciate is that:

> The food we call "tasty" gives vital clues as to what is missing in our psyches [and] not just our stomachs. It's in the power of food to help us be more rounded versions of ourselves.

Mind you, maybe that last phrase is a little unfortunate.

Chapter 31

Indulge Yourself

On their arrival in the Americas in the seventeenth century, the Spanish quickly identified chocolate as a very classy drink, and it is not irrelevant to note that the first chocolate pods that arrived in France crossed the Pyrenees in no less posh company than that of Anne of Austria, wife of Louis XIII. For centuries after, chocolate basked in a reputation for being sophisticated in a way that coffee, for example, which was discovered around the same time in the Americas, never quite managed to equal.

A big part of chocolate's original appeal was its supposed health-giving properties. Real chocolate (as opposed to today's sugary substitutes) is full of some very valuable substances: antioxidants, which soak up damaged molecules in the bloodstream; plant sterols, which help regulate cholesterol levels; and cocoa flavanols, which improve blood circulation. (Hence chocolate's racy reputation.)

A respected seventeenth-century Spanish physician, Dr. Juanes de Barrios, once recommended consuming chocolate for breakfast, saying that after eating "the Indian nectar," one needed no further meat, bread, or drink.

Other Spanish physicians of the period praised chocolate, including an unnamed doctor from Seville, who noted that "… no one hath been known to live above seven days by drinking wine alone, [however] one may live months, and years using nothing but chocolate." The doctor further testified that he himself:

> … saw a childe weaned, which could not be brought by any artifice to take any food, and for

four months space he was preserved alive by giving him *chocolata* only, mixing now and then some crumbs of bread therewith.

In eighteenth-century France, the popular view was that this new chocolate was a kind of superfood. In his Natural Hisory of Chocolate and Sugar (1719), Doctor de Quélus provided testimonial evidence that chocolate was more than beneficial for health and that its use extended longevity:

> There recently died at Martinico a councilor aged about a hundred years, who, for thirty years past, lived on nothing but chocolate and biscuit. He sometimes, indeed, had a little soup at dinner, but never any fish, flesh, or other victuals: he was, nevertheless, so vigorous and nimble, that at fourscore and five, he could get on horseback without stirrups.

No wonder that when a Spanish military doctor, Antonio Lavedán, compared various Western weaknesses in his influential 1796 treatise *On Coffee, Tea, Chocolate and Tobacco*, he closed by saying:

> It is possible for chocolate alone to keep a man robust and healthy for many years, if he takes it three times a day, that is, in the morning, at noon and at night.

Today, potential benefits claimed for chocolate include lower cholesterol levels, prevention of cognitive decline, and reduced risk of cardiovascular problems. But most surprising of all may be the accumulating evidence that consuming a bit of chocolate, especially dark chocolate, can be part of a diet regimen!

Diet Tip: Chocolate-Eating Strategies

Nibble on organic dark chocolate.

Drink hot chocolate made with raw milk and real cacao.

Hint: real chocolate is very hard to find; the big multinationals long ago decided that selling sugary fats was much more profitable, but the French do know it (sourced from one of their jealously guarded colonies) and you can buy specialty cocoa for drinks or cooking in supermarkets now if you know where to look.

Chili non Carne y Chocolate

- 2 tablespoons olive oil
- 2 medium onions, finely chopped
- 1 leek, white part only, finely chopped
- 1 large zucchini, finely chopped
- 1 large carrot, peeled and finely chopped
- 1 fresh red chili pepper, finely chopped
- 4 cloves garlic, minced
- Herbs and spices to taste (e.g., regular ones like oregano, basil,and thyme; exotic ones like cumin, ground coriander, paprika, cinnamon, and nutmeg)
- Salt (preferably "real" salt, freshly ground)
- Black pepper (freshly ground)
- 2 tablespoons tomato purée
- $2^1/2$ cups (500g) dried lentils, red, green, or a mixture
- 1 15-ounce (400g) can red kidney beans, drained and rinsed (I use fewer of these than some people, as to be honest, a few are good and a lot are dull.)
- 2 15-ounce cans chopped or sieved tomatoes
- 1 tablespoon butter

Chili non Carne y Chocolate (cont.)

- Spoonful of honey, splash of wine (optional)

- 2 ounces (60 g) bittersweet chocolate

- $1/4$ cup grated Cheddar cheese, for garnish

In a large saucepan, heat the oil till shimmering. Add the finely chopped vegetables, regular herbs, salt, and pepper; cook over medium heat until the vegetables are softened. Add the exotic spices, including a grating of nutmeg if desired; cook for a few minutes. Stir in the tomato purée and cook over moderately low heat for five minutes. Stir in the lentils, kidney beans, and tomatoes. Add butter, and (if desired) a spoonful of honey and a splash of wine. Finally, add the all-important chocolate, stirring until it's melted. Simmer for five minutes. Reduce to low heat and cook very gently for at least half an hour (until lentils are tender), stirring occasionally. Serve with rice, and maybe add banana slices and chocolate buttons. Garnish with grated Cheddar cheese.

Chapter 32

Chocolate Money Really Does Grow on Trees

We've all been told endlessly at school about Christopher Columbus sailing the ocean blue and "discovering" the Americas (even though he didn't really), but hardly anyone is taught about his discovery of chocolate. This came some ten years later, in 1502, when Columbus and his men captured a canoe at the Caribbean island of Guanaja that contained a quantity of mysterious-looking "almonds." They were, in fact, cacao beans, which the explorers later discovered were used as a unit of currency in Mesoamerica, although they never managed to solve the riddle of what use they had and why they were so valued.

What Columbus did soon find out was that the Aztec rulers fought wars with neighbors solely in order to acquire chocolate plants, that they demanded taxes from the Mayans that were paid in cocoa, and that the pods of the plant were transported back to the Aztec court along special trails. Still, he remained unaware of the complicated rituals of the beans' preparation and exact ceremonial use.

It was only later, when Europeans were invited to witness the grandest ceremonies of the time, that cocoa's special place in Aztec life become apparent. It's a story that presents another side of "food as therapy": as for the Aztecs, chocolate was large-scale therapy for the state! Bernal Díaz del Castillo, a Spanish conquistador who participated as a foot soldier in the conquest of Mexico with Hernán Cortés, described one such event in the court of the famous Montezuma, king of the Aztecs:

From time to time the guards brought him, in cups
of pure gold, a drink made from the cocoa-plant,
which they said he took before visiting his wives.
We did not take much notice of this at the time,
though I saw them bring in a good fifty large jugs
of chocolate, all frothed up, of which he would
drink a little. As soon as the great Montezuma
had dined, all the guards and many more of his
household servants ate in their turn. I think more
than a thousand plates of food must have been
brought in for them, and more than two thousand
jugs of chocolate frothed up in the Mexican style.

Westerners being Westerners, they immediately set about
growing more of this "rare currency." However, *Theobroma
cacao* is hard to grow. It requires particular soils, particular
rainfall—and it even needs the shade of particular companion
trees. The breakthrough came in 1674, when a Jesuit priest,
Joao Felipe Bettendorff, traveled with several cocoa pods by
canoe from Para, where he had been administering several
Jesuit missions, and tried growing them in Santa Lucia. The
exercise was so successful that within three years the Jesuits
there had more than a thousand healthy cacao plants. As early
as 1693, a letter from Alfonso Avirrillaga, a Jesuit priest, to the
Provincial Father reports that the college of Chiapas in Mexico
had two plantations made up of no fewer than 75,000 trees! A
third plantation with yet more plants even had a millstone and
was efficiently grinding and processing the cacao.

The Jesuits shipped their chocolate back from the Americas
to Italy by way of Spain. Like the Franciscans, they were deeply
involved in the cacao trade between Brazil, Paraguay, and
Mexico on the one hand and California and Western Europe
on the other. The churches established plantations in Brazil,
forcibly relocating the locals, and imported slaves to work
on them. Some priests objected on ethical grounds but were

overruled, illustrating a pattern that continues today where local priests are kept in line by a remote Catholic hierarchy.

Speaking of hierarchies, among this Church elite, senior Jesuits sent each other packets of chocolate scented in a variety of fragrances. Naturally, the different sects had different opinions about how chocolate should be made. The Dominicans objected to the introduction of "aromatic plants" in hot chocolate, and the Benedictines were appalled by chocolate sauce. To some extent, this Jesuit influence lives on in attitudes toward chocolate. If in sophisticated circles choc-exotica flourishes these days and in France, chocolate experts have long mixed flavors freely, for many people chocolate is reduced to just two variants: milk or dark, with added bits in it, like nuts and raisins, or maybe peppermint chunks, the only embellishments. In this way, a vast range of chocolatey experiences is excluded.

But somewhere along the line 'hot chocolate' lost some of its cachet – particularly in the Anglosphere, where it became strongly associated with children's treats. In countries like France, by contrast, 'chocolateries' continue to exist as high-class (and expensive) places to pause for a hot chocolate. Because although today few people will grab a quick 'chocolate drink' in the office, or even at Starbucks, it is also to the rituals of the South American chocolate drinkers that we owe us our coffee house tradition, perhaps even more so than those of the Oriental tea drinkers.

Recall that the first coffeehouse in London was opened in 1652; the first teahouse followed in 1657 (when tea was fabulously expensive), and in the same year a Frenchman opened the first chocolate house. This was in Queen's Head Alley, Bishopsgate Street. A drink produced in appalling conditions by slaves in the West Indies, chocolate thus ended up being drunk in the most exclusive corners of England by the crème de la crème of society. The habit immediately caught on. The famous diarist of the Great Fire of London, Samuel Pepys, records in his entry for November 24, 1664: "To a coffee house to drink jocolatte." This, he says, was "very good" and credits with relieving his "sad head" and "imbecilic stomach" the day after apparently overdoing it at parties celebrating Charles II's coronation.

Chocolate Ganache with Juniper Berries

Ganache is a posh French word for what is basically a sauce, or, in thicker form, a paste. It is made of just two ingredients, chocolate and cream, to which can be added flavorings, including alcoholic ones. Ganache is often used as a filling for cakes and pastries but can also be used inside chocolate truffles and as an ingredient in savory dishes—for example with salmon. Nothing could be easier to prepare; it is basically the same as a hot chocolate made with cream rather than milk.

3½ fluid ounces (100 ml, about ½ cup) heavy cream

2 tablespoons dried juniper berries, finely chopped

4 ounces (100g) high-quality dark chocolate, chopped

In a medium saucepan over moderately low heat, cook the cream to just before boiling. Add the juniper berries, and simmer to infuse the flavors, about 2 minutes. Don't allow the mixture to reach a boil. Add the chocolate, stirring gently until it is melted.

Pour the ganache into a bowl, allow to cool at room temperature, and then chill in the refrigerator for at least an hour.

Sipping chocolate in public was considered a mark of sophistication and culture, and one Chocolate House in Pall Mall, famous in the days of Queen Anne, under its sign of the "Cocoa Tree," became the center of both gambling and political intrigues before settling down as a literary club. This would

Plato's Noble Cakes

These thoroughly "noble" cakes are made with chocolate, honey, and barley flour, and are definitely not sinful at all. Enjoy them at tea time.

A bar of dark chocolate

1 tablespoon butter (⅛ stick)

½ cup honey

½ cup granulated sugar

¼ cup unsweetened cocoa powder

Seeds from 1 vanilla pod

1 cup applesauce (best if homemade from stewing fresh apples)

¼ cup water

1 cup barley flour

1 teaspoon baking powder

½ cup chopped nuts

Dash of salt

Preheat oven to 350°F. Grease an 8-inch square Pyrex baking dish; set aside. In a large bowl, using low heat, melt the chocolate and butter. Stir in the honey, sugar, cocoa powder, vanilla seeds, applesauce, and water; whisk the mixture until smooth. With a wooden spoon, gently stir in the barley flour, followed by the baking powder, chopped nuts, and salt. Pour the batter into the prepared baking dish and bake until the cake springs back when pressed with a finger in the middle, 35 to 40 minutes. Remove from oven and allow to cool completely in the baking dish. Cut into squares.

include amongst its members Edward Gibbon, the historian who wrote The History of the Decline and Fall of the Roman Empire, and Baron George Byron, the poet, usually known as 'Lord Byron'. He seems to have had some body-image issues, being self indulgent in every way and naturally putting on weight. He then became stricly abstemious, as far as food was concerned anyway, in order to take it off again. In this sense, chocolatein a poem entitled "To Caroline":

> Oh! then let us drain, while we may, draughts of pleasure,
>
> Which from passion like ours may unceasingly flow;
>
> Let us pass round the cup of love's bliss in full measure,
>
> And quaff the contents as our nectar below.

*(From Hours of Idleness, published 1807, composed 1805)

Chapter 33
Darker Chocolate

Long before the Europeans arrived and turned chocolate into both a lucrative business and a lubricant in rowdy drinking clubs, the peoples of South and Central America used it for spiritual and religious purposes. They believed that cacao created a balance between earth, sky, and underworld and that God created man out of maize and chocolate. The cacao tree itself was the first tree, the origin of the universe. And their chocolate rituals related to the underworld, water, and death.

Indeed, chocolate was a central part of the rituals for human sacrifices. One panel of the *Madrid Codex*, one of only four surviving books attributed to the ancient Mayan culture, depicts priests lancing their ear lobes and covering the cacao with blood. Yuck! But there's worse. According to the Mayan and Mexican traditions, the Sovereign Plumed Serpent gave cacao to the Mayan people after humans were created from maize by the divine grandmother goddess, Xmucane. The ceremony to celebrate this event included the sacrifice of a dog with chocolate-colored markings. This was to be just part of the price paid by humanity to the gods of chocolate. More famous amongst the traditions was the one in which a slave was kept in a cage and fed a mix of chocolate and blood before eventually being sacrificed precisely at midnight.

The most important of all the Aztec myths concerning food is a cautionary tale involving theft and punishment. It tells of how the god Quetzalcóatl, the god of air, wind, and medicine, also called Plumed or Feathered Serpent, smuggled cacao beans—the food of the gods—down from the heavens and gave them to the humans, along with the sacred knowledge of how to prepare it for consumption: the process of growing the pods; fermenting, drying, roasting the beans; winnowing and then beating them into paste with water in gourds.

According to legend, Quetzalcóatl stole the small bush with dark red flowers that later became dark fruits. He planted the bush and asked Tláloc, god of rain, to water it and Xochiquetzal, goddess of fertility, to tend it and make it beautiful with flowers. The little tree flowered incessantly. Quetzalcóatl harvested the pods, roasted the kernels, and taught the Toltec women to grind them into a fine powder. The women mixed the powder with water and whipped the blend into a frothy drink which they called *chocolatl*. In the beginning it was only consumed by priests and royalty. It was drunk without being sweetened; hence, the Mayas called it *kahau*, which means bitter.

Inevitably, Quetzalcoatl's fellow gods were angry at this sharing of their food with mortals, but what really made them mad (according to legend) was how much *pleasure* the chocolate gave the humans.

The Feast of the Chocolate Gods

During the month of "raising of the banners" (which runs on the Western calendar from about November 21 to December 10), the Mexicans celebrate a festival in honor of Huitzilopochtli, god of war and the sun, which includes sacrifices to Yacatecuhtli, also known as "Lord of the Nose" and god of travelers. Centuries ago, on the festival eve, cacao beverages were served to the individuals slated to be killed as sacrifices to the god.

Another ritual, still practiced today in Mexico at harvest time, involved feeding the cocoa flowers with blood from cuts made on celebrants' ears and arms.

Death by Chocolate Cake

To perform this important Western ritual, you will need a chocolate cake. These days, there are lots of possible sources—including recipes for ones made from scratch (for a good one, see Appendix E), bakery cakes and brownies (unfrosted), and that excellent fallback: the mix. To qualify as a true "death by" cake, you need to add a very rich topping and filling. A recipe for a suitable one is offered below. Select a high-quality dark chocolate that is at least 70 percent cocoa solids, either semi-sweet or unsweetened. If unsweetened, add a bit of honey.

The topping

In a medium saucepan, heat ⅔ cup heavy cream. Remove from heat. Add 9 ounces (260 g) of finely chopped dark chocolate (remembering the caution above regarding sweetening) and a dash of rum (optional). Stir until smooth and let the mixture cool until it thickens but remains spreadable.

Remove the crusted surface from the top of the cake and cut it in half horizontally. Spread the topping on each of the two layers. Some might spread it on the sides of the cake too, but personally I think this is a vulgarization. If desired, garnish the top with chocolate chips or other small chocolate candies. Refrigerate the cake to harden the frosting but serve at room temperature.

Chapter 34

From Death by Chocolate to Survival by K Rations

And so they were happy over the provisions of the good mountain, filled with sweet things, ... thick with pataxte and cacao... the rich foods filling up the citadel named Broken Place, Bitter Water Place.

High praise for chocolate from the *Popol Vuh*, sacred book of the Maya. (Quoted by Dennis Tedlock in his 1985 book of the same name)

In Central America, chocolate has long been much more than a snack—instead often part of the main dish. It is a key ingredient in savory stews, and in a kind of soup drink made out of a mix of cocoa butter and hot peppers. In a learned account called *The Indian Nectar, Or A Discourse Concerning Chocolata* (1662), an English doctor and writer named Henry Stubbe recorded that Indian women ate chocolate so often that they scarcely consumed any solid meat yet did not exhibit a decline in strength. The book also describes how English soldiers stationed in Jamaica lived on cacao nut paste mixed with sugar that the troops dissolved in water; this was how the soldiers sustained themselves for long seasons.

When chocolate arrived in Europe in the seventeenth century, the Italians experimented originally with it as an ingredient for main courses. Ironically, given their name, the Italian Futurists revived this ancient tradition in the twentieth century with their flamboyant recipes. When Cadbury opened a café in Birmingham in 1824 and sold, alongside tea and coffee, "cocoa nibs," it was advertised as a "nutritious beverage for breakfast," following this long tradition of chocolate as a healthy food.

When the Europeans discovered that in its native Mesoamerica cacao was so valued for its medicinal and nutritional properties that only priests, high government officials, and distinguished warriors got to taste it, chocolate acquired a very different aura. Not to mention the small but important fact that cocoa was the last drink given to sacrificial victims. This history of chocolate has skewed our perceptions ever since.

These days Western culture has decided that chocolate is really only suitable for dessert. People who snack on chocolate instead of having "normal food" are criticized for not eating properly. Not even a slice of chocolate gateau will count as a suitable dinner!

Cultural norms aside, the fact remains that for those on a diet or with limited access to food, chocolate is an excellent, concentrated food source, containing fats, sugar, protein, and iron. It thus deserves its place in emergency rations quite apart from any of its other qualities. That's not just my humble opinion, but that of the American food scientist Ancel Keys—the same Ancel Keys who created a dietary orthodoxy in the mid-twentieth century by producing a spurious list of countries and thereby linking heart disease to eating too much fat. Before his battles on that front, though, he was given the task of designing basic rations for millions of soldiers in World War II. Keys was wrong about fatty food but spot on about the nutritional value of chocolate. The "K Rations," named after him, consisted of hard biscuits, dry sausage, hard candy—and chocolate.

Part VII
Letting Logic Choose the Menu

Chapter 35

The Method of Doubt

The Great Cupboard Clearout

... my method imitates that of the architect. When an architect wants to build a house which is stable on ground where there is a sandy topsoil over underlying rock, or clay, or some other firm base, he begins by digging out a set of trenches from which he removes the sand, and anything resting on or mixed in with the sand, so that he can lay his foundations on firm soil. In the same way, I began by taking everything that was doubtful and throwing it out, like sand ...

René Descartes, from his replies, in the *Meditations*

Modern Philosophy starts with Descartes spending time in his French oven room (appropriately enough for a book on food) meditating quietly on how to avoid the pitfalls of believing things that are, in fact, not true. Anyone who has ever tried to follow a weight-loss diet will have had a similar feeling: wondering if they can really believe the claims of the diet gurus and nutritionists. Here are some of the questionable claims that have been made:

- *Fat not only makes you fat but raises cholesterol and gives you heart disease.*
- *Sugar not only makes you fat but gives you diabetes.*
- *Carbohydrates in things like bread and potatoes not only make you fat but give you heart disease* and *diabetes!*

Might it all be misinformation—or even some kind of grand deception?

"What is there, then, that can be esteemed true? Perhaps this only, that there is absolutely nothing certain." That's how Descartes put it all those centuries ago. In his philosophical view the doubt is so sweeping that out goes *all* knowledge of the external world, not merely dietary tips. Iron rules about physical objects, cause and effect, and so on are suspected and are instead to be replaced with knowledge of God.

That's not our project though; we just want to know what is healthy to eat, although this seems just as hard to pin down. Yet Descartes, who was short and plump himself, might well have been talking of food matters when he wrote, "The senses deceive from time to time, and it is prudent never to trust wholly those who have deceived us even once."

And it is Descartes' *method* that is really the thing for healthy eaters—the one which involves throwing away all your previous beliefs (or meal plans) until you find the few that you can be absolutely certain of. In Descartes' case, he famously ended up with only the following statement:

I think, therefore I am.

Like Descartes, we must be radical and we must be skeptical of much more than just the claims of supermarket foods, or even advice from celebrity diet gurus. We have to suspect *the entire edifice of nutritional advice*, whether it be from governments or doctors or *even* from slick internet sites. All theories and rules are to be considered "doubtful until proven."

The practical application of this principle would be to go to your refrigerator and food pantry and *clear them all out*, putting all the doubtful things into a box or maybe the compartment at the bottom of the fridge previously reserved for unwanted vegetables, and leave them there until you are sure what's in them. Descartes took six days to systematically reject all his old lazy assumptions and find certainty (that was a literary device—in reality it took him years, but whatever), so we should not expect to obtain clarification on what to eat in just half an hour. Instead assume that *all* foods are dodgy, with the exception—because I don't want you to starve!—of nature's most humble foods, leaves and fruits. Don't worry, you can soon expand your diet—once you have uncovered, in food matters at least, that crystal-clear perception of truth and falsity that only a little bit of philosophizing can bring.

Applying Descartes' Method of Doubt to Your Diet

Go through your cupboards and throw out all the junk foods:

Cookies, chips, pastries, and cakes

Ready-made, prepackaged meals

Anything marked low-fat, low-sugar, or "high in" something unintelligible.

Don't accept the claims on the packaging at face value. Indeed, treat them as suspicious. Why would a healthy product need to hide behind all this marketing talk?

Check the sell-by date. If the product is dried, pickled, or fermented—the traditional ways to preserve food—there's no need to worry. Otherwise, the farther out the sell-by date is, the less goodness there likely is left in the food. (Milk is a good example of this.) Actually, the smart way to use such dates is as a guide to how many nutrients remain in the food. The longer the shelf life, the more processed the food usually is, and the less nutritious.

Chapter 36

Correlation Is Not Causation

One of my friends was a nutritionist, indeed, I imagine she still is, and her job was to persuade people to eliminate sugar and fat from their diets. She was rather thin and, if anything, looked unhealthy. But I said she was thin—right? So, the advice must have worked. Wrong! That's fallacy number one, assuming that someone's low-fat, low-sugar diet made them thin, because there are any number of other factors that might have really been responsible. It's what philosophers rather grandly call the "fallacy of affirming the consequent" and it is a reasoning error which, long name or not, crops up again and again in dietary advice. Take a deep breath and allow an example to illustrate the point.

Suppose you're talking about Paris. A correct argument proceeds like this:

> If it's December then the coffee will be cold in the sidewalk cafés.
>
> It is December.
>
> Therefore, the coffee will be cold in the sidewalk cafés.

The conclusion is true because the premises are taken to be true. Basically, a logically valid argument just repeats the information in its assumptions in the conclusion. *If A then B, and we do have A, therefore B.* It says nothing really.

What is more useful about philosophical logic, as Aristotle rightly spotted, is helping you to identify bad arguments. For example, look at what happens if the above argument has been mangled:

> If it's December then the coffee will be cold in the sidewalk cafés.
>
> The coffee *is* cold in the sidewalk cafés.
>
> Therefore, it must be December.

But no! It can be a cold day in January or in almost any month—or the coffee maker could be broken.

With matters of food and health, we often look for something that the healthy person does that is conspicuously different from what we do—and then we assume that's their secret! But just as with the coffee being cold, there are many reasons that could explain the phenomenon. (Realizing this is another element in the method of doubting everything.)

For logicians, it would be a silly mistake to make. But it's one we all make about lots of things. If we see someone who has some attribute we admire—say they are slim and healthy, or fit and youthful looking—and they tell us one unusual thing that they do which is distinctively different from us ("Well, you see, I always drink one gallon of water before going to bed," or "Well, you see, I always eat tuna fish for breakfast"), we tend to think that must be it. And we imagine that if only we, too, did exactly the same thing, we'd become like them.

Philosophy highlights that such reasoning is invalid, which is useful, but (despite what professors may tell their introductory students) it's not quite the same thing as saying it is wrong. Because even an invalid argument is a way of offering evidence for a particular belief. Why do you think your friend is on a fruits-only diet? Because they are thin. Recognizing that such reasoning is dodgy can spare you wasted energies and disappointment later.

Affirming the Consequent

Post hoc ergo propter hoc is Latin for "after this, therefore because of this."

A celebrity explains that they always wake up at 5:00 a.m. and go for a run to the beach—followed by a lettuce salad and an hour lifting weights. And they're thin! So we link the two things. But there's no logical connection. Assuming that an effect—being thin in this case—is caused by something else is a common assumption in many dietary, and indeed health, matters. But often it is the wrong assumption.

For philosophers it is a logic reversal. People who affirm the consequent imagine that the effect of a cause is also the cause of the cause. But it's not!

Here's another example that may make it easier to see the problem with this very common kind of reasoning.

Premise: If you eat pizza every evening you will get fat.

Premise: I do not want to get fat.

Therefore (this is the logical bit): I should compensate for eating this helping of pizza by having no milk in my coffee afterward.

Is the argument valid? Not sure? Then you may as well have the milk in the coffee—and eat the pizza! But that's psychology, not logic. And indeed, it's not really logical thinking, although it's certainly how we do think. It's what I'd call warped thinking. And understanding how it's warped can help you make those endless little life decisions. (Speaking of "warps" reminds me—have you noticed how the famously logical Mr.

Spock of *Star Trek* always looked very smart in his clingy tunic, whereas poor Captain Kirk struggled to avoid looking pot-bellied? Being logical and being thin seem to go together like strawberries and cream, or maybe we should say like arugula leaves and olive oil.)

One reason why nutritional science struggles to offer good advice is that the human organism is very complex, and eating healthily is about the right lifestyle balance, rather than following one simple linear rule. To understand this, recall that suggestions that may be good in principle often come with contrary feedback effects. Take, for example, the evergreen advice to reduce the amount of fat in one's diet. It seems obvious that eating less fat will make you less fat, but human biology doesn't do "obvious." And one thing that fat is vital for is the production of testosterone, the male hormone that both genders rely on as part of the mechanism for regulating the amount of—wait for it!—*fat* the body stores, as opposed to, say, making muscle. This is why diets that accidentally upset the body's hormonal balance can speedily and directly result in people losing muscle mass and putting on pounds around the tummy. (If you're curious for more details, I mention one study in the notes.) Or take the advice to exercise more. People often offset increased exercise by increasing their intake of energy drinks or snacks, or by a need (quite possibly legitimate) to rest afterward. Some find after a while that their exercise regimen becomes extremely boring. This is why many health gurus recommend short bouts of intense exercise—but that's exactly the sort of activity that can potentially cause injuries to the body, requiring rest.

There's another way—a more important one than logic—in which philosophy and healthy eating go hand in hand. And that's because healthy eating is about choices. Choices are often complicated things. They may involve assessing, sifting through, and evaluating evidence and claims. "Oh, I don't have time for all that!" I hear you say. Indeed, most of us outsource our decisions, particularly on food, to other people. Unfortunately for that strategy, nutritional science is full of experts whose advice is contradictory and demands skepticism. One expert rails against fats, another says that the problem is sugars, and a third warns against relying on proteins. And despite all the millions of dollars of research, it's a staggering fact that in the wide world today one billion people are said to be chronically overweight or obese. (Not to forget the 5 percent in the West who are chronically underweight from anorexia.) There's never been a period in history like it. Something odd has happened to the way we eat, and our bodies are the irrefutable evidence.

When there's no shortage of advice and opinions about healthy eating and diets, much of which is wrong and the rest contradictory, finding your way through it requires a bit of logic as well as a bucket-load of skepticism.

Most of this book has been about separating fact and fiction, along with a little flavoring of logic and arguments. The science of nutrition is, unfortunately, filled with examples of bad science and dangerous dogmas. Take the following apparently golden rules, often handed down to us by well-meaning folk:

- Fats are always bad, and while low-fat is a little better, really only "no-fat" will do.

- Refined sugar—misleadingly often categorized just as "carbs"—is pure evil, but also beware hidden sugar in apparently healthy fruits.

- On the other hand, protein makes you healthy and strong—all you need is a few vitamins in addition. (Buy separately.)

They're all plausible, and plenty of nutritionists, dieticians, doctors—whatever—will offer this kind of advice. Who am I to disagree? Who are you to? But recall that first rule of philosophy, at least since Descartes, which is: "doubt everything." Forget what everyone else has told you about healthy eating and diets as "doubtful" and "unproven." (That's the easy bit.) Then, stage two, build up from the few facts that seem to be beyond doubt your own approach. This illustrates why the philosophical way to make your way through the food, health, and dieting maze is to become an active thinker. And even if we are still wrong about our choices as to what to eat, whether to walk to the shop or to drive, or whatever—at least as long as we do think about what we are eating, we become a little more human and a little less like a machine.

Wittgenstein Sandwich

Ludwig Wittgenstein, the twentieth-century logician and dissector of language, is associated with strict diets. His biographer tells us that he "did not care what he ate so long as it was always the same." For many years his diet consisted of pork pies, although on one occasion the wife of his friend Noel Malcolm served him a particular kind of rye bread with Swiss cheese. When she brought it in, he exclaimed, "Hot Ziggety!" It is said that he liked the simple sandwich so much that for a while he insisted on having it every day. It's not particularly tasty, but it's very practical, or "functional," as Wittgenstein put it (when he wasn't designing cast-iron radiators).

Spread butter on two slices of sourdough rye bread. Layer slices of Swiss cheese between them. (For Wittgenstein, only Emmental would do—none of the other "sort-of-Swiss" cheeses sold nowadays.)

Afterword: Existential Reflections in a Fast-Food Restaurant

Logic has spoiled many a promising soirée—and if you don't believe me, just look at what Wittgenstein insisted on for dinner: pork pie. *Every* dinner. On the other hand, there is something to be said for applying Descartes' famous "method of doubt" when faced with food items you don't know much about—and it's absolutely essential if you're trying to separate the unhealthy, fake foods from the authentic, delicious ones. All of which brings us eventually to McDonald's, where things are far from as simple as they seem, and a little philosophical skepticism is very, well, *wise*.

For me, a trip to McDonald's is a very philosophical occasion. There's the ethics, of course—just how much rainforest had to be chopped down to produce not only the beef in the burger but also the soy hidden in the fries? The social justice issues—can it really be right that the staff have a clock ticking away to make them scurry around to get your meal ready in less than a minute? But much more interesting than all these is how McDonald's challenges definitions of things. What it is to be burger, to be a fry… to be a salad?

Now don't get me wrong. When I was very, very young (sometime in the last century) I remember how much pleasure I got from my first McDonald's meal. I loved the way the food tasted—especially the little fries, and the cheeseburger, with its special mix of sauces. I even liked the decor! On reflection, that should have been the giveaway that maybe my judgments were a bit naive.

Nowadays, I have an aversion to the places and the giant plastic clown, but let's try to be open minded. If you want fast food, McDonald's is, if anything, at the "quality" end of it. So, what today, in health terms, will you get if you drop by there?

First of all, let's suppose you try to stick to the healthy eating and buy a salad. McDonald's salads are often pushed as a healthier alternative to other fast-food items on the menu like Chicken McNuggets or McGriddles. The firm will happily explain that Premium Salads are a mixture of iceberg lettuce and a special lettuce assortment (romaine, etc.), with cherry tomatoes. Less well explained is that it also contains cilantro lime glaze and orange glaze. Within these glazes lies propylene glycol—a viscous, colorless liquid which is nearly odorless but has a faintly sweet taste. It is produced on an industrial scale mainly for the production of polymers, but within the food industry it lurks in various edible items such as coffee-based drinks, ice cream, whipped dairy products (in the EU, it is identified as E1520). It is considered a "safe" additive, although some people may be allergic, in which case, look out for inflamed dry skin in the facial area, or small red dots on the body.

Besides a possible allergic reaction to propylene glycol, other side effects of your healthy salad could be:

- Headache
- Flushing
- Sweating
- Facial pressure or tightness
- Numbness, tingling, or burning in the face, neck, and other areas
- Rapid, fluttering heartbeats (heart palpitations)

Could be, I say, because these are the classic signs of the MSG symptom complex. MSG (monosodium glutamate) is the chemical freely used in a lot of Chinese restaurants. Researchers still argue about it, of course, but I've had a nasty attack once myself, and it was enough to nudge my eating habits. Classic

McDonald's recipes from the '50s through the '70s reveal enthusiastic use of monosodium glutamate in the innocent years before its potential health effects caused controversy. Today, however, officially McDonald's does not use MSG— so why should we worry? Turns out that McDonald's salads contain two ingredients that, according to Anthony Gucciardi, a food writer and co-founder of the Natural Society, "divulge the presence of MSG": disodium inosinate and disodium guanylate.

MSG and Chinese Restaurant Syndrome

Although MSG sounds like a terrible and thoroughly unnatural food, it occurs entirely naturally in certain foods, including tomatoes and anchovies. The commercial variety is made via fermentation, and as far as so-called Chinese Restaurant Syndrome goes, the villain may be other fermented ingredients in the dish, like soy sauce or shellfish sauce.

Critics today say that Grilled Chicken Filet, Sausage Patty, and yes, the French fries contain MSG, perhaps hidden as "natural flavors" or "hydrolyzed protein"—but no one is claiming that those items are healthy anyway. Or maybe they would if they believed a McDonald's commercial: "after selecting certain potatoes," "we peel them, slice them, fry them and that's it." The ad, by the way, was withdrawn after it failed an investigation by the British Advertising Standards Authority.

But now, *to the meat*, to coin a phrase. Hamburgers, in this case. McDonald's burgers are advertised as "100% beef patty" topped with melted cheese, tangy pickles, minced onions, and (of course) ketchup and mustard.

Sounds pretty good, right? But philosophers won't settle for what things *sound* like; we want to know what they really are. And hamburger meat is almost invariably made from cows that have not been grazing peacefully in fields but in what are called CAFOs—Concentrated Agricultural Feeding Operations. And for each burger, it is "cows" plural, not because there's so much meat in it, but cows plural because even if it's not the dreaded pink slime that it used to be (until the media caught hold of it), it's lots of bits of meat from many cows—cows maybe from all around the world.

McDonald's U.S., "like many other food retailers," acknowledges that it *used to* put pink slime in its burgers between 2004 and 2011, but now it says that it's seen the light and just uses meaty bits. Alas, the cows will have been treated with antibiotics and hormones, and the meaty bits come with unknown bacteria. "Most of the cattle we get our beef from are treated with added hormones, a common practice in the U.S. that ranchers use to promote growth," says McDonald's complacently. Last but not least, because fast food raises global demand for beef, and McDonald's is the word's largest beef buyer, it does put pressure on rainforests, which are cleared for cattle, even if McDonald's makes a big point of their policy being to source their beef elsewhere.

Okay, so the beef is bad but still better than it used to be, even if the rainforests are paying the price. But what about the bun? As everyone seems to worry these days, bread is often the fattening ingredient in a meal. And some breads are worse than others. How does a McDonald's burger bun compare? Well, each one comes with a long list of ingredients:

> Enriched flour (bleached wheat flour, malted
> barley flour, niacin, reduced iron, thiamin
> mononitrate, riboflavin, folic acid), water,
> high-fructose corn syrup and/or sugar, yeast,
> soybean oil and/or canola oil, contains 2% or
> less of the following: salt, wheat gluten, calcium

sulfate, calcium carbonate, ammonium sulfate, ammonium chloride, dough conditioners (may contain one or more of the following: sodium stearoyl lactylate, datem, ascorbic acid, azodicarbonamide, mono- and diglycerides, ethoxylated monoglycerides, monocalcium phosphate, enzymes, guar gum, calcium peroxide), sorbic acid, calcium propionate and/or sodium propionate (preservatives), soy lecithin.

Just the length of the list makes me feel queasy! Perhaps the most alarming elements, though, are all the oils: soybean, canola—and the high-fructose corn syrup. (More HFCS is included in the ketchup, and with the regular corn syrup.)

So there's a few good reasons *not* to drop by a burger bar for lunch: the burgers, the buns, even the salads in McDonald's are a big Mistake, with a double-arches capital *M*. But what about just a teeny-weeny portion of those golden Freedom Fries?

It would seem logical to assume that there are only three ingredients in McDonald's "not very French" fries: potatoes, oil, and salt. And potatoes, in themselves are quite a good thing to eat, as long as you can burn the calories off later. But if logic gets you the right answer in computing and math, it doesn't get you very far in fast-food restaurants.

Starting in 2015, McDonald's began a transparency campaign. As a result, the previously secret ingredient lists and processing techniques are now freely available. It's certainly nice of them to share the secret of those tasty, golden fries. Because it turns out that there is much more going on there than you could possibly have imagined. For a start, there are another sixteen key ingredients!

The good news is that potato is still the main ingredient, reassuringly. But there is a whole lot of other stuff that you might not expect to be eating. Starting with canola oil. This is not just for frying but for "color, flavor and texture" as a helpful handout explains. Indeed, these days cooking oil in many professional kitchens is a mix of 25 percent olive oil to 75 percent canola oil. In my local health food shop, next to one's for olive and sunflower, there's a large glass jar of the oil, a sort of dirty brown color, with a note saying it is 'cold-pressed'. This is a mark of how successful the rebranding of the oil has been. Yet most canola oil is now genetically modified, indeed the rapeseed crop itself is a hybridized version of the bright yellow mustard flower, but claims to be healthy as it contains monounsaturated fatty acids, like the ones contained in olive oil. This despite the fact that the whole saturated/ unsaturated fat thing (that for years justified a drive to switch consumers from dairy to factory products like margarine) is – if not bogus- certainly unproven. What is clear is that it has a mild taste and is ultra cheap. In these last two respects, canola oil is a far cry from lovely olive oil...and sure enough, it seems to come with quite a different health profile too. John Moody, writing for the Healthy Home Economist, sees big health issues about canola. He reminds us that it was originally called LEAR for Low Erucic Acid Rapeseed oil. The thing about rapeseed oil was that it was full of this erucic acid—and the acid was causing heart and kidney damage. Canola is the end product of research to develop, via genetic modification, a version that was less dangerous. As John says, the final step was for the researchers, backed by the Canadian government and some $50 million, GRAS status for the new oil. *GRAS* stands for Generally Recognized as Safe, and that's what it is—plus canola nowadays comes with the blessing of popular health books like those by Andrew Weil and Barry Seals. "If health gurus promote it in bestselling books, Canola must be healthy, right?" says John, rather sardonically.

But I personally wouldn't want all this talk about canola oil to distract from another important ingredient in the fries, which is the oil made from Big Ag's favorite standby, soybeans: hydrogenated soy oil. But hang on, what is all this "hydrogenation" stuff anyway? Hydrogenation is the process of heating the beans in the presence of hydrogen and a catalyst. This converts some polyunsaturated fatty acids in the beans into monounsaturated and saturated fatty acids, producing the health distinction just mentioned above that has served canola oil so well. But from a chemical standpoint, saturated fats are simply fat molecules that have no double bonds between carbon molecules because they are saturated with hydrogen molecules. Clear? Not at all. Does it matter? Does the body consider saturated oils bad and unsaturated good? That certainly was the expert view for many years. That is, until the data from actual studies were collated by researchers, who found no health benefits from the decades of the "butter is bad/ margarine is good" advice. They also uncovered alarming signs that it was having the reverse health effects, including increased mortality.

Having carefully surveyed the to-and-fro of the good fat/ bad fat debates over decades, I can sigh that the only thing that is clear is that nothing is clear. Even the latest airy talk about saturated fats "maybe" turning on genes that block fat burning and promote fat storage, or "maybe" turning off genes that do the opposite is just that—airy. Or maybe it's a kind of "more research money, please," talk. The practical point to note is that both butter and extra-virgin olive oil (see nearby sidebar), which were condemned in the past, have now been rehabilitated for both eating and cooking—which is certainly very good as far as convenience and taste go.

As far as I can see, the advice of the food writer Michael Pollan, along with many others today, is good: ignore the chemistry jargon, and stick to talking about actual foods. And, to borrow his measure, rapeseed is not something anyone's great-grandma would have been munching on.

Actually, McDonald's is not content to leave matters there—it wants to add another ingredient to its recipe for unhealthy eating and global deforestation: safflower oil. However, safflower is actually a rather lovely plant with spiked leaves and yellow or orange flowers that long ago (before McDonald's) were used as a dye for clothing. It's reassuring to hear that garlands of safflower were found in King Tut's tomb in ancient Egypt. Oh, and another thing that sounds nice: this oil is claimed to actually help reduce body fat! So, go on, Ronald, throw it in to the fries' mix.

Let's say something positive about the fries, and this is surely that there are zero grams of sugar in the fries. Unfortunately, McDonald's spoils that by spraying the dextrose onto the potato sticks at the last moment. This is to help them maintain a gold color, as is a dash of sodium acid pyrophosphate, used to prevent the potato mix from turning gray. Speaking of which, the chemical industry's safety data sheets list sodium acid pyrophosphate as hazardous for ingestion. In its bulk state, it even merits a printed warning that it may be very hazardous upon skin or eye contact, inhalation, or ingestion, and may cause severe inflammation. However, the U.S. Food and Drug Administration considers if safe for human consumption, in a dispersed state as a food ingredient.

So, for a truly natural ingredient, let's go with citric acid, used as a preservative. The mention of acid always sounds scary, but this one is just lemon juice. One teaspoon of powdered citric acid is equivalent to four tablespoons of juice. Indeed, the human body even makes its own supply of the acid.

So, citric acid gets the all-clear, but the same can't be said for dimethylpolysiloxane. Never heard of it? Actually, it has some non-food uses—it is the kind of silicon ingredient that is used in breast implants and as silly putty. In industrial processes it's used as an anti-foaming agent. In food, though, it does come accompanied by a long list of safety concerns. You may have heard about the risk of breast implants "leaking" into the blood stream? But how about the risk of eating the same chemical while you eat your French fries?

The terrifying truth is that the oil that is used for frying is a mix of seven ingredients, including canola oil, corn oil, soybean oil, hydrogenated soybean oil, citric acid, and

Olive Oil

These days, olive oil is back in favor. It is credited with lots of healthy properties, including a reduced risk of rheumatoid arthritis, heart disease, and cancer—this last due to its high level of antioxidants. The final plaudit came with a Spanish study in 2015, which found that consuming a little olive oil every day was associated with a 68 percent reduction in breast cancer. (Curious to note that the control group in the study were given canned low-fat foods and books on how to eat a low-fat diet. It's quite possible that this bad advice increased their cancer risks. Perhaps I should mention, too, that there is currently no way of distinguishing between harmless, benign breast cancers and the kind that spread and thus need treatment.) To get the most benefit, though, you have to buy extra-virgin, cold pressed oils. Yes, yes, the most expensive kind. But when you don't have any particular information to direct you otherwise, price is actually a useful indicator of quality when faced with apparently equivalent foods, at least once you discount the price hike of heavily advertised brands. The process by which this oil is made leaves it full of disease-fighting polyphenols.

This is (as ever) a technical term dragged into dietary daylight as a source of the most abundant natural antioxidants, from chemistry, where it signifies membership of the family of organic compounds characterized by their having a hydroxyl ($-OH$) group attached to a carbon atom that is part of an aromatic ring. Good, I'm glad that's all clear now. For us, the concept of polyphenols brings together certain foods that all seem to have this cancer-fighting quality, such as tea and red wine, along with traditionally therapeutic herbs like rosemary, thyme, oregano, sage, and peppermint. For plants, polyphenols help defend against attack by insects and give plants their color, and indeed, with olive oil, a strong color is a positive indicator of its nutritive value.

dimethylpolysiloxane—with a dash of tert-butylhydroquinone (TBHQ) thrown in. This is a petroleum-based relative of butane—yes, lighter fluid! As a food additive (with an E number in the EU of E319) it is added to a wide range of foods, with the highest limits for frozen fish and fish products. Its function is to extend storage life. Both the European Food Safety Authority (EFSA) and the United States Food and Drug Administration have evaluated TBHQ and determined that it is safe to consume, in teeny-weeny amounts. In excess, though, it has been linked to asthma, skin conditions, hormone disruption, and cancer.

Thus, it will be seen that in these cunning ways McDonald's regularly manages to upturn the three fundamental laws of logic:

- The law of contradiction: by making it possible for Freedom Fries to both be sugar-free and yet contain sugar
- The law of excluded middle: by creating a world in which producing its burgers both involves chopping down rainforests and definitely doesn't involve chopping them down (the truth is somewhere in between)
- The principle of identity: which assures you, for example, that your salad really is salad and not a dodgy mix of chemicals

My logical shortcut—and a wise general strategy for eating—is: don't be too quick to supersize your fries.

Okay, so what this chapter has done, indeed most of the book has done, is look at the food question, very, very closely. I've taken apart ideas and issues in order to take a closer look at them, to try to understand better what we're eating, and in the process to see how the modern food industry works. That's a traditional philosophical task: of analysis—pulling apart something complex to examine the pieces. But what about the existentialism? This imposing term implies something a bit more, and indeed, I think there is. What a modern-day fast-food restaurant, or a convenient ready-made meal in a supermarket, shows us is that we're no longer in control of what we eat. We don't actually know what's in it, far less what the effects of the various elements on our health might be. How could it have come about that the most commonly used cooking oil could have been invented in a laboratory at a cost of tens of millions of dollars? How could it be that the taste of food is decided not by chefs in funny white hats, but chemists in funny white lab coats?

We are what we eat. But, that means that somewhere along the line, what we are became someone else's decision.

Biographical Notes

A bit of extra background on people mentioned in the book, both famous philosophers and current researchers.

The Philosophical Experts

René Descartes (1595–1650)

If you think of food merely as something that has to be eaten in order to keep doing more important things, then René Descartes has a lot to do with it. After all, in one of the most famous philosophy books of them all, the Frenchman wrote:

> I perceived that I had a head, hands, feet and other members composing that body which I considered as part, or perhaps even as the whole, of myself. I perceived further, that that body was placed among many others, by which it was capable of being affected in diverse ways, both beneficial and hurtful; and what was beneficial I remarked by a certain sensation of pleasure, and what was hurtful by a sensation of pain. And besides this pleasure and pain, I was likewise conscious of hunger, thirst, and other appetites, as well as certain corporeal inclinations toward joy, sadness, anger, and similar passions.

—*Meditations* (1641)

Actually, Descartes doesn't really have much to say about food, other than noting hunger as one of those "corporeal inclinations." Nonetheless, he is one of those philosophers who have had a profound influence on both what we do and what we think. In particular, where many ancients tended toward empathy with the animal kingdom and advocated what we would now consider to be healthy diets containing plenty of fruit and vegetables, the French philosopher insisted, really rather absurdly, that animals were essentially clockwork machines, without any awareness or feelings. He is for this reason considered something of an extreme "anti-vegetarian," the Father of Factory Farming, and a contributor to the idea that food is a mere necessity—fit for animals!—rather than the stuff of "thinking beings."

If you know but one philosophical quote, it is likely to be from Descartes, for it was the French philosopher who wrote "I think, therefore I am," the aphorism I make a little play on in the title of this book. This statement appears in *Meditations*, where it is presented as the sole fact that Descartes can rely on in a world where so many things turn out to be not quite certain and dependent on other (equally shaky) assumptions.

It is Descartes' approach rather than his actual arguments that is more important. After all, his famous dictum was not even original to him, but borrowed barely changed from his Jesuit teachers who taught the advice of Saint Augustine:

"He who is not, cannot be deceived: therefore, if I am deceived, I am."

If in many other ways Descartes' philosophy turns out to be rather unoriginal, rather shallow—and even plain silly—on closer inspection, his books remain some of the most influential philosophical texts ever written, widely read to this day. In food matters his most valuable contribution would, however, surely be this intellectual invitation to "reject all that we have been told" and instead seek out a few things, a few broad food principles, that we can know with reasonable certainty.

John Locke (1632–1704)

"He that is nourished by the Acorns he picked up
under an Oak, or the Apples he gathered from
the Trees in the Wood, has certainly appropriated
them to himself. Nobody can deny but the
nourishment is his. I ask then, When did they
begin to be his? When he digested? Or when he
eat? Or when he boiled? Or when he brought
them home? Or when he picked them up?"

—*Second Treatise of Government* (1689)

It's a typical philosopher's question, but Locke's ideas on not
so much the scrounging of acorns and apples, but the nature
of private property and ownership have echoed down the
centuries. As have his views on human perception and what
philosophers grandly call epistemology.

According to Locke, ideas are imprinted on our minds as
we grow and experience our surroundings in the world from
childhood to adulthood—and nowhere is this insight more
apposite than in food and diet matters.

But food? How influential have Locke's writings been on
the food question? If he (rather unfortunately) spent the early
part of his career coming up with justifications for slavery in
the plantations of the New World, at least Locke also produced
the influential argument that if someone took more food than
they could actually consume and let it go to waste, in so doing
"he took more than his share, and robbed others."

If, on the other hand, such a person consumed, traded, or
even gave away his surplus food, Locke considered that "he
did no injury; he wasted not the common stock; destroyed no
part of the portion of goods that belonged to others, so long as
nothing perished uselessly in his hands."

As a philosopher Locke is particularly remembered for applying logic to political science, but he was also very influential in his discussion of how the mind perceives and makes use of the stream of experience that he presented as "sense datums." And yet John Locke also talked of introspection, which he called "reflection," defining it as the "notice which the mind takes of its own operations, and the manner of them."

With the so-called Enlightenment, rationality came back in favor, and thinkers such as Locke, as well as fellow philosophers Leibniz, Bentham, and Spinoza, all set about trying to achieve well-ordered systems for processing information and obtaining sound conclusions.

However, what I love about John Locke's style of philosophy is that he passes effortlessly from advising nations on human rights to advising neighbors on wrapping up warm against the frost.

Here's a typical passage from his much under-appreciated essay "Some Thoughts Concerning Education," penned in 1692 but still as fresh as a daisy. (Well, maybe it does begin to sound a little bit crusty, but still: not 450 years crusty!)

> "And thus I have done with what concerns the body and health, which reduces itself to these few and easy observable rules: plenty of open air, exercise, and sleep, plain diet, no wine or strong drink, and very little or no *physick* [medicine], not too warm and strait clothing, especially the head and feet kept cold, and the feet often used to cold water, and exposed to wet."

In actual fact, Locke suffered from health problems for most of his adult life, including respiratory ailments which were exacerbated by his visits to London, where the air quality was very poor. All of this fragility, rather than his more philosophical theories, tended to guide him toward the plain and simple repast and all those healthful apples.

Karl Marx (1818–83)

> "Hunger is hunger; but the hunger that is satisfied
> by cooked meat eaten with a knife and fork differs
> from hunger that devours raw meat with the help
> of hands, nails and teeth."
>
> —*Grundrisse*, or "Critique of Political Economy,"
> penned in 1861

Marx the revolutionary is known as the man who inspired a wave of workers' revolutions across Europe in the nineteenth century. Marx the philosopher is know for a veritable mini-industry of books on political theory that were supposed to build upon an already incomprehensible theory of one G. W. Hegel.

However, in food matters, it is Marx the individual who is most important.

Revolutionary or not, he was the son of a wealthy German lawyer who had renounced his Jewish faith in order to progress in his career. His comfortable origins enabled him to marry the "most beautiful girl in Trier," this being Jenny, the daughter of the baron of Westphalen, a family connection which not least enabled the Marxes to later pawn the family silver—marked with the crest of the Dukes of Argyll.

Nonetheless, despite his comfortable origins and even a substantial inheritance, Marx lived a rather sad and lonely life of straitened circumstances, if not true poverty, tragically punctuated by the early deaths of four of his seven children from malnutrition and poor living conditions. Did this personal insight into the problems of food and diet alert Marx to the serious questions of food politics? It seems not.

But then, Marx always saw himself as a philosopher rather than a practical technician. He vowed never to allow "bourgeois society" to make him into a "money-making machine," and surely he kept that vow, while money that was given to him or otherwise came to the family was frequently expended ineffectually on revolutionary projects, school fees, wine, or parties! Indeed, I think that in many ways Marx's writings are a substitute for practical activity—revolutionary or otherwise. So, it is not in the writings of Marx himself that food advice can be found, even if many have found lessons in his broader ideas for deconstructing how the "food machine" today works.

Friedrich Nietzsche (1844–1900)

"I am much more interested in a question on which the 'salvation of humanity' depends far more than on any theologian's credo; the question of nutrition."

—*Ecce Homo* (1908)

Nietzsche is that wild-eyed bearded sage known to many as a great aphorist. Born in the Prussian town of Röcken during a period of political and economic ferment that makes today's Trumpian dramatics look like mere tweets, his central interests—being the "death of God" and politics—reflected the gloom of the times. In this regard, Nietzsche invariably sought controversy, decrying, as he put it, the "slave morality" of Christianity with its elevation of self-sacrifice and pity and praising instead what he considered the true virtue: the pursuit of power.

No surprise, then, that, of all the movies other people tell you about, or indeed all the movies made, Nietzsche appears more often than any other philosopher. This is because he is both very quotable and very much misrepresented. You can't have one without the other, I guess. Anyway, at least according to my Google-based research methods, out of all the philosophers, he is the philosopher-du-jour of the movie industry.

There was even a movie made in his honor in 2003 called simply *Nietzsche*, which has as the opening line: "God is dead." This Nietzscheism is so famous that it's even got its own 2000-odd-word Wikipedia entry, for God's sake! Or should I say, for evil's sake...

You have to admire the brevity in that saying. A whole lot of ideas encapsulated in one bitter pill.

Here are a few more catchy Nietzscheisms, judged by that dubious yardstick that they appear in popular movies:

In *Enter the Matrix* (2003), the character Ghost recalls Nietzsche's advice that:

"One must want nothing to be different—not forward, not backward, not in all eternity. Not only bear what is necessary, but to love it."

In *The Doors* (1991) as part of a discussion of Jim Morrison's film class project, the soon-to-be-pop-star Morrison reports Nietzsche's words that

"All great things must first wear terrifying and monstrous masks in order to inscribe themselves on the hearts of humanity."

And in *Smallville* (2001), Lana says: "Nietzsche? I didn't know you have a dark side, Clark." To which Clark (aka Superman) says "Doesn't everyone?" Lana then asks, "So what are you: Man or Superman?" The punch line is Clark's droller than droll (or is it 'duller than dull'?) reply: "I haven't figured it out yet."

Of course, this exchange has nothing to do with Nietzsche's philosophy. But the connection pleases the film maker and the audience alike. Because, to movie director, philosophy professors, and aphorists alike, Nietzsche is a hero. All cherish the way that he wrote wildly opinionated texts on religion, morality, contemporary culture, philosophy, and science, without doing anything dull like thinking about the practical, social consequences.

As explained in chapter 7, much of Nietzsche's philosophy is concerned with the philosophical problem of free will, and whether or not we really have any. Food choices were a good example for him of how we may have less freedom than we imagine, for many of us cannot eat what we want but instead have to bend toward what our body tolerates. So, against those who, ever since Pythagoras, have recommended eating particular foods in particular ways in order to enjoy good health and long life, Nietzsche argued the opposite. In this crusade, he was at least consistent, as his general approach to all things ethical was to reverse orthodoxy and—quite literally—to make "good" bad, and "bad" good.

Nietzsche's own life is a tragicomedy. A creative and brilliant mind turned bitter by professional failure and long-running physical illness, he is forever trapped in the contrast, sadly familiar to many of us, between aspirations and achievements.

Plato (427–347 BCE)

Plato's views on most things vary depending on what exactly you are reading. However, according to his most definitive works, a healthy diet consists of cereals, legumes, fruits, helped down by milk, honey, and regular helpings of fish. Meat and wine are rather frowned upon and certainly should be consumed only in moderate quantities.

Worse, in one alarming passage of Plato's, food, and especially nice food, is the enemy of philosophy and of culture— no less than a hindrance to reason!

> "In order then that disease might not quickly
> destroy us, and lest our mortal race should perish
> without fulfilling its end—intending to provide
> against this, the gods made what is called the
> lower belly, to be a receptacle for the superfluous

meat and drink, and formed the convolution of the bowels, so that the food might be prevented from passing quickly through and compelling the body to require more food, thus producing insatiable gluttony and making the whole race an enemy to philosophy and culture, and rebellious against the divinest element within us."

—*Timaeus*, 72e-73a (*circa* 360 BCE)

Plato is generally considered the greatest of all the great philosophers. He has the remarkable compliment paid to him by history of being considered to make something philosophy just by talking about it. And indeed, Plato's views roam far and wide, and certainly included that perennial question of what to eat. As far as *highfalutin* metaphysical matters go, he offers his own very opaque theories, even as he terms those who he says baffle others through "empty tricks with words" as "sophists" and charlatans.

Plato was born, studied, taught, and died in Athens, albeit with some traveling in between. His dialogues, apparently recording historical conversations between Socrates and various fellow citizens of the city, range widely, from the distinction between mind and matter, echoed later by Descartes, to the strange theory of heavenly ideas, or forms, one of which exists for every concept we have. However, it is clear from his elevation of the "Form of the Good" and his metaphor of the Cave (both of which appear in his most famous dialogue, "The Republic") that ethics is the central concern to which he always returns. The shackled prisoners he uses as a metaphor for ordinary folk like us (as opposed to the true philosophers) can only be "set free" when they let the light thrown out by knowledge of the good illuminate their miserable earthbound existence.

Pythagoras (around 500 BCE)

For his followers, Pythagoras lived toward the end of the sixth century BCE somewhere in the Mediterranean region and was a key figure in the development of mathematical thinking. For his detractors he never existed at all, but for someone who never existed he's still been pretty influential. Anyway, a cult around him certainly existed.

The Pythagoreans followed strict rules in which food was central. Rule number 1 was no flesh—no slaughtered animals. Pythagoreans followed strict injunctions not to kill living creatures and to abstain from "harsh-sounding bloodshed"—thinking in particular of animal sacrifice rituals.

Instead, the diet Pythagoras followed was lacto-vegetarian. Fruits, vegetables, cereals, nuts, legumes, and a little bit of dairy. Like me, the Pythagoreans treated fish as not quite animals and even them in small quantities. But nuts and cereals were the basis of the diet and the staple food of the Pythagoreans. "For lunch the Pythagoreans used only bread and honey," the Roman commentator Iamblichus later noted in one of his writings, "On Long Pythagoras."

Jean-Jacques Rousseau (1712–78)

"The further we remove from a natural mode of living the more we lose our natural tastes; or rather habit makes a second nature, which we substitute to such a degree for the first that none among us any longer knows what the latter is. It follows from this that the most simple tastes must also be the most natural, for they are those which are most easily changed, while being sharpened and by being irritated by our whims they assume a form which never changes."

—*Émile* (1762)

Like many a great thinker, Rousseau fights against conventional philosophy on every front. Rousseau's gentle and insightful book on education and child development, *Émile*, includes a characteristic confession that one day, with his mind fixated on fantasies of female dominatrices, he felt a compulsion to expose his rear end to strangers, and one day he actually did so, near a well where a group of young women were collected. "What they saw wasn't the obscene object; I didn't even dream of that; it was the ridiculous one. The foolish pleasure I took in exposing it to their eyes cannot be described." Recalling the episode, the academic Leo Damrosch says, "some of the women laughed, some screamed, and Rousseau rushed away."

Rousseau's influence as a philosopher is inseparable from his colorful life. He disdains all artificiality, even in matters of the palate, while retaining in other ways a sense of grand style. His writings are liberally sprinkled with grand, rhetorical appeals for liberty and equality.

As a *philosophe*, musician, novelist, and autobiographer, he is quite distinct from what was even in his times becoming the standard model of philosophy: a rather dry study grounded in mathematics, physics, and sobriety.

Jean-Paul Sartre (1905–80)

Would Sartre really have preferred to eat insects to going hungry? Assuredly this is the kind of choice that his existential philosophy is all about.

For Jean-Paul Sartre, food was both sustenance and symbol. "It is not a matter of indifference whether we like oysters or clams, snails or shrimp, if only we know how to unravel the existential significance of these foods," the French philosopher wrote. And indeed, Sartre's diet said a lot about him. He found crabs and lobsters revolting precisely because they reminded him of insects. Conversely, he liked cakes and pastries because "the appearance, the putting together, and even the taste have been thought out by man and made on purpose." The more processed the food, the better, in fact—an approach that runs contrary, of course, to today's dietary wisdom. Ecology be damned, Sartre defiantly preferred canned fruits and vegetables to fresh produce, thinking that the processing made the food more of a man-made product, and therefore better. Fresh produce, he believed, was "too natural."

Sartre's views on food don't seem to have been taken very seriously, anyway. However, in one area, his philosophy does matter: in the question of what it is to be true to ourselves. Here, I think you might just as well consider a little joke as one of his long philosophical tomes:

Sartre Orders a Coffee

A man is sitting at a French cafe, reading (or at least pretending to) a long, complicated philosophy book. After a time, the waitress comes over to take his order. He orders a cup of coffee, with no cream. The waitress disappears for a minute and then returns apologetically, "I'm sorry, Monsieur, but we're out of cream. Will a coffee with no milk do instead?"

The amusement, for students of philosophy anyway, is that in his long, windy book, *Being and Nothingness*, Sartre explains that an absence of something is still something.

Personally, what I like about the story is that it echoes the very real existential (life-changing) choices we all have to make—and then later often wonder why we got them wrong. Understanding our choices, how we make them and where we go wrong, is the question at the heart of his book.

Henry David Thoreau (1817–1862)

"I came to love my rows, my beans... They attached me to the earth, and so I got strength

like Antaeus. But why should I raise them? Only
Heaven knows. This was my curious labor all
summer—to make this portion of the earth's
surface, which had yielded only cinquefoil,
blackberries, johnswort, and the like, before,
sweet wild fruits and pleasant flowers, produce
instead this pulse. What shall I learn of beans or
beans of me? I cherish them, I hoe them, early
and late I have an eye to them; and this is my
day's work."

　　　—*Walden* (1854)

As I noted earlier in the book, many of the philosophers
whom we rely on to represent little oases of good sense and
rationality in a disorganized world disappointingly turn out, on
closer inspection, to be not only rather eccentric, but downright
irrational. Henry David Thoreau, an anarchist who eked out a
living by making pencils while living in a shed by a pond, on the
other hand, appears even at first glance to be rather eccentric.
At least, unlike many other thinkers, he recognizes this. In his
Journal entry for January 7, 1857, Thoreau says of himself:

"In the streets and in society I am almost
invariably cheap and dissipated, my life is
unspeakably mean. No amount of gold or
respectability would in the least redeem it—dining
with the Governor or a member of Congress!
But alone in the distant woods or fields, in
unpretending sprout-lands or pastures tracked by
rabbits, even in a bleak and, to most, cheerless
day, like this, when a villager would be thinking of
his inn, I come to myself, I once more feel myself
grandly related, and that cold and solitude are
friends of mine.

I suppose that this value, in my case, is equivalent
to what others get by churchgoing and prayer.

I come home to my solitary woodland walk as
the homesick go home. I thus dispose of the
superfluous and see things as they are, grand and
beautiful. . ."

Thoreau was born in Concord, Massachusetts, on the eastern
coast of North America. Being a political radical, Thoreau
naturally studied at Harvard, but then, having acquired the
foundations for a very conventional philosopher (rhetoric,
classics, mathematics, and so on), returned to his native town,
where he became part of a group of writers that included Ralph
Waldo Emerson, the leading light of a movement called New
England Transcendentalism. This cult-like movement held
that it is through nature that we come into touch with our
essential soul. For many of his admirers today, Thoreau is the
first true ecologist.

In fact, his interests in nature really only started in 1845,
when he relocated himself about half an hour's walk from
his main home to a small wooden shed, that he fondly but
inaccurately called a "log-cabin," on the shores of Walden Pond,
which is not a pond but a lake set in some forest. Ponds, after
all, are defined by being small, and this one the locals said
was bottomless. Thoreau can at least be allowed this small
contribution to human knowledge: he determined that the
lake at its deepest point was one hundred feet. Whatever his
motives for moving there, it was not particularly secluded, as
it was very close to the town; indeed, Thoreau praises not only
wilderness in some supposed pure state, but also "partially
cultivated countryside." One of the notes in his diary gives
surely a timeless piece of advice:

"Take the shortest way round and stay at home. A
man dwells in his native valley like a corolla in its
calyx, like an acorn in its cup. Here, of course, is
all that you love, all that you expect, all that you
are. Here is your bride elect, as close to you as she

can be got. Here is all the best and all the worst
you can imagine. What more do you want? Bear
her away then! Foolish people imagine that what
they imagine is somewhere else.

—*Journal*, November 1, 1858"

His most famous book, *Walden, or Life in the Woods*, combines complimentary descriptions of the woods with disparaging observations on human nature and society. He starts by saying that most people waste their time by trying to acquire material goods instead of living simply (which is Plato's ancient lament too), and that even those who rise above that waste time reading modern fiction instead of Homer and Aeschylus. That, we might say, must be the Harvard influence coming out. Fortunately, the influence was only superficial, and Thoreau soon stresses that nature in all her mystery and splendor are even more interesting than the Greek classics. Over time, he recorded a wealth of detail on the forest and the lake, and how nature changes, adapts, and regenerates. Thoreau's nature diary offers a possible idea for a food diary, because for him each entry was a two-step process. First, Thoreau would carefully record his observations, such as the weather for the day, which flowers were in blossom, how deep was the water of Walden Pond, and the behavior of any animals he saw. But then, after this, he would attempt to identify and describe the spiritual and the aesthetic significance of what he had seen. We might borrow this idea and record our most interesting meals or dishes, noting the superficial aspects first, but then moving on to consider the more philosophical aspects and significance.

Current Researchers and Writers on Food and Policy

In writing this book, I have been greatly helped by a wide network of food writers and experts—several of whom have even checked aspects of the book and offered tips and guidance.

Listed below are some of those whose work I have found most helpful and revealing.

Michael Moss, journalist and author

Michael Moss is the author of popular books on food matters like *Salt Sugar Fat: How the Food Giants Hooked Us* (Random House, 2013) as well as a Pulitzer Prize winner for his reporting at the *New York Times*. His line is that by concentrating fat, salt, and sugar in products formulated for maximum "bliss," Big Food has spent almost a century distorting the American diet in particular in favor of calorie-dense products which can but lead to obesity.

It was Michael Moss who brought us the evocative term "pink slime" in relation to beef-burger production in a 2009 article on beef safety. In all his work he deftly lays out the complicated links between science and marketing that both create today's food industry and skew the public understanding of food issues.

With his friend and colleague David A. Kessler, a former Food and Drug Administration director, he has tried to warn the public about the dangers of "conditioned hyper-eating" driven by the food industry's deliberate manipulation of the brain's pleasure centers, where sugar and fat "sing their siren songs."

Jennie Brand-Miller, nutritionist and author

"GI Jennie" is an Australian professor, author, and food expert whose ground-breaking work on how the body absorbs carbohydrates—especially French baguettes!—has spawned the new "GI diets."

Professor Brand-Miller holds a personal chair in human nutrition in the School of Molecular Biosciences at the University of Sydney, where she has delved into the mysteries of how the body copes with carbohydrates—blood sugars—

with a particular focus on finding foods that the body copes with best. She has a special interest in evolutionary nutrition, and it was while she was investigating Aboriginal bush-food (the diet of Australian Aborigines) as a nutrition lecturer in 1981 that she came across the glycemic index—a concept originally devised by David J. Jenkins and colleagues from the University of Toronto. The index has profoundly influenced the way nutritional experts think about food and dieting.

Brand-Miller's influence has been to spread the idea of the GI through books like *The New Glucose Revolution: Low GI Eating Made Easy* (Da Capo Lifelong Books 2005), which sold more than two million copies, and the more recent *The Low GI Diet* (2004)—as well as in more than 200 journal articles.

Refreshingly, Brand-Miller says that it's the message, not the money, that is important to her and she is more than happy for her university to take the lion's share of any profits to be made from her work related to the glycemic index. "I've never believed money would make me happy," she says, "and the bottom line is that my university salary is paid by the tax-payer. I am a public servant and it's my duty to inform, not to make a profit.

She's quite happy just doing the talking. "It's so important to spread the word, she says. "Food companies spend millions advertising their processed rubbish and we don't have the budget to compete. All we can do is talk as loudly as possible to as wide an audience as we can reach and hope the message gets across."

Richard McKenzie, free-market economist and author

As well as holding many distinguished honorary titles in the field of economics, Richard McKenzie is the author of numerous books, including *HEAVY! The Surprising Reasons America Is the Land of the Free—and the Home of the Fat*. He retired from UC Irvine in 2011 after a forty-five-year academic career, but continues to pursue an array of academic and non-academic ventures, including the development of his online video lecture course, involving fifty-eight thirty-minute lectures, on microeconomics.

As mentioned in chapter 19, on the economics of obesity, in his book *HEAVY!*, Richard McKenzie discusses the economic causes and consequences of America's dramatic weight gain over the past half century. Relating weight gain to the growth in world trade freedom, the downfall of communism, the spread of free-market economics, and so on reveals a key, statistical link between time spent preparing meals and weight, and lower food prices relating to higher food consumption.

Valter Longo, biochemist

Longo is a cutting-edge researcher on food issues who has discovered a link between periodic fasting and cell repair. In a piece for *STAT* magazine (June 13, 2017), Usha Lee McFarling wrote:

> "It's not every day that a tenured professor at a prestigious university starts peddling a mail-order diet to melt away belly fat, rejuvenate worn-out cells, prevent diseases ranging from diabetes to cancer — and, for good measure, turn back the clock on aging ... "

But that's exactly what Valter Longo, a young Italian biochemist until recently based in California, has done. Longo, who patiently explained to me by email that the important thing about yeast is that they are not bacteria but are microorganisms, has moved on from pure science to a little bit of practical application by packing precise quantities of kale chips, quinoa soup, hibiscus tea, and the like into boxes that altogether make up what he calls his ProLon diet (short for "pro-longevity") and cost hundreds of dollars.

These days, Longo runs labs at both the University of Southern California and at the IFOM cancer institute in Milan and believes he has found out why the ancient practice of fasting can give cells a chance to rest, renew, and rebuild themselves. Animal studies are never conclusive, but as for Longo himself, well, it seems that he uses his own diet every few months—especially to lose weight after returning from stays in pasta-loving Italy. And in general, he often eats just two meals a day.

Robert Shiller, economics professor, Nobel Laureate, and best-selling author

Bob Shiller was formerly a professor of economics at Yale University and is currently a fellow at the Yale School of Management's International Center for Finance. He is far from being a food guru, but rather his interest is in rational decision making—and his painstaking, detailed, and innovative studies of economic data earned him the Nobel Prize for Economics in 2013.

In a Q&A with the *Wall Street Journal*'s Jason Zweig discussing his new book *Phishing for Phools* (2015)—which he co-wrote with George Akerlof—Shiller disclosed that he ate cat food to see if the different flavors marketed to cat owners really tasted any different. The answer? They don't. Here's how he reported the fact:

> "The labels on the cans said things like "roast beef paté"; things that we would see in a restaurant. So I said, if they say that, it must be something like that. I tried tasting it, and they all tasted pretty much the same. They tasted like cat food. There is an artificial reality that is created by marketing."

That's dedication! I'm a particular fan of Shiller's earlier book, *Irrational Exuberance* (2000), whose introduction of the notion of "animal spirits" driving supposedly "rational" human decision-making dovetailed with other things I had been thinking about, particularly in relation to situations ostensibly involving ethical principles. In an email to me Bob Shiller pointed out how, for example, religious codes still determine many people's dietary choices.

Marlene Zuk, biologist and author

Marlene Zuk is a bestselling author of books including *Paleofantasy: What Evolution Really Tells Us About Sex, Diet, and How We Live* (2014). She has been critical of the Paleo diet approach. *Paleofantasy* is a lively but scholarly debunking of what she sees as the central myths lying behind the enormously popular Paleo diet lifestyle movement.

As explained in chapter 4 of this book, *Paleofantasy* challenges the persistent philosophical notion that there is a "natural state" for humanity, any departure from which entails great dangers, mentioning, in passing, that certain philosophers have promoted this view. This reminded me of the views of Jean-Jacques Rousseau, featured prominently in my own book here, who talks of the nobility of man in his natural state and presents the development of agriculture writ large as humanity's biggest-ever mistake. Zuk notes how:

> "It is indeed during the blink of an eye, relatively speaking, that people settled down from nomadism to permanent settlements, developed agriculture, lived in towns and then cities, and acquired the ability to fly to the moon, create embryos in the lab, and store enormous amounts of information in a space the size of our handily opposable thumbs."

The seemingly plausible idea that we evolved for one set of circumstances and struggle to adapt to the rapidly changing current context is, Marlene Zuk argues, false. It is a "paleofantasy," to borrow the phrase of the anthropologist Leslie Aiello. Those who advocate "slow-food or no-food diets, barefoot running" and so on, rest their recommendations at least partly on the idea that we belong biologically in a bygone age, that technologies have outstripped evolutionary change.

Zuk says such talk rests on a gross misrepresentation of how evolution works. Far from receding in micro steps over eons, it can be "fast, slow or in-between." Furthermore, evolutionary adaptation is all about compromise; an adaptation that allows for faster running, for example, may become a handicap in terms of conserving body heat, as husky dogs demonstrate. That strange physical anomaly the hiccup is a reminder of the "imperfect transfer of anatomical technology" from our fishy ancestors. The hiccup is a reminder that evolution follows the principle "If it ain't broken, don't fix it."

In terms of diet, it is simply false to imagine that we once ate foods that exactly matched the requirements of our bodies. Nor were the food resources constant; ancient peoples would have faced changes in their environments, "shifting from warm to cool, from savanna to forest."

Professor Zuk reflects the thinking of anthropologist William Leonard, of Northwestern University, who wrote in *Scientific American* in 2002:

> "Too often modern health problems are portrayed as the result of eating "bad" foods that are departures from the natural human diet...This is a fundamentally flawed approach to assessing human nutritional needs. Our species was not designed to subsist on a single, optimal diet. What is remarkable about human beings is the extraordinary variety of what we eat."

Leonard adds, "Each of us is a dynamic assemblage of inherited traits that have been tweaked, transformed, lost and regained since the beginning of life itself. Such changes have not ceased in the past 10,000 years."

As an academic researcher, Zuk focuses on insect behavior—and then draws on the evidence she uncovers in that discipline to theorize about how humans use animal behavior. She told me by email that she was still a little puzzled at the public focus on the relatively minor aspect of the Paleo controversy as opposed to the broad and timeless issues of evolutionary adaptation. It appears that in food matters we can afford to be a little parochial!

Part VIII
Appendices

Appendix A

"Like Cures Like"? Foods That Give Clues to Their Health Properties

Back in the fourth century BCE the Father of Modern Medicine, Hippocrates, offered his famous advice to "let your food be your medicine and your medicine be your food" But don't take the first part of this too quickly and start quaffing cough medicine and gulping down handfuls of aspirins. Rather, what Hippocrates meant is that real food—meaning naturally produced, locally sourced—has amazing, unique, and definitely underappreciated healing properties!

What both Paracelsus and Hippocrates add to this insight is a theory that some foods give clues as to their healing properties in their appearance. A bizarre notion? Certainly. But even if taken solely as an *aide-memoire* (memory device), the idea is fascinating. Below are described some of the food "resemblances" claimed by adherents of the idea that in food and health matters, "like cures like." And in at least some circles, people hold that 2,500 years on, modern scientific studies increasingly point at evidence to support this idea.

The simple approach is to consider the appearance of foods. Strawberries, for example, are considered to resemble little edible hearts. Could eating them be good for the heart by promoting blood flow? Could they promote amorous feelings? The idea is that every fruit and vegetable has a certain shape that resembles a bodily organ, and that this appearance acts as a signal to us of what that fruit or vegetable's benefit might be.

To the evidence then, and you must be the judge!

1. Tomatoes

Tomatoes are said to bring to mind the human heart. Slice open a tomato, and you will observe that the red fruit (yes fruit, because strictly speaking that is what they are) contains multiple chambers that mimic the structure of the human heart. Tomatoes contain many nutrients that are good for your overall health, including:

- Lycopene
- Folate
- Potassium
- Good helpings of the vitamins A, C, E, and some of the B vitamins

Lycopene is the chemical that gives tomatoes their red color and is also a powerful antioxidant: a substance that helps keep cells from becoming damaged. Some research shows that lycopene also helps reduce "bad" cholesterol and keeps blood from clotting, all of which promotes heart health. Fancy that!

2. Walnuts

The characteristic brown, wrinkly folds of the walnut certainly bring to mind images of the brain. That said, how many people living in times prior to paper images of any kind would have seen an actual brain?

But put that quibble aside, and the fact is that the shape of the walnut does approximate the organ, including having both a left and right hemisphere. Grant this and then ask, could walnuts be good for the brain? And yes, it seems that walnuts have a very high content of omega-3 fatty acids, nutrients known nowadays to be of particular importance in supporting brain function, as well as to be a rich source of vitamin E, which some research indicates can help prevent neurological disorders and diseases such as Alzheimer's.

3. Carrots

The resemblance here is less obvious. In fact, you have to slice a carrot in half crosswise to get it. When you do so, a kind of "eye" appears, right down to a pattern of radiating lines that mimic the pupil and iris of the human eye.

So, are carrots good for eye health? You betcha! The old tale told to countless generations of children reluctant to eat their carrots is true, because carrots contain a whacking dose of beta-carotene (the name comes from the vegetable itself), which is a precursor to vitamin A. Regular helpings of beta-carotene combat dryness on the surface of the eye (the cornea). For older people, carrots can stave off macular degeneration, the irreversible and most frequent cause of vision loss in older people.

4. Red Kidney Beans

There's a tiny clue in the name, isn't there? They resemble the human kidney—and because (if rather unexpectedly) they contain so many essential nutrients, they are extremely good for the kidneys.

Kidney beans are an excellent source of molybdenum, an element that has been dubbed the "most important mineral you've never heard of." Too little of it causes uric acid to build up in the blood, which leads to inflamed and painful joints at best and, at worst, damages the nervous system.

Kidney beans contain a host of other goodies including folate, copper, manganese, phosphorus, vitamin B1, iron, potassium, and magnesium.

In short, these beans are manna for kidneys.

5. Ginger

For people familiar with the shapes of their internal organs, the root of this herb looks a bit like the human stomach. And—sure enough!—ginger has some very particular health benefits for stomachs. Gingerol, the ingredient responsible for ginger's pungent scent and taste, is credited by the United States Department of Agriculture as one of a small number of phytochemicals having the ability to prevent nausea and vomiting. Ginger is also known to prevent stomach cramps and even to combat stomach ulcers.

6. Sweet Potatoes

Sweet potatoes apparently look like the pancreas, an important gland that helps in digestion and also has a function in regulating levels of (wait for it) blood sugar. The pancreas is where insulin is produced. Sweet potatoes, like carrots, are high in beta-carotene, the potent antioxidant that protects all tissues of the body, including the pancreas.

7. Celery

The pale, whitish stalks not only resemble bones but are very good for them. This is mainly because they contain a good dose of the mineral silicon. While many nutrients can reduce bone breakdown or stimulate new bone formation, only silicon can do both.

8. Avocados

This fruit resembles the female uterus. Avocados are something of a miracle food, packed with unusual nutrients. Turns out they are also beneficial for the human reproductive system, particularly because they contain a good helping of folic acid, or vitamin B9. This vitamin is so important in preventing birth defects that in the United States (since 1998) and many other countries it is added by law to processed foods like breads and cereals.

9. Oranges, Lemons, and Grapefruits

Here the link seems particularly, ah, subjective, but nonetheless, for some people there is a significant resemblance between grapefruits and women's breasts. Be that as it may, the idea can serve as a useful reminder that grapefruits, along with many other citrus fruits (e.g., oranges, lemons) contain substances called limonoids, which are thought to protect against cancer. Of course, all these fruits also contain vitamin C, which has long been known to protect against immune system deficiencies (hence warding off seasonal flus and colds), cardiovascular disease, and prenatal health problems, and promoting both eye and skin health. Whether you can see all that just by looking at citrus fruits is not immediately demonstrated—but surely these fruits do look like they ought to be good for you.

10. Figs

It is claimed, rather implausibly I think, that figs recall the male testicles. Certainly, figs are full of seeds and hang in twos when they grow. Anyway, it seems that eating them affords considerable benefits in terms of both the numbers of and mobility of male sperm.

11. Mushrooms

They resemble ears. Well, not all mushrooms look like ears, but some do. More scientifically (if such an unscientific approach can be taken more scientifically), slice most ordinary mushrooms in half lengthwise, and they resemble a human ear with its attached canal.

And indeed, mushrooms have been found to improve hearing, as they contain ergosterol, a precursor to vitamin D. This particular vitamin—sometimes called the "sunshine vitamin," since we can make it ourselves if we allow our skin to absorb sunlight—is important for healthy bones, including the tiny ones in the ear that transmit sound to the brain.

12. *Grapes*

Finally (although one could go on with intriguing examples), grapes, or to be precise bunches of grapes, look a little like lungs, which are made up of branches of ever-smaller airways that end in bunches of tiny air sacs called alveoli. These are what allow oxygen to pass from the lungs to the bloodstream. Grapes offer an incredible range of health benefits, including promoting heart health and regulating blood pressure. Perhaps most curious of all, grape seeds contain proanthocyanidin, a chemical that is believed to reduce the severity of asthma attacks.

Appendix B

10 Snack-Busting Foods

The biggest challenge for many people is that they are just too busy to cook. "People really are stressed out with all that they have to do, and they don't want to," says Julie Guthman, author of *Weighing In: Obesity, Food Justice, and the Limits of Capitalism* (2012). As everyone knows, it is quick to heat a supermarket pizza, but a lot of bother to prepare ingredients, stew them, add rice, etc., as so much healthy-eating advice demands.

But if you clear your pantry of all the sugary/salty junk (as suggested in chapter 35), what can you replace it with for a quick snack? Here are ten foods that keep a long time and yet contain many of the nutrients of a healthy meal.

1. Salted Pistachios

Salted, definitely. Because it is salt cravings that drive a lot of snacking. Pistachios are one of those paradoxical fatty goods that are not fattening. They contain "heart-healthy" unsaturated fats, and minerals like potassium. Each nut provides 4 calories of useful energy which somehow, by the wonders of our complex metabolism, is slow to convert into fat stores in the body. Of course, buy the nuts in the shells.

2. Dried Tomatoes

Tomatoes are one of those miracle foods that afford all sorts of unexpected health properties. But more than that, they are a very flexible food, suitable for salads, sandwiches, side dishes—whatever. Dried tomatoes packed in oil actually taste better than fresh ones. Spend a bit on them—the cheap stuff may well be covered in chemicals.

3. Nuts and Raisins (aka Trail Mix)

The ideal hunger-fighter is a handful (or two) of nuts and raisins. Some variations on trail mix contain other ingredients, like sunflower seeds or dried cranberries. Nuts are full of fat, yes, but not fattening, and dried fruits are full of sugars, but they're "good sugars."

4. Apples

Apples may seem boring, but there are actually many different kinds. Purchase a few unfamiliar varieties and you won't mind snacking on them—and indeed cooking with them. Slice them into salads or munch on them with fish, nuts, or cheese. Stew them with raisins for a sweet dessert. If the apples are organic and fresh when you get them, they should stay good for weeks, making them a very convenient food—although eating them won't mean you can skip showering. I mention this because of a curious fact about Steve Jobs, the computer wonk and marketing genius behind the world's most successful computer company. He was a vegetarian who named his firm after his favorite fruit. Before he moved on to higher things, Jobs even worked in an apple orchard. And during a low point in his life, shortly after dropping out of college after just one semester, he experimented with an all-apple diet, thinking it might cleanse his body and even eliminate the need for him to bathe. It didn't, but the "Apple" logo and concept proved to be powerful in many other ways.

5. Pine Nuts

Another flexible food friend, pine nuts are delicious, especially if fried on fish, but they can be sprinkled on salads or added to stews too. They are said to actually suppress appetite, and they certainly provide an energy boost that watery "diet" foods fail to. They are good sources of minerals like iron and magnesium, which are reputed to combat feelings of fatigue.

6. Pickled Herrings

Vegetarians and some ecologists may not approve, but herrings—"the Little Fish That Feeds Multitudes," as the *National Geographic* once rather nicely put it—is a very healthy snack. As well as being very filling, herrings are one of the best food sources of precursors to vitamin D, the vitamin that the human body can make for itself in sunlight. In practice, given lousy weather or too much time spent indoors, many of us fail to get enough of this vital nutrient, which is involved in important bodily processes besides helping to strengthen teeth and bones.

Herring (like many fish) is also loaded with certain fatty acids that help prevent heart disease and keep the brain functioning properly. For the same reason, it also seems to combat inflammatory conditions, such as Crohn's disease and arthritis. In fact, probably because herring have for centuries been considered the food of the poor, they are still often undervalued as part of a healthy diet.

There is a huge range of quality in pickled herring. They usually come in jars with sliced onion; better versions come with slices of pickle and carrot too. Instant dinners.

7. Eggs

Madonna probably would not approve (she follows a macrobiotic diet*), but eggs do belong in your refrigerator as they are not fattening and are highly nutritious. More than that they are extremely easy to cook with. If you think eggs are boring—boiled, scrambled, fried—try calling them by their French names instead: *oeuf à la coque, oeufs brouillés*. And hard-boiled eggs are portable.

Tip: Always eat eggs from hens that have been allowed to roam freely: healthy, happy birds lay healthy, "happy" eggs. You can tell a good egg from a bad one by its shell. The shell should be attractive—smooth and shiny, with a carton of eggs including a range of delicate colors from white to brown. Factory-farmed eggs give themselves away by being dull, slightly pink, and mottled.

8. *Mushrooms*

How do you keep mushrooms in a pantry? They will last only one day before they go bad. The solution is dried mushrooms, which also have the advantage that dried ones are often better mushrooms—exotic varieties like shiitakes, porcini, morels, and chanterelles. The flavor of dried mushrooms is concentrated and intense, and they provide a substitute for meat in sauces or as a meal themselves with vegetables. Literally, just add water!

9. *Baked Beans*

Surprised by my listing this British favorite? Skeptical even? After all, they are a bit sugary and salty, and they're certainly mass-produced. Yet baked beans are also a source of fiber and lean protein along with useful vitamins and minerals, and they have been used successfully in weight-loss diets. In April 2008, a British newspaper reported that a 40-year-old man had devised a diet consisting only of baked beans, which (dreadful to imagine) he followed for nine months, at the end of which he had lost 140 lbs. Since he also stopped drinking beer the experiment was even less scientific than it sounds, but there we are—baked beans are not actually fattening and they certainly are very convenient.

If serving them with toast, it must be thinly sliced whole-grain bread, not the fake white stuff.

The best beans are made by Heinz, an American company, which for some reason really found its home in the UK. These days its factory in Kitt Green, Wigan, is the largest food factory in Europe, and produces more than one billion cans of baked beans every year. Like Coca-Cola, the company tells some grand story about its special recipe, which does (oh dear) contain sugar and modified corn flour, so the beans are not really the stuff of celebrity diets, but for practical emergency eating they're a great fallback.

The question remains, what exactly *is* a "baked bean"? The answer is a haricot bean, also known as a Navy bean. They are considered to have a good influence on lowering cholesterol levels, and their high fiber content prevents the body's all-important blood sugar levels from rising too rapidly after a meal, reducing the desire to eat other foods later, as happens when elevated sugar levels drop suddenly. (For these reasons, beans are a good choice for individuals with diabetes.) The beans are a good source of folate (vitamin B9, essential for cell growth), manganese, thiamin (vitamin B1), potassium, phosphorus, copper, magnesium, zinc—and a bit of selenium too.

10. Canned Vegetables

Yes, canned veggies are inferior to fresh ones, but they're still worth keeping in the pantry. As with dried mushrooms, they'll stay good for several years. Good ones to have on hand are spinach, peas, and carrots (which can be poured into a saucepan and called "soup") and tomatoes, diced or sieved. Bonus: the combination can be made into almost anything in about five minutes. All these vegetables keep you thin by keeping meals excellently watery, while providing little doses of goodness.

*The macrobiotic diet is a strange eating plan supposedly based on certain Buddhist philosophies. It replaces eating for pleasure with eating and drinking only what is necessary to sustain one's life, with an eye on maintaining balance between yin and yang. In practice, it comes down to eating whole grains, vegetables, beans, and sea vegetables.

Recipes

Appendix D

A Selection of Traditional Health Claims Made for Chocolate

The *Florentine Codex*, a sixteenth-century account of Mesoamerica by the Franciscan friar Bernardino de Sahagún (originally titled *The Universal History of the Things of New Spain*) describes in detail the preparation of various cacao decoctions and identifies the illnesses appropriate for treatment with cacao. These include cacao flowers to treat fatigue, and cacao beans to alleviate fever and to treat the faint of heart.

In ancient Mexican tradition, health was perceived as "balance," whereas illness and disease were "imbalance." The Spanish system of medicine had evolved from earlier Greek–Roman, Christian–Jewish–Muslim concepts, in which all diseases were perceived as either hot or cold, wet or dry, and all available foods and medicines were perceived as either hot or cold, wet or dry. Hot diseases were treated using cold foods/medicines; dry diseases were treated using wet foods/ medicines. This healing system was called allopathy.

Manuscripts produced in Europe and New Spain from the sixteenth to the early twentieth century describe more than one hundred medicinal uses for cacao, including treatment for poor appetite, mental fatigue, kidney stones, and "poor sexual appetite." See the list of examples below.

Cacao/chocolate in medical treatment: An historical summary of positive claims and uses

Cacao bean/nut/seed prepared as chocolate

- Appetite: awakens/improves (Lavedan, 1796)
- Digestion: improves/promotes
- Hair (white hair): delays growth of (Lavedan, 1796)
- Irritation (mental): reduces (Brillat–Savarin, 1825, p. 100)
- Labor/childbirth/delivery: facilitates (Buchan, 1792, p. 224)
- Longevity: improves/lengthens/prolongs (Quélus, 1730, pp. 45, 58)
- Moral nature: improves (Saint–Arroman, 1846, p. 86)
- Nerves (delicate)/nervous distress: calms/improves (Brillat–Savarin, 1825)
- Rheumatism: reduces (Blégny 1687, pp. 282–85, Hughes, 1672, p. 146)
- Sleep: both aids and prevents

Appendix E

How to Make a Chocolate Cake

This cake, like any rich dessert, isn't intended to be consumed in large portions as part of a strict weight-loss regimen. Still, many people who are watching their intake of sweets, or calories overall, recognize the need for an occasional treat, taken in moderation. The recipe makes eight generous servings, each of which contains about 20 grams of sugar—roughly the same as a medium-sized apple.

- 8 oz (225 g) dark chocolate with a high percentage of cocoa solids
- ⅔ cup (140 g) butter, plus butter to greasing pan
- 4 eggs
- 1 cup (210 g) sugar
- 4 heaping tablespoons self-rising flour
- 4 tablespoons unsweetened cocoa powder
- 1½ teaspoon baking powder
- 1 teaspoon vanilla extract
- 4 tablespoons sour cream

Preheat oven to 350°F (gas mark 4 or 180°C). Grease a large cake pan with butter, or line with parchment paper.

Melt the dark chocolate in a mug over hot water and stir in the butter to make a chocolate sauce.

In a large bowl, beat the eggs with the sugar, and then mix in the flour, cocoa powder, baking powder, and vanilla extract. Slowly stir in the chocolate sauce, and then the sour cream.

Pour the batter into the prepared cake pan. Bake for approximately 40 minutes or until a knife inserted in the center comes out clean. Cool the cake to room temperature in the pan. Then place in the refrigerator for at least 30 minutes. Slice and enjoy!

Further Reading

Many of the sociological and scientific books on food seem to have been written by people who, we suspect, don't cook much. On the other hand, clearly most of us *don't* cook much, and so I think books on food should not be excessively gourmandizing. My book is very much a practical guide to food for people, like myself, who enjoy their food but don't want to devote their leisure time, let alone their lives, exclusively to it. So I will start this notes section off with just a few suggestions for foodie books for general readers, and then step through each chapter saying where I found the data and the views that make up the book.

But if I imagine the reader having food only as one of many interests in life, the first book I'd like to recommend for additional reading is that of Larry Olmsted, who is very much a food connoisseur, a gourmet. His book, *Real Food/Fake Food: Why You Don't Know What You're Eating and What You Can Do About It* (Algonquin Books, 2016), combines a searing critique of "lousy food" and the people producing it, from industrial farmers to restaurant chefs, with an evangelical mission to get people eating and enjoying "real food." In it, he skewers many "fake foods" and offers detailed chapters on his favorites, which seem to be meat (with two entire chapters devoted to the subject) and champagne and Scotch, which are surely relatively specialist interests. Wines he also treats as a grand theme, which is allowed to consume a full chapter.

I recognize the importance of this gourmandizing and of the love of good food, in my extensive discussion of the Italian slow-food movement, among other things, but the note my book strikes is much more democratic, much more everyman. First of all, the recipes detailed are all variations on well-known themes and are things either I, or my family, have tried, with the exception of David Hume's "Sheep's Head Broth" (mentioned in chapter 5 although not described, but yes, it involves boiling a sheep's head for ten hours in a large pan). If you do try this one, please don't write to tell me about it—I'm a sensitive soul.

Listed here are some suggestions for reading more on broader food issues. There have always been huge numbers of books about food written from a practical perspective—cookbooks and diet books—but nowadays there are lots of books about food written from theoretical perspectives too: ranging from social science to philosophy and even anthropology. Some are sociological, some are highly political, some seek to combine theory with practical advice—and some are polemical. Books like these cross the gender barrier by appealing to both male and female readerships, and although these disciplines are traditionally dominated by male professors and male readers, it is notable that many of the authors of the scientific and the sociological studies of food are in fact women.

This category includes the following titles:

- *Paleofantasy: What Evolution Really Tells Us About Sex, Diet, and How We Live,* by Marlene Zuk (W.W. Norton, 2013)

- *In Defense of Food: An Eater's Manifesto,* by Michael Pollan (Penguin, 2008)

- *Food Politics: How the Food Industry Influences Nutrition and Health,* by Marion Nestle (University of California Press, 2002)

- *Appetite for Profit: How the Food Industry Undermines Our Health and How to Fight Back,* by Michele Simon (Nation Books, 2006)

- *Death by Food Pyramid: How Shoddy Science, Sketchy Politics and Shady Special Interests Have Ruined Our Health,* by Denise Minger (Primal Nutrition Inc., 2014)

As this list demonstrates, the food industry has plenty of critics, but without doubt two of the most effective are Michael Pollan and Michael Moss, whose ideas I reference in the main text. Michael Moss is the author of popular books on food matters like *Salt Sugar Fat: How the Food Giants Hooked Us* (Random House, 2013), as well as a Pulitzer Prize winner for his reporting at the *New York Times*. His line is that by manipulating fat, salt, and sugar levels in products to create a maximum "bliss" sensation, Big Food distorted food choices in countries like America in particular in favor of calorie-dense products which can lead to obesity. For the book, Michael Moss spent nearly four years interviewing hundreds of food industry insiders—chemists, nutritionists, behavioural biologists, food technologists, package designers, and senior company executives. It all makes a great detective story as well as a guide to better eating!

Michael Pollan's book, *In Defense of Food: An Eater's Manifesto*, is also a nicely written while extremely serious (one might almost say "unrelenting") examination of the food industry. Its central theme is that we need to eat more like our great-grandparents and be more distrustful of modern food production techniques.

Pollan is the author of several other, similar books, including *Food Rules: An Eater's Manual* (Penguin, 2009), which is described as focusing a bit more on the "implementation" issues. However, some readers have complained that it is also a re-tread of *In Defense of Food*. The fact that the *Eater's Manual* exists illustrates the importance of the "how to" aspect. For that reason, I've tried to offer plenty of practical strategies and not just theoretical debates here.

The food industry is also the bogeyman of *The End of Overeating: Taking Control of the Insatiable American Appetite* by David Kessler (Roedale, 2010). Kessler, formerly of the U.S. Food and Drug Administration, is focused on the corporate malfeasance of the food industry, which is pushing nutritionally unbalanced foods on people who already tend to eat more than they need. In other words, the book is long on the uncontrolled behavior patterns of irrational eating, or what Kessler terms "conditioned hypereating." At the end, he concludes that overeating is a disease rather than a failure of willpower. This book focuses very much on the "thin" theme.

I hope my book makes a gentle case for more environmental awareness, and in this sense a companion read is the venerable classic *Silent Spring* by Rachel Carson (Houghton Mifflin, 1962).

For publishers *Silent Spring* started a new interest in issues that had previously been the province of a minority of middle-class intellectuals, not to say hippies. Rachel Carson used the language of literature and of the heart to describe and explain issues that otherwise had been presented through dry statistical findings and austere political pronouncements. *Silent Spring* gave political and social trends a poetical dimension, presenting decisions about food as emotional prerogatives.

The style reflected its first incarnation as a serialization in the *New Yorker* in June of 1962. Interest was immediately so great that when the book appeared in September of that year, it sparked an outcry that forced the banning of DDT and changes in laws affecting "our air, land, and water." The *New York Times* Book Review said her book was "a cry" to the public to take on and oppose policies "which by use of poisons will end by destroying life on earth" "to save nature and mankind no less." Unlike the great bulk of the food radicals, I have also campaigned in many practical areas for environmental causes— even (mainly by writing a critical "expert" report) successfully stopping a motorway though a national park in the UK!

Anyway, philosophers will recognize that, in fact, Rachel Carson was only following a long tradition of such ecologically aware writing, of which the great Henry Thoreau's book *Walden, or Life in the Woods* (Ticknor and Fields, 1854) is a prime example. My book continues in this philosophical–literary tradition, of discussing big issues in ethics, social science, and economics without losing sight of the personal, the emotional, and the profound. Indeed, my book is actually continuing this philosophical tradition, and reconnecting with it.

Notes and Sources

Introduction

The general claims in the introduction are referring to topics discussed in detail in the book proper, and more details, as well as the sources for these claims, are given in the relevant chapters. The particular discussion of reasons people have for not cooking (and eating badly), as well as the sneaky infiltration of soy and corn oil, is taken up in Chapter 19: The Economics of Obesity. The cited figures on reasons not to eat healthily come from a ShopSmart Poll, reported by PRNewswire. The emphasis of this report was on cost, not time, with the report entitled: "57 percent of women say cost of food keeps them from eating healthy."

http://www.prnewswire.com/news-releases/shopsmart-poll-57-percent-of-women-say-cost-of-food-keeps-them-from-eating-healthy-151343115.html

Is it really true that: "Farmers were spreading industrial waste"? Indeed, it is almost commonplace in many parts of the world. I came across evidence of these kinds of practices in my time in Australia, but additional alarming "fertilization" practices of world farmers is indicated by this 2008 report, for example: "Human Waste Used by 200 Million Farmers, Study Says," by Tasha Eichenseher for *National Geographic News*, available online at

http://news.nationalgeographic.com/news/2008/08/080821-human-waste.html.

"Bitter fruit: The truth about supermarket pineapples," is a related and definitely scary tale of pineapple production in Costa Rica, written by Felicity Lawrence, that was published in *The Guardian* (London) in 2010. The main focus of this article is the widespread application of hazardous and toxic pesticides as a risk to both the farmworkers and the eventual consumers.

https://www.theguardian.com/business/2010/oct/02/truth-about-pineapple-production

"The so-called obesity epidemic." So-called, but the problem is very real. The figures quoted, roughly $2 trillion, or 2.8 percent of global GDP, are from an article called: "The Obesity Crisis," by Richard Dobbs and James Manyika, originally in *The Cairo Review of Global Affairs*, July 5, 2015, and now available online at http://www.mckinsey.com/mgi/overview/in-the-news/the-obesity-crisis.

I myself wrote a short overview of the economic aspects of the obesity epidemic for *The Guardian* (November 24, 2016): "The obesity epidemic is an economic issue," which is online at https://www.theguardian.com/business/economics-blog/2016/nov/24/obesity-epidemic-economic-market-junk-food.

Anyone trying to make sense of the obesity epidemic should also consider the damning relationship of child obesity to social inequality. I wrote an article in February 2018 exploring this for The Conversation website. It's at: https://theconversation.com/its-poverty-not-individual-choice-that-is-driving-extraordinary-obesity-levels-91447.

But back to this book and some more sources for particular claims in the introduction:

"In 2005 and 2006, research convincingly demonstrated that the claimed health advantages of dietary fiber (preventing certain cancers and heart disease) seemed to be bogus, and that even more extraordinarily, that 'low fat' diets actually increased the individual's risks of heart disease and, wait for it, made people put on weight!"

For more on dietary fiber see "The hot air and cold facts of dietary fibre" published in the *Canadian Journal of Gastroenterology*, by Carla S. Coffin and Eldon A. Shaffer in April 2006.

Harvard Medical School expert and "Obesity Warrior" Dr. David Ludwig explains all about the low-fat diet paradox is in his popular book *Always Hungry?* (Grand Central Life & Style, 2016)

For the background to the statement that "$4.6 billion was spent just on *advertising* by American *fast food* restaurants in 2012," see this article published by Yale News: "Fast food companies still target kids with marketing for unhealthy products" by Megan Orciari, November 4, 2013. Online at: https://news.yale.edu/2013/11/04/fast-food-companies-still-target-kids-marketing-unhealthy-products

Part I. Separating Food Fact from Food Fiction

Chapter 1. Searching Out Imitation Foods

John Locke was writing in a pamphlet called "Some Thoughts Concerning Education" (1692). The full text is available online from Fordham University at http://legacy.fordham.edu/halsall/mod/1692locke-education.asp.

Read more of the food industry's sneaky ways in *Swallow This: Serving Up The Food Industry's Darkest Secrets*, by Joanna Blythman. And there's a rather chirpy version of a 1969 advert for Mothers Pride bread, sung by Dusty Springfield, on YouTube at https://www.youtube.com/watch?v=-Pu8E-KCEik ("I'm a happy knocker-upper and I'm popular beside/ 'Cos I wake 'em with a cuppa ... and tasty Mothers Pride!")

The critic quoted in the text is Joseph Mercola, who runs a comprehensive website at http://www.mercola.com/ outlining his views on many food matters.

The complexity of testing products with mice is discussed in "Laboratory animals as surrogate models of human obesity": *Acta Pharmacologica Sinica* (2012) 33: 173–181; doi: 10.1038/aps.2011.203 by Cecilia Nilsson, Kirsten Raun, Fei-fei Yan, Marianne O Larsen, and Mads Tang-Christensen.

The "Markets and Markets" claim referenced in the text is available online at http://www.marketsandmarkets.com/PressReleases/functional-flour.asp.

More on the critique of "Ingredion" is at the "Know What's In Your Food" website, for example here: http://knowwhatsinyourfood.com/2013/05/19/starchology-its-not-your-grandmothers-kitchen-anymore/.

For more on the claim, "*Fooducate* recently analyzed the ingredient lists of over 2,000 breads. Their survey found that the average mix had around twenty ingredients," see: Fooducate, "The Top 20 Ingredients Used in Bread," November 4, 2010, online at https://www.fooducate.com/app#!page=post&id=57A3337E-D661-889F-44BF-BD45913618E8.

For more on the claim that: "in fact research has found that barely 10% of those who think they have a gluten intolerance really do" see: "'Gluten Sensitivity' May Not Actually Be Caused By Gluten" by Jonathan O'Callaghan, November 13, 2017, for iFL Science, online at http://www.iflscience.com/health-and-medicine/gluten-sensitivity-may-not-actually-be-caused-by-gluten/.

For more on the claim that: "the US-based Environmental Working Group in 2014, found that additives were actually themselves a potential health risk" see "EWG's Dirty Dozen Guide to Food Additives: Food Additives Linked to Health Concerns," published November 12, 2014, and online at: https://www.ewg.org/research/ewg-s-dirty-dozen-guide-food-additives/food-additives-linked-health-risks#.WpRvkdfjJek.

For more on the claim that: "Soybean oil is much, much cheaper. Just a pity that it is also more fattening, and researchers believe may even be cancerous," see Kaayla Daniels in an article for the Weston A. Price Organization called "Soybesity: Soy and Weight Gain," published March 4, 2014, as well as more on the problem that "Soy protein is fattening despite its reputation as a low-carb, low-fat, low-glycemic index, high protein ingredient."

As to cancer, an article published in the September 4, 2014, issue of the *Journal of the National Cancer Institute* called "The Effects of Soy Supplementation on Gene Expression in Breast Cancer: A Randomized Placebo-Controlled Study" found soy in diets could turn on the genes that can cause cancer to grow. See: http://www.breastcancer.org/research-news/soy-may-turn-on-genes-linked-to-cancer for more details.

Similarly, the "health library" of the Dana Farber organization advises that women should avoid soy isoflavones supplements, soy protein powder, and soy protein until more is known about their impacts on breast cancer. See: http://www.dana-farber.org/health-library/articles/supplements-with-soybean-oil/.

Chapter 2. Don't Forget to Check What's Not *in the Ingredients*

"Ingredion" has a whole website to itself, http://www.ingredion.com, which just underlines how pervasive food technology is and how little we know about it. Rowing back, though, on behalf of the naive consumer, are sites like Know What's in Your Food, which has a special investigation of the matter: https://knowwhatsinyourfood.wordpress.com/tag/ingredion/.

Coca-Cola's "bromate" disaster, mentioned in the text, is described in more detail by Felicity Lawrence in an article for *The Guardian*, March 20, 2004, entitled "Things get worse with Coke." It is available online at https://www.theguardian.com/business/2004/mar/20/medicineandhealth.lifeandhealth.

The claim that: "The market for functional flours is projected to exceed $800 billion by 2019" is based on the figure reported by *PR Newwire* May 8, 2015.

The claim "A survey by the Environmental Working Group in 2016 found Bromates present in a long list of everyday supermarket products" was press released by the EWG, October 14, 2015, and is available online at https://www.ewg.org/release/scores-baked-goods-contain-possible-cancer-causing-additive#.WpR3MNfjJek.

Chapter 3. Eat Like a Horse

Our horsey expert, Karen Briggs, has written a whole book on this, called *Understanding Equine Nutrition: Your Guide to Horse Health Care and Management*, part of the "Horse Health Care Library" (Eclipse Press, 2007).

The claim that "Old hay, like old prepackaged salad or other vegetables, loses most of its goodness and vitamins" is detailed by *The Horse* magazine, which has the full story, "Nutrition Loss in Stored Hay," written by Clair Thunes, PhD February 13, 2017. Online at: https://thehorse.com/19685/nutrition-loss-in-stored-hay/.

Henry David Thoreau and the goodness in green beans is all described, as the main text says, in his *Journal*. This can be read either in a manuscript or in the dedicated online library: http://thoreau.library.ucsb.edu/writings_journals.html.

The text of this is at http://thoreau.eserver.org/walden00.html.

Chapter 4. The Caveman Diet

"When vocal supporters of the Paleo diet, such as Mark Sisson, a 'fitness trainer' in Malibu, California, proclaim on their websites that 'while the world has changed in innumerable ways in the last 10,000 years (for better and worse), the human genome has changed very little and thus only thrives under similar conditions,' they ignore the detail and appeal to popular myths."

The quote is from "Primal Blueprint," a website and book (published by Primal Nutrition, Inc., as an updated edition in 2016) by Mark Sisson.

Why You Can't Rely on Safety Tests

The problem of inappropriate conclusions drawn from tests on rats was discussed, for example, by Cecilia Nilsson and other scientists in a 2012 *Acta Pharmacol Sinic* journal review titled: "Laboratory animals as surrogate models of human obesity" by Cecilia Nilsson, Kirsten Raun, Fei-fei Yan, Marianne O Larsen, and Mads Tang-Christensen. Published online February 3, 2012, at https://www.ncbi.nlm.nih.gov/pmc/articles/PMC4010334/.

On the issue of just how emulsifiers may be impacting gut microbiota, the "Civil Eats" (a campaign group) website has a scary article publicizing a study in *Nature* concerned with the potential health risks of all kinds of emulsifiers. The original article (paywall protected) is here: http://www.nature.com/articles/nature14232 and the Civil Eats summary is here: https://civileats.com/2015/02/25/how-emulsifiers-are-messing-with-our-guts-and-making-us-fat/.

As to enzymes like amylase and protease see, for example, "Enzyme Technology: Safety and regulatory aspects of enzyme use," a neutral overview at http://www1.lsbu.ac.uk/water/enztech/safety.html.

In an article simply called "Digestive Enzymes," *RxList* lists (naturally enough) some of the long list of potential hazards of enzymes here: https://www.rxlist.com/consumer_digestive_enzymes_zenpep/drugs-condition.htm.

As mentioned in the text, *Paleofantasy: What Evolution Really Tells Us about Sex, Diet, and How We Live,* is by Marlene Zuk and was published by W.W. Norton in 2014.

Other key sources are the *Scientific American*: "How to Really Eat Like a Hunter-Gatherer: Why the Paleo Diet Is Half-Baked," by Ferris Jabr, published on June 3, 2013, and *The Paleo Diet: Lose Weight and Get Healthy by Eating the Foods You Were Designed to Eat* by Loren Cordain (2002).

The British Dietetic Associations warnings were part of a survey of contemporary diet plans, the conclusions of which are published online athttp://www.nhs.uk/Livewell/loseweight/Pages/top-10-most-popular-diets-review.aspx.

Hume on "Sheep's Head Broth" is described in more detail in my book *How to Live* (Media Studies Unit, 2012).

George Akerlof and Robert Shiller's views on food, including that "Free markets, as bountiful as they may be, will not only provide us with what we want, as long as we can pay for it; they will also tempt us into buying things that are bad for us, whatever the costs" is drawn from their book *Phishing for Phools: The Economics of Manipulation and Deception*, (Princeton University Press, 2015)

Chapter 5. The Energy Balance

The opening source is "Energy balance and its components: implications for body weight regulation." Authors: Kevin D. Hall, Steven B. Heymsfield, Joseph W. Kemnitz, Samuel Klein, Dale A. Schoeller, and John R. Speakman, *American Journal of Clinical Nutrition*. 2012 Apr; 95(4): 989–994. doi: 10.3945/ajcn.112.036350 PMCID: PMC3302369

For more on the claim: "Take some of the statistics gathered by a large American research initiative called the Healthy Eating Index. Their research shows that adults with a body mass index of 20 or less and those with a BMI of more than 30 (which is the line for being clinically obese) have similar caloric intakes," see: "Food intake patterns and body mass index in observational studies" by P. Togo, M. Osler, T.I.A. Sørensen & B.L. Heitmann in *The International Journal of Obesity* volume 25, pages 1741–1751 (2001).

For more on the claim "that one pound of body weight lost or gained corresponds to 3,500 calories eaten or not eaten," see the following article: "Time to Correctly Predict the Amount of Weight Loss with Dieting," from the *Journal of the Academy of Nutrition and Dietetics*, describing and discussing Max Wishnofsky's equation in detail for readers who want to delve more deeply: https://www.ncbi.nlm.nih.gov/pmc/articles/PMC4035446/

"It's mind-boggling to discover that 90% of the ten thousand weight conscious members of the U.S. National Weight Control Registry were exercising for one hour every day in their bid to 'burn off' extra calories." This is from "NWCR Facts" archived online at: http://www.nwcr.ws/research/default.htm.

"It has been estimated that the normal, lean adult human body contains 130,000 calories of stored energy made up of about 38% muscle, 20% fat and everything else as the balance." That is Joseph Castro's calculation for the *Quora* website anyway: https://www.quora.com/How-many-calories-are-there-in-the-average-human-body, with Castro calculating (for convenience) with a rather slim 100-pound person. The crucial statistic is that one pound of fat (0.45 kilogram) is calculated to be the equivalent of 3,500 calories.

In a December 2011 article called "The Fat Trap," the *New York Times* offers a snapshot of an assortment of moderately obese adults carrying about 60 excess pounds each—which corresponds to another 210,000 more calories on top of the original 13,000. However, as I say in the main text, the idea that eating 3,500 calories, or (more likely) not eating 3,500 calories, corresponds to a pound of fat gained or lost is just a myth. The *New England Journal of Medicine* explodes it in a special article, "Myths, Presumptions, and Facts about Obesity" here: http://www.nejm.org/doi/full/10.1056/NEJMsa1208051

For more on the claim: "When a team of researchers at Harvard University in 2009 specifically looked at the effects of different 'kinds of calories' and weight loss, they found a complete mismatch," see "Diets that reduce calories lead to weight loss, regardless of carbohydrate, protein or fat content," Harvard T.H. Chan School of Health press release February 25, 2009, online at https://www.hsph.harvard.edu/news/press-releases/diets-weight-loss-carbohydrate-protein-fat/.

For more on the claim: "Another study by researchers at Arizona State University found that an 8-week high-carbohydrate, low-fat, low-protein diet was equally effective (or if you like 'ineffective') in terms of weight loss" see the study entitled: "Effects of an 8-Week High-Protein or High-Carbohydrate Diet in Adults With Hyperinsulinemia" for the journal *Medscape General Medicine* 2006; 8(4): 39. Published online November 22, 2006 at https://www.ncbi.nlm.nih.gov/pmc/articles/PMC1868379/.

For more on the claim: "Put on the same diet regimens, some individuals will lose significant amounts of weight and some will actually gain weight" see, for example, an article entitled "Does Metabolism Matter in Weight Loss?" Published July 2015 by Harvard Health Publishing, online at: https://www.health.harvard.edu/diet-and-weight-loss/does-metabolism-matter-in-weight-loss.

The claimed 'leptin cure' by Professor Farooqi can be read about in this article published online by the *Scientific American*: "Appetite-Killing Hormone Negates Joy of Eating" By J R Minkel and publsiehd on August 9, 2007. See: https://www.scientificamerican.com/article/appetite-killing-hormone-negates-joy-eating/

A full list of Farooqi's scientific papers are on her page at the Cambridge Neuroscience website: http://www.neuroscience.cam.ac.uk/directory/profile.php?isf20

Lastly, the quotation from Aristotle on beauty comes from his *Rhetoric, book 1, chapter 5*

Chapter 6. The Salt Paradox

The cat is really out of the bag now on this health myth. See for example, "Study Linking Illness and Salt Leaves Researchers Doubtful" by Nicholas Bakalar April 22, 2014, at the *New York Times*

Online at: http://www.nytimes.com/2014/04/22/health/study-linking-illness-and-salt-leaves-researchers-doubtful.html

Another nice overview comes in an article entitled "Why Everything We Know About Salt May Be Wrong," by Gina Kolata on May 8, 2017, in the *New York Times* again. This one describes how researchers are having to rethink basic assumptions about salt.

https://www.nytimes.com/2017/05/08/health/salt-health-effects.html

For more on the claim: "A study published in the *Journal of the American Medical Association* in 2011 found that low-salt diets actually *increased* the risk of death from heart attacks and strokes" see an article entitled: "Study calls sodium intake guidelines into question," published on November 23, 2011, with the source credited as the National University of Ireland, Galway. It is described by the *Science Daily* online at https://www.sciencedaily.com/releases/2011/11/111123132935.htm.

The claim: "I cannot see why the society should spend billions on sodium reduction" by Professor Graudal is from the Wonkblog entitled: "Could 95 percent of the world's people be wrong about salt?" by Peter Whoriskey, published May 26, 2015. This is online at https://www.washingtonpost.com/news/wonk/wp/2015/05/26/could-95-percent-of-the-worlds-people-be-wrong-about-salt/?utm_term=.00bba9c747dd.

The claim that "There is a distinct and growing lack of scientific consensus on making a single sodium consumption recommendation for all Americans," of Academy president Sonja L. Connor is also from Wonkblog.

For more on the claim that low-salt diets actually increased the risk of death from heart attacks and stroke see Section V" "V. Cross-Cutting Topics of Public Health Importance" in DGAC Scientific Report, May 8, 2015, published online at https://www.eatrightpro.org/news-center/on-the-pulse-of-public-policy/regulatory-comments/dgac-scientific-report.

For more on Niels Graudal's view that "there is any reason to believe there is a net benefit of decreasing sodium intake in the general population" see the Reuters report November 9, 2011, entitled "New review questions benefit of cutting down on salt," by Kate Kelland, online at https://www.reuters.com/article/us-salt-health/new-review-questions-benefit-of-cutting-down-on-salt-idUSTRE7A84HS20111109.

"Another paper, published around the same time, in the *New England Journal of Medicine*, equally firmly announced a salt-related toll of 44,000 lives a year, thereby saving 106,000 lives with the stroke of a pen, or more precisely the pressing of some keys on a calculator. A later editorial (dated August 14, 2014) concluded that the research linking salt consumption to adverse health effects rested largely on *statistical correlations* and needed to be taken, ahem, with a pinch of salt."

The NEJM Editorial was entitled: "Low Sodium Intake—Cardiovascular Health Benefit or Risk?" and is online at http://www.nejm.org/doi/full/10.1056/NEJMe1407695.

Illustrating the wild range of salt mortality estimates is a paper entitled "Global Sodium Consumption and Death from Cardiovascular Causes" by Dariush Mozaffarian, and collaborators in the *New England Journal of Medicine* (August 2014) which estimates between

1.1 million to 2.22 million deaths from too much salt! The article is online at http://www.nejm.org/doi/full/10.1056/NEJMoa1304127.

For more on the claim that "Researchers at the Universities of California and Washington accused the British authorities of cherry-picking their salt surveys to produce the reduction, while ignoring other studies that found no change in people's consumption" see an article in *Health Policy and Planning*, February 2016, entitled "Cardiovascular disease and impoverishment averted due to a salt reduction policy in South Africa: an extended cost-effectiveness analysis" by D. A. Watkins and collaborators. This is online at https://www.ncbi.nlm.nih.gov/pubmed/25841771.

For more on the claim that: "When American 'pro-salt researchers' analyzed surveys from over thirty countries and cultures, they found that despite wide differences in diet and medical opinion, people all consumed about the same amount of salt!" see "The Paradox And Mystery Of Our Taste For Salt" by Dan Charles, December 20, 2012, online at https://www.npr.org/sections/thesalt/2012/12/20/167619010/the-paradox-and-mystery-of-our-taste-for-salt.

Part II. Philosophical Eating Strategies

Chapter 7. Nietzsche On the Nutritional Excellence of Industrial Meat Broth

Surprisingly, there is a whole academic literature on Nietzsche and food, including the aptly entitled: "Nietzsche and Food," by Robert T. Valgenti, published in the *Encyclopedia of Food and Agricultural Ethics*, pp. 1440-1446 (November 21, 2014)—and this rather disproving report, too, from the *Souvenir Book of the 1957 International Vegetarian Union Congress in India* (author unknown): https://ivu.org/history/europe19b/nietzsche.html.

Nietzsche's breakfast and other fascinating dietary details are revealed by Julian Young in his book, *Friedrich Nietzsche: A Philosophical Biography* (Cambridge University Press, 2010).

My tale of Nietzsche draws in part from a very unusual book called *What the Great Ate: A Curious History of Food and Fame*, by Matthew and Mark Jacob (Crown, 2010).

But does boiling beef extract destroy all the goodness? Well, yes and no. It is actually a bit of a folk myth, that boiling destroys all the goodness in food, and it's not always true. Vitamin C, some of the B vitamins, and certain other phytonutrients are vulnerable to destruction by heat. But even they aren't *completely* lost—just partially. And the fat-soluble vitamins aren't especially vulnerable to heat or oxidation. But as for Liebig's extract, well you can't argue with Edward Kemmerich's dog test. Except on ethical grounds.

Chapter 8. Blessed are the Cheese-makers

Rousseau expounds on the virtues of dairy in his book *Emile or On Education* (1762) Being a great philosopher, and safely out of copyright, many of Rousseau's writings, such as *Émile, or On Education* and on to his *Confessions*, are all available online, for example at the Project Gutenberg site. But in looking at Rousseau's love of dairy products, I was informed and influenced by a very nice essay on a website punningly entitled "Culture Magazine: The Word on Cheese" dated December 10, 2010. The essay itself was called "Rousseau's Perception on Milk and Human Nature," but try as I might, I could not find the name of the author who appears to be more of a cheesemaker than a writer! As far as the Freudian claim that control of the milk supply brings power goes, it is said that in the Zulu kingdom of southern Africa the kings' control of the flow of milk in society was the source of his power and the mechanism by which he controlled the state. However, as the kings also used more conventional tools such as mass executions, it is not clear how much overlap there is between the Zulu and Romantic philosophies. See: http://culturecheesemag. com/blog/mbshrem_rousseau.

The counter-charge to claims about dietary fat and heart disease in *Science* Magazine was led by Gary Taubes, then a correspondent for the magazine and later an author of a book on the subject, "Good Calories, Bad Calories" (Knopf, 2007). His arguments and the American Heart Associations retreat on the issue was discussed by the *New York Times* in an article "Diet and Fat: A Severe Case of Mistaken Consensus", by John Tierney, on October 9, 2007.

Chapter 9. The Paracelsus Principle: Eat Fat to Get Thin

For the background on Ancel Keys and starting diet fads, see my own book *Paradigm Shift: How expert opinions keep changing on life, the universe, and everything* (Imprint Academic, 2015).

An interesting and clear article on the "Inuit Paradox" is at *Discovery Magazine*: http://discovermagazine.com/2004/oct/inuit-paradox.

The quote is from the U.S. National Library of Medicine article at https://www.ncbi.nlm.nih.gov/pmc/articles/PMC3005482/ for which the

citation details are: "Reduction in the Incidence of Type 2 Diabetes With the Mediterranean Diet, results of the PREDIMED-Reus nutrition intervention randomized trial" in the Journal *Diabetes Care*, published online before print October 7, 2010, doi: 10.2337/dc10-1288 Diabetes Care January 2011 vol. 34 no. 1 14-19.

Dr. Mark Hyman's book extolling the virtues of fat is called: *Eat Fat, Get Thin: Why the Fat We Eat Is the Key to Sustained Weight Loss and Vibrant Health* (Little Brown & Co., 2016)

The so-called Inuit Paradox concerns the question of just how the Inuit people (Eskimos), who gorge on fat and rarely see a vegetable, can be healthier than we are. The issue was explored by *Discover Magazine* in an article by Patricia Gadsby and Leon Steele for their October 2004 issue: see http://discovermagazine.com/2004/oct/inuit-paradox.

Chapter 10. Banquet Like a Pythagorean

The opening quote on Pythagoras is from *Ovid, Metamorphoses, Book XV:60-142, Pythagoras's Teachings*. Later on in the chapter, Russell's view is, as noted in the text, from *History of Western Philosophy* (1945)

Although I say it myself, a good overview of Pythagoras can be found in my *Philosophical Tales* (yes, because you see, everything is in there) but otherwise the great thinker's views on food are much misunderstood. Recently, Wendy Cook for example, even though she has taken the time to write a whole book about such things called *Foodwise: Understanding What We Eat and How it Affects Us: the Story of Human Nutrition* (Clairview, 2003), manages to both misquote Pythagoras on not defiling the body with "sinful foods" and misunderstand the significance of "beans." Ms. Cook says, in learned fashion, that "during digestion" the beans interfered with the "creative perception of numbers," whereas in all likelihood, Pythagoras's rule against such things had nothing to do with *eating* beans but was rather to do with gambling, which in those days involved choosing different colored beans. Bertrand Russell deliberately perpetuated the bean myth (and other negative views of Pythagoras) in his *History of Western Philosophy*, first published in 1947. Don't be one of his victims!

Lastly, for this chapter, for the claim that "Doctor Xand van Tulleken has made rejecting the tyranny of three meals a day the central idea of his so-called Definitive Diet" see: http://www.dailymail.co.uk/health/article-4100646/Lose-stone-two-weeks-Dr-Xand-van-Tulleken-offers-tips-tricks-just-selection-recipes-Definitive-Diet.html.

The *Daily Mail* (London) seems to have a small franchise on Dr. Xand, but this is enough to get the general thesis.

If you really want to find out more about that 'Definitive Diet, it is all in the book, 'How To Lose Weight Well: Keep Weight Off Forever, The Healthy, Simple Way' by Dr Xand van Tulleken with recipes by Georgina Davies (Quadrille, 2017)

And, by way of a contrast, Digones' diet is described by Dio Chrysostom in Discourse 6 of *The Discourses*

Chapter 11. Jean-Jacques Rousseau and the Importance of Eating Fresh Fruits in Season

As mentioned in the chapter, Rousseau's views including his taste for seasonal fruits, are drawn from his short book to his book *Emile, de ou l'Education*, translated in English as *Emile, or On Education*. The book was published originally in 1762, and is nowadays available both online and as a budget Dover text.

Chapter 12. Philosophers Still Arguing Over the Veggies

You can read more on the philosophical issues in Nietzsche's *Thus Spoke Zarathustra: An Edinburgh Philosophical Guide,* by Douglas Burnham and Martin Jesinghausen (Edinburgh University Press, 2010)

A great essay extending Zarathustra and the wicked way we eat into the future is "Thousand Words: Thus Steak Zarathustra: food in 2001: A Space Odyssey," by Jez Conolly, posted online in 2011 at http://thebigpicturemagazine.com/thus-steak-zarathustra-food-in-2001-a-space-odyssey/.

Part III. Food Myths and Legends

Chapter 13. Sugar Is Good

Several large-scale studies have found a correlation between artificial sweetener consumption and weight gain.

See: "Artificial Sweeteners Are Linked to Weight Gain—Not Weight Loss," by Alexandra Sifferlin, July 17, 2017, for *Time* Health. Online at: http://time.com/4859012/artificial-sweeteners-weight-loss/.

Mark Hyman, a food blogger, health campaigner, and practicing family physician (how does he fit it all in?), warned that "… we are eating huge doses of sugar" in "Why You Should Never Eat High Fructose Corn Syrup" (November 12, 2013) and on the *Huffington Post* health blog too: https://www.huffingtonpost.com/dr-mark-hyman/high-fructose-corn-syrup_b_4256220.html.

For more on the claim that: "From 1963 through 1968, diet soda's share of the soft-drink market shot from four percent to fifteen percent" see the December 2012 issue of *Mother Jones*, "Big Sugar's Sweet Little Lies," by Gary Taubes, https://www.motherjones.com/environment/2012/10/sugar-industry-lies-campaign/300/.

The view of Independent Social Research Foundation vice president and research director John Hickson that "A dollar's worth of sugar could be replaced with a dime's worth" of sugar alternatives is in the book *Fizz: How Soda Shook Up the World* by Tristan Donovan (Chicago Review Press, 2013).

"A new report came along in 1996 highlighting a rise in the number of Americans with (untested for) brain tumors that went in lockstep with the introduction and use of this sweetener." For more on the links between artificial sweeteners and neurological illness see section 3.2.2.3 of the book *Cancer Mortality and Morbidity Patterns in the U.S. Population: An Interdisciplinary Approach* by K. G. Manton et al (Springer Science & Business Media, 2008).

Some nice images of sugar industry advertisements are online, for example at http://www.theatlantic.com/entertainment/archive/2015/06/if-sugar-is-fattening-how-come-so-many-kids-are-thin/396380/.

Food Myth: Drink More Water

Rachel Vreeman and Aaron Carroll's look at medical myths appeared as a "Festive Feature" for Christmas 2008: Seasonal Fayre, in the *British Medical Journal* 2008; 337:a2769. The paper can be found at http://www.bmj.com/content/337/bmj.a2769.

Diogenes's Diet Tip is from a book called the *Discourses*, by Dio Chrysostom. The Loeb Classical Library has the full text online—in the original Greek too! See https://www.loebclassics.com

For more on the claim that: "Half the population is (water) malnourished. One study even found a quarter of American children drinking no water at all!" see the Harvard T.H. Chan School of Public Health press release for June 11, 2015: "Study finds inadequate hydration among U.S. children." Online at: https://www.hsph.harvard.edu/news/press-releases/study-finds-inadequate-hydration-among-u-s-children/

Chapter 14. In Praise of Not Eating

The source for the quote is "Autophagy in the Pathogenesis of Disease," *Cell* Volume 132, Issue 1, pp. 1-162.

A technical discussion of the "microbiota that the human large intestine contains" is in the *Journal of Parenteral and Enteral Nutrition*: "Collaborative JPEN-Clinical Nutrition Scientific Publications Role of intestinal bacteria in nutrient metabolism," by J.H. Cummings and G.T. Macfarlane, both of the Medical Research Council Dunn Clinical Nutrition Centre, Hills Road, Cambridge, UK.

Chapter 15. Eat Dirty and Chapter 16 Eat Something While It Is Still Alive

For an expert overview on this, see, for example, the paper "Did you know that your cravings might be microbes controlling your mind?" by A. Zakrisson, *Acta Physiologica*, Volume 215, Issue 4, pp. 165–166, December 2015. For more on the unexpected ways that "microorganisms are able to affect the way our brains work", see also an article entitled "Human memory may be the result of a 400-million-year-old viral infection" by Thomas MacMullan for the journal *Bioscience*, 11 January 2018, online at http://www.alphr.com/

bioscience/1008172/human-memory-arc-protein-400-million-year-old-viral-infection.

The "Diet Tips of the Nazis" is (as you might expect) a popular subject. A nice piece on it appeared online in October 2014 at the BBC website *History Extra*, called "When Hitler took cocaine" and it includes an account of the flatulence ritual. The piece was written by the historian Giles Milton who has also written on related matters in a series of ebooks. See: http://www.historyextra.com/feature/second-world-war/when-hitler-took-cocaine.

There are many fine videos of related historical events, too, including one by the UK Channel 4 "Secret History" series at YouTube: https://www.youtube.com/watch?v=8DJr5q4Bf_s called "Hitler's Hidden Drug Habit: Secret History."

The story of bacteria is a very recent and rather technical one, but there are many summaries online and in magazine or newspaper articles. Michael Pollan offers one on the importance of feeding our internal bugs entitled "Some of My Best Friends Are Germs" for the *New York Times* (May 15, 2013). And a detailed book is *Probiotic Bacteria and Their Effect on Human Health and Well-Being* edited by A. Guarino, E. M. M. Quigley, and W. A Walker (Karger, 2013).

Reuters news agency has covered the "stealth fiber" threat in articles including: "Popular food additive can cause stomach ache," published July 8, 2010, and online at http://www.reuters.com/article/us-popular-food-additive-can-cause-stoma-idUSTRE6675QC20100708.

And the source for the claim about the epidemiology of "most cases of e-coli" is the *Journal of Emerging Infectious Diseases*, Volume 11, Number 4, April 2005 entitled "Epidemiology of *Escherichia coli* O157:H7 Outbreaks, United States, 1982–2002" online at

https://wwwnc.cdc.gov/eid/article/11/4/04-0739_article.

Martin Blaser's comments on antibiotics were summarised in an article for *The Observer* newspaper (London) called "Why antibiotics are making us all ill," on June 1, 2014. Blaser mentions the baby milk aspect briefly, but for more detail go to the East Cheshire NHS Trust (part of the British national health service) webpage entitled: "What is the difference between breast milk and formula milk?" which is online at http://www.eastcheshire.nhs.uk/Our-Services/differences-in-baby-milk.htm.

Part IV. The Economics of Eating

Chapter 17. The Marxist Theory of Snacks

This story can be put in context by reading the chapter on Marx and Engels in my *Philosophical Tales*, (Blackwell, 2008). The actual Marxist quote is from *Capital*, Volume 2, pp. 257–8. For in-depth analysis see, for example, "Understanding Capital: Marx's Economic Theory" by Duncan K. Foley. Marx on the necessities of life: is from Economic Manuscripts (1894): in *Capital*, Vol.3, Chapter 15

There's more on the health benefits of beer at sites like Organic Facts; see https://www.organicfacts.net/health-benefits/beverage/health-benefits-of-beer.html and books like *Beer in Health and Disease Prevention* by Victor R. Preedy. Regarding the report that "Xanthohumol has also been said to boost neurons in the brain," see the article "Can beer boost brain power," published December 26, 2014, by Calaveras Enterprise and online at http://www.calaverasenterprise.com/health/article_f79ba902-8ba9-11e4-84df-a390de9458c8.html.

More health benefits for beer were described in the *Journal of Agriculture and Food Chemistry*, "Xanthohumol, a Polyphenol Chalcone Present in Hops, Activating Nrf2 Enzymes To Confer Protection against Oxidative Damage in PC12 Cells' by Juan Yao et al, published online on January 14, 2015, at: https://pubs.acs.org/doi/abs/10.1021/jf505075n.

Chapter 18. The Ethics of the Dinner Plate

Barack Obama's auobiographical food recollections are from *Dreams from My Father: A Story of Race and Inheritance* (Times Books, 1995).

Is food 'addictive'? The website 'Tedmed' has links to academic papers on the ways it just might be, at https://www.tedmed.com/speakers/show?id=309051

One such is "Addiction and brain reward and anti-reward pathways" which is at: https://www.ncbi.nlm.nih.gov/pubmed/21508625

The quote from Akerlof and Shiller on free markets is from the article "The dark side of free markets" published 21 October 2015 by 'The Conversation' website, online at https://theconversation.com/the-dark-side-of-free-markets-48862

I wrote an essay early on in the Obama presidency, entitled "Primary Colors" for reasons I still have not worked out, (the subeditor's title, I mean, not the essay!) critiquing Obama's ethics, which is available at the *Times Higher* website: https://www.timeshighereducation.com/features/primary-colours/407459.article.

The BBC offers lots more ideas for harmless barbecues at http://www.bbcgoodfood.com/recipes/collection/vegetarian-barbecue.

Chapter 19. The Economics of Obesity

Everyone is talking about obesity! "Obesity Now Costs the World $2 Trillion a Year" is the actual headline, for example, in this overview in *Time* magazine by Tessa Berenson, November 20, 2014.

The background on "Obesity now accounts for almost 21 percent of U.S. health care costs—more than twice the previous estimates, reports a new study" is at the *Science Daily*, April 9, 2012, online at https://www.sciencedaily.com/releases/2012/04/120409103247.htm.

A good place to start finding out more about soybeans is this 2013 online article: "Is Soy Bad For You, or Good? The Shocking Truth," by Kris Gunnars, on the website *Authority Nutrition*, which takes "An Evidence Based Approach," which certainly sounds a good idea. See: http://authoritynutrition.com/is-soy-bad-for-you-or-good/

This chapter expands on the article (already mentioned above) I wrote for *The Guardian*, "The obesity epidemic is an economic issue": https://www.theguardian.com/business/economics-blog/2016/nov/24/obesity-epidemic-economic-market-junk-food, and a second one for *The Conversation* website, which gives further sources, including the European Association for the Study of Obesity (http://easo.org/education-portal/obesity-facts-figures/), which has the key data. "It's poverty, not individual choice, that is driving extraordinary obesity levels," published February 19, 2018, is online at https://theconversation.com/its-poverty-not-individual-choice-that-is-driving-extraordinary-obesity-levels-91447.

"One study cites more than a $1.3 billion in the US in just the year 2011." See, for example: "Billions In Farm Subsidies Underwrite Junk Food, Study Finds" in the *Huffington Post*, December 6, 2017, online at https://www.huffingtonpost.com/2011/09/22/farm-subsidies-junk-food_n_975711.html.

Mark Bittman's article "Is Junk Food Really Cheaper?" for the *New York Times* was published on September 24, 2011, and is online at http://www.nytimes.com/2011/09/25/opinion/sunday/is-junk-food-really-cheaper.html.

Still on chapter 19 and the obesity epidemic, the claim that "Americans are so short of time that, as another of those peculiarly revealing studies found, those between the ages of 18 and 50 now consume one-fifth of their daily food while driving!" comes via the United States Department of Agriculture report "How Much Time Do Americans Spend on Food?" by Karen Hamrick et al, (November 2011), which draws on data from the 2006-08 ERS Eating & Health Module of the American Time Use Survey online athttps://www.ers.usda.gov/webdocs/publications/44607/8864_eib86.pdf?v=41136.

Backing for the ideas here: "It's estimated that three-quarters of the vegetable oils in the average American's daily diet come from soy" and that "half of the sweeteners consumed each day, the ones put into food to replace supposedly evil natural sugars, come from corn," comes from Dr. Axe, who has a nice clear set of charts based on the official U.S. government date, such as Chart 8: "The Prevalence of GMO Foods in Our Diet" at https://draxe.com/charts-american-diet/.

For background on the claim that "Soy and corn are the two cheapest and most profitable crops for agriculture" see, for example, this interesting snapshot view: North Dakota's most profitable crops for 2017 (January 16, 2017) online at http://www.dakotafarmer.com/crops/north-dakota-s-most-profitable-crops-2017.

For more on the claim that: "Worldwide, soy oil is the food industry's most widely used plant oil," see, the Soy Connection webpage "Soybean Oil Uses & Overview," at http://www.soyconnection.com/soybean-oil/soybean-oil-overview.

And for more on "Why, in the U.S. alone, the retail soy-foods industry is worth more than $5 billion a year" see the SoyFoods webpage: "Sales and Trends: Sales Data," at http://www.soyfoods.org/soy-products/sales-and-trends.

As to those soy health risks? *The Observer* Sunday newspaper in the UK devoted several pages to the story back in 2004, noting how the food had been heavily promoted for years as a "wonder food" but was increasingly associated with deforestation in the Amazon and health issues. Their article, entitled "They hailed it as a wonder food. Soya not only destroys forests and small farmers—it can also be bad for your health" by Anthony Barnett published November 7, 2004, is available online at https://www.theguardian.com/lifeandstyle/2004/nov/07/foodanddrink.features7.

If you like to wallow in the bad news, then *hey*! Kaayla T. Daniel has written a book on the subject called *The Whole Soy Story: The Dark Side of America's Favorite Health Food* (NewTrends Publishing, 2005) in which she details everything she doesn't like about soy (which is a lot). Here's a brief extract to give the, er, flavor:

The soybean was a modest and unpopular crop until food manufacturers intent on creating cheap vegetable oils convinced the U.S. government to start subsidizing it. The soy was turned into oil, and the industry was left with an industrial waste product. Then somebody had a brilliant idea: Let's take this industrial waste product full of toxins and carcinogens—isolated soy protein—and turn it into food that people will eat!

Joseph Mercola was allowed to give the anti-soy case a good run by the *Huffington Post* in an article headed "The Health Dangers of Soy" on August 23, 2012. It is online at https://www.huffingtonpost.com/dr-mercola/soy-health_b_1822466.html.

Actual research studies of the health risks of soy are, however, completely split between the pros and the antis. For example, these two studies found a link between soy and cancer:

de Lemos, M.L., Effects of soy phytoestrogens genistein and daidzein on breast cancer growth. Ann Pharmacother, 2001. 35(9): p. 1118-21

Allred, C.D., et al., Soy diets containing varying amounts of genistein stimulate growth of estrogen-dependent (MCF-7) tumors in a dose-dependent manner. Cancer Res, 2001. 61(13): p. 5045-50

But numerous others have not. Indeed, some studies posit a *protective* role for soy in preventing cancer. Fortunately, a very good summary of the present state of knowledge called "Straight talk about soy" is published online by *The Nutrition Source*, part of the Harvard T. H. Chan School of Public Health, at https://www.hsph.harvard.edu/nutritionsource/2014/02/12/straight-talk-about-soy/#ref31.

This bears out that some studies have linked soy to health problems like memory loss, "cardiovascular mortality" and breast cancer—but equally other studies have not. *The Nutrition Source*'s conclusion is that... more research is needed. It always is.

Some studies have linked soy to thyroid problems and impaired endocrine function as well as harmful effects on reproductive development—but a *PubMed* review found no evidence for the claims except perhaps for those with pre-existing problems with their thyroid. The summary by Messina M. and Redmond G.: "Effects of soy protein and soybean isoflavones on thyroid function in healthy adults and hypothyroid patients: a review of the relevant literature March 2006; 16(3):249-58 is available online at https://www.ncbi.nlm.nih.gov/pubmed/16571087.

For the background to my claim that: "Over the last fifty years been busy pouring public money into farming in such a way that the price of soy and corn have dropped by about a third while the price of real foods like real vegetables and real fruit have increased by 40%" see the article for *Time* magazine, "Getting Real About the High Price of Cheap Food," August 21, 2009, by Bryan Walsh, in which he bemoans the state of farming. It is online at http://content.time.com/time/magazine/article/0,9171,1917726,00.html.

If you only read one thing on soy though (apart from my book!), it could be this nice article by Mark Hyman, who also surveys the clinical literature but (unlike me) concludes that it's pretty much half a dozen on one side and six on the other. What he does clearly recommend though is to try to avoid junk, mass-produced soy in whatever form. See "How Soy Can Kill You and Save Your Life," online at http://drhyman.com/blog/2010/08/06/how-soy-can-kill-you-and-save-your-life/.

Chapter 20. Eat Out and Only Snack at Home

Dieters Making Their Excuses? The May 14, 2012 Shopsmart survey is archivbed at https://www.prnewswire.com/news-releases/shopsmart-poll-57-percent-of-women-say-cost-of-food-keeps-them-from-eating-healthy-151343115.html under the title 'ShopSmart Poll: 57 percent of women say cost of food keeps them from eating healthy'.

The extracts quoted are from (in sequence) the books by Sartre himself, *War Diaries: Notebooks from a Phony War*, November 1939–March 1940; by Simone de Beauvoir herself, *She Comes to Stay* (1943) and *Sartre: A Life* by Annie Cohen-Solal; translated by Anna Cancogni; Pantheon (1988, it was originally published earlier, though in French).

For more on the claim that "Binge-eating diets linked to weight loss" see a study mentioned in *Science Daily* called, yes, "Binge eating linked to weight-loss challenges" by researchers at the University of Pennsylvania. It is reported by *Science Daily*, December 5, 2017, and online at https://www.sciencedaily.com/releases/2017/12/171205115949.htm.

If you want to find out more about Simone de Beauvoir and Jean Paul Sartre, the de Beauvoir–Sartre relationship and the similarities between their works are explained in detail in *Simone de Beauvoir and Jean-Paul Sartre*, by Kate and Howard Fullbrook (Basic Books/ Harper Collins, 1994), and the "alternative explanation" offered is theirs. Sartre's autobiography, *The Words*, was published in 1963; *She Came to Stay*, de Beauvoir's first published work, came out in 1943. Sartre's War Diaries: Notebooks from a Phoney War is available in a 2012 edition translated by

Quintin Hoare and published by Verso. Annie Cohen-Solal's biography is Sartre: A Life, (Pantheon) translated into English by Anna Cancogni;, Plus! I offer a *spicy* chapter on the two in my book *Philosophical Tales*, (Blackwell, 2008).

Chapter 21. "Mindful" Eating

This chapter came about as a blog that I wrote originally for the European food start-up "Stop My Craving." Full disclosure, I've been a kind of pro-bono advisor to the start-up and modestly remunerated blogger working under the great Tania Birral on the website in the past, as I like the idea of breaking the monopoly of the big food producers, particularly in the area of office snacks. The idea of Sofie Dralle, CEO and founder of the start-up, is to effortlessly deliver healthy snacks ordered online direct to the masses—which I think is a winning idea whose time has come, although I'm not so sure about the 'healthy bit'. Anyway, quite how a food approach based on spending an hour to eat one nut fits in, I don't really know, but Tania wanted something on "mindfulness" and this is where the research led. The raisin quote though, "I can still remember the raisin from that first mindfulness class I took..." and the other quotes are from an article at Mindful called "6 Ways to Practice Mindful Eating" by Christopher Willard. It was published online on October 13, 2016. The closing quote from Thich Nhat Hanh, who says, "Drink your tea slowly and reverently, as if it is the axis on which the world earth revolves," however, goes back further. Plum Village Mindfulness Center has a story by Dianna

Bonny called "Meditating on a Hillside with Thich Nhat Hanh" published online November 21, 2013; see https://plumvillage.org/blog/friends/meditating-on-a-hillside-with-thich-nhat-hanh/.

Part V. Futurist Eating

Chapter 22. Inventing a New Cuisine and Chapter 23 Back to the Future with the Slow-Food Movement

As well as the recipe book *Italian Food* (1974) by the food writer Elizabeth David, mentioned in the text, there is the original Futurist Food Manifesto, and a whole series of books essentially on Marinetti, the author of countless poems, plays, and most notably, the more general tract the *Futurist Manifesto* of 1909, wherein he advocated an art of violence, cruelty, and injustice. Another interesting perspective is offered by John F. Mariani in *How Italian Food Conquered the World* (Palgrave Macmillan, 2011) and then there is *The Taste of Art: Cooking, Food, and Counterculture* by Silvia Bottinelli and ▯Margherita d'Ayala Valva (2017) which describes how the Futurist diner:

delicately passes the tips of the index and middle fingers of his left hand over a rectangular device, made of a swatch of red damask, a little square of black velvet and a tiny piece of sandpaper....

Philip McCouat was giving his assessment in an article: "The Futurists declare war on pasta" for the online *Journal of Art in Society*, www.artinsociety.com in 2014.

The sidebar on supplements says that: "According to the *Readers Digest*, in any given week, "nearly a third of adult Britons take some sort of supplement in the hope that they will feel healthier." For the background to this see, for example, the article "The Vitamin Myth" by Neena Samuel online at https://www.rd.com/health/wellness/are-vitamins-really-that-good-for-you/.

The back story on the claim that "Weight-loss supplements seem to be particularly dodgy" is research by Pieter Cohen (no relation) in the U.S. Cohen has identified popular supplements that contain things like anti-depressants, laxatives, and thyroid hormones. *Science Magazine* has the details in a special feature: "Revealing the hidden dangers of dietary supplements" by Jennifer Couzin-Frankel, published August 20, 2015. It is online at http://www.sciencemag.org/news/2015/08/feature-revealing-hidden-dangers-dietary-supplements.

Slow Food

The slow-food movement, founded by Carlo Petrini in Italy in 1986, is today an international organization: www.slowfood.com.

"Pasta is made of long silent archaeological worms," writes Fillia, Marinetti's co-campaigner in *The Futurist Cookbook*, "which, like their brothers living in the dungeons of history, weigh down the stomach make it ill render it useless. You mustn't introduce these white worms into the body unless you want to make it as closed dark and immobile as a museum." Quoted in *Histories of the Future* by Susan Harding and Daniel Rosenberg (Duke University Press, 2009).

For the background to the claim "At least according to one of those rather dodgy surveys, most Britons only spend six minutes on breakfast," see *The Daily Mirror* (London) https://www.mirror.co.uk/news/uk-news/great-british-breakfast-heres-how-7302638.

For the detail on why John Nihoff, a professor of gastronomy at the Culinary Institute of America, "has estimated that about one in five American meals are now consumed in cars," see the story on CBS News by Jaclyn Schiff via AP, November 9, 2005, called "Car Cuisine" online at https://www.cbsnews.com/news/car-cuisine/.

For more on the claim that "It's snack foods that very often replace meals... so nutritionally [people are] not really getting what they need," made by that spokeswoman for the American Dietetic Association, see NBC News, "Food Industry Catering for Hungry Drivers," via AP November 22, 2005, online at http://www.nbcnews.com/id/10154905/ns/health-fitness/t/food-industry-catering-hungry-drivers/.

Some of the artistic flourishes in this piece come from the elegant article "The Futurists Declare War on Pasta" by Philip McCouat in the *Journal of Art in Society*, 2014. It is online at www.artinsociety.com/the-futurists-declare-war-on-pasta.html.

Chapter 24. Counter-Revolutionary Eating

The claim that by June 2014 Mad Cow Disease had killed 177 people in the United Kingdom alone is from news reports. See, for example, the *Daily Mirror* (London) report "Mad Cow Disease returns to the UK after dead cow tests positive for BSE," by Richard Smith and David Ottewell, October 1, 2015, online at https://www.mirror.co.uk/news/uk-news/mad-cow-disease-returns-uk-6554649.

For more on the historical claim that between 1845 and 1852, the population of Ireland fell nearly 25 percent, see, for example, Christine Kinealy's book, *This Great Calamity* (Gill & Macmillan, 1994).

Food Myth: There Is a Pill for That

The background on the claims in the Food Myth: "There is a Pill for That" are as follows:

"A 25-year-old woman from Worthing, West Sussex, took the substance and was dead a few weeks later. Her inquest was told she may as well have been 'taking rat poison.' Another tragic victim, 26 years old, was found dead in a cold bath, after trying desperately to reduce her body temperature." The sad story is told by the *Daily Mail*, (UK) which knows very well the value of sad stories, and indeed emphasizes all the piquant elements, even in the headlines. See "Slimmer, 25, died after taking controversial 'rat poison' diet pill because she was worried she had eaten too much at her birthday dinner." The story was by Lucy Crossley, December 15, 2015, and is online at http://www.dailymail.co.uk/news/article-3360973/Slimmer-25-died-taking-controversial-rat-poison-diet-pill-worried-eaten-birthday-dinner.html#ixzz58QNbflPa.

Monoculture

The quotes are from an essay by Dena Rash Guzman called "Monoculture In Farming: The First In A Series On The Food Industry" published online for *Stir Journal*, March 31, 2014. See http://www.stirjournal.com/2014/03/31/monoculture-in-farming-the-first-in-a-series-on-the-food-industry/ for the fuller account, well worth a read.

Read more: *Monocultures of the Mind: Perspectives on Biodiversity and Biotechnology*, by Vandana Shiva (Zed Books Ltd., 1993).

Rousseau's views, as mentioned in the text, are from *Emile, or Concerning Education*. Project Gutenberg offers a translation (by Eleanor Worthington). See https://www.gutenberg.org/files/30433/30433-h/30433-h.htm

For the back story on Tam Fry, from the UK's National Obesity Forum, saying that, "People are taking drugs that put their lives at risk in order to look their best at a party," see this story, in another UK tabloid, *The Sun*, entitled: "Diet pills likened to rat poison by coroner as they claim another life." The piece is by Jane Atkinson and Rachel Spencer and was published on December 13, 2015. It is online at https://www.thesun.co.uk/archives/news/858457/diet-pills-likened-to-rat-poison-by-coroner-as-they-claim-another-life/.

More on the diet pills danger is at the *Daily Mirror* (London) in a piece called "Diet pills danger: Surge of women desperate to lose weight putting lives at risk with online tablets" by Caroline Jones, published July 18, 2013, online at https://www.mirror.co.uk/lifestyle/health/diet-pills-danger-surge-women-2060938.

Chapter 25. Living in an Obesogenic Environment

Read more on the obesogenic environment in the journal the *Lancet*'s profile on "Boyd Swinburn: combating obesity at the community level." This is available online at http://www.thelancet.com/pdfs/journals/lancet/PIIS0140-6736(11)61364-0.pdf.

For more on obesogens and the claim that "About half a billion kilos of phthalates are made each year worldwide" see: "Obesogens: A Worldwide Issue," by Dr. Edward Group, online at: http://www.globalhealingcenter.com/natural-health/whats-the-deal-with-obesogens/.

For the back story on Animal feed supplementation, see the SoyINfo center's book: *History Of Industrial Uses Of Soybeans (660 CE–2017)* by William Shurtleff and Akiko Aoyagi (ISBN: 978-1-928914-98-3). For more on the problem of plastics in wild fish, visit https://www.npr.org/sections/thesalt/2013/12/12/250438904/how-plastic-in-the-ocean-is-contaminating-your-seafood.

The claim that "Sales of organic food in the United States increased from approximately $11 billion in 2004 to an estimated $27 billion in 2012," was according to the *Nutrition Business Journal*. See the paper "Attitudes and Willingness to Pay More for Organic Foods by Tennessee Consumers" by Hiren Bhavsar et al, November 2017, online at: https://www.researchgate.net/ as a PDF.

The use of pesticides is in fact allowed in organic farming, although there are rules about what's allowed. See https://blogs.scientificamerican.com/science-sushi/httpblogsscientificamericancomscience-sushi20110718mythbusting-101-organic-farming-conventional-agriculture for more.

Oh, and Sartre's own views on eating are featured prominently in his otherwise unreadable book *Being and Nothingness* (1943).

Chapter 26. *The Future of Food Is Vegetables*

This claim that "The Future of Food is… Vegetables" returns us, as indicated in the text, to Marinetti's *Futurist Cookbook*.

Part VI. Secrets of the Chocolate Tree

Chapter 27. *A Believer's History of Chocolate and Chapter 28 Chocolate Lovers*

For more "dabbling in the murky history of Cadburys, but an entirely healthy description of company's sexy advertising" see the "Top 25 Cadbury's Adverts of all time" by Ola Agbaimoni for Eelan Media (posted February 6, 2014). Article online at http://www.eelanmedia.com/top-25-cadburys-adverts-of-all-time/

The source for the claim: "Chocolate snacks make you thin?" is *Obesity* (Silver Spring). December 2013; 21(12):2504-12. doi: 10.1002/oby.20460. Epub July 2, 2013. High caloric intake at breakfast vs. dinner differentially influences weight loss of overweight and obese women. D. Jakubowicz, M. Barnea, J. Wainstein, O. Froy.

The backstory on Irene Rosenfeld, the Kraft chief executive who authorized this kind gesture, at the same time allocated $10 million extra for herself as a pay raise—taking her annual remuneration to $21 million is at http://www.chicagobusiness.com/article/20150327/NEWS07/150329833/pay-rises-big-time-for-mondelez-ceo-rosenfeld.

Published, March 27, 2015, as "Pay rises big time for Mondelez CEO Rosenfeld," and written by Peter Frost.

Chapter 29. *Chocolate for Stimulation and Reassurance*

On the issue of chocolate's properties as a drug—the research cited was published in *Nature*. August 22, 1996; 382(6593):677-8 as "Brain cannabinoids in chocolate" by E. di Tomaso, M. Beltramo, D. Piomelli.

Read more on the history of chocolate: Sophie D. and Michael D. Coe, *The True History of Chocolate*. London: Thames and Hudson, 1996.

For a bit more on the weird psychology of what we like, I looked into the work of Clotaire Rapaille, and its philosophical underpinnings, in my book *Mind Games* (Blackwell, 2010).

Doctor de Quélus' book on chocolate is written in French under the title: *Histoire Naturelle Du Cacao Et Du Sucre* (1719). Antonio Lavedán, compared various Western weaknesses in his 1796 treatise *On Coffee, Tea, Chocolate and Tobacco* which was written in Spanish as *Tratado de los Usos, Abusos, Propiedades y Virtudes del Tabaco, Cafe, Te, y Chocolate.* Hernán Cortés was writing about the chocolate rituals in *The True History of the Conquest of New Spain* (published in 1552)

Chapter 30. Food Therapy

The School of Life website has several more examples, indeed an app at its website: http://www.thebookoflife.org/food-as-therapy/.

Chapter 31. Indulge Yourself and Chapter 32: Chocolate Money Really Does Grow on Trees

Dennis Tedlock is the translator of *Popol Vuh: The Mayan Book Of The Dawn Of Life* which can be downloaded online as a PDF file from holybooks.com:

http://www.holybooks.com/wp-content/uploads/popol-vuh-the-mayan-book-of-the-dawn-of-life-translated-by-Dennis-Tedlock.pdf.

There are also some very through scholarly accounts of the "origins of chocolate," including *Time Among the Maya: Travels in Belize, Guatemala, and Mexico*, by Ronald Wright (Grove Press, 2000).

Doctor de Quélus' strict advice to eat chocolate at breakfast appears in *Histoire Naturelle Du Cacao Et Du Sucre* (1719). Additional information from: *On the Chocolate Trail: A Delicious Adventure Connecting Jews, Religions, History, Travel, Rituals and Recipes to the Magic of Cacao* by Deborah Prinz (who is a Rabbi, no less). The book was published by an obscure outfit called Jewish Lights Publishing in 2013.

For the backstory on this: "There recently died at Martinico a councilor aged about a hundred years, who, for thirty years past, lived on nothing but chocolate and biscuit. He sometimes, indeed, had a little soup at dinner, but never any fish, flesh, or other victuals: he was, nevertheless, so vigorous and nimble, that at fourscore and five, he could get on horseback without stirrups," see: *Histoire Naturelle Du Cacao Et Du Sucre,* by by D. de Quelus (1719).

Similarly, for more on this tale: "From time to time the guards brought him, in cups of pure gold, a drink made from the cocoa-plant, which they said he took before visiting his wives. We did not take much notice of this at the time, though I saw them bring in a good fifty large jugs of chocolate, all frothed up, of which he would drink a little. As soon as the great Montezuma had dined, all the guards and many more of his household servants ate in their turn. I think more than a thousand plates of food must have been brought in for them, and more than two thousand jugs of chocolate frothed up in the Mexican style" see *The True History of the Conquest of New Spain* by Bernal Díaz del Castillo (published in 1552).

Chapter 33. Darker Chocolate

This just touches on some of the spooky traditions of the Aztecs and Maya. See, for example, *The Return of Quetzalcoatl. Ancient Mesoamerica* by William Ringle, Tomás Gallareta Negrón, George Bey (Cambridge University Press, 1998). Unreliable but indefatigable Wikipedia has quite a thorough exploration of all the South American gods and traditions.

Chapter 34. From Death by Chocolate to Survival by K Rations

"The lemonade powder in the K-ration, the sole source of vitamin C, was so acidic that soldiers commonly joked that it worked better as a floor cleaner than as a drink." A playful discussion of K-rations is here: http://www.uh.edu/engines/epi1324.htm.

More on the health properties of chocolate can be found in *Chocolate: Healthfood of the Gods: Unwrap the Secrets of Chocolate for Health, Beauty, and Longevity* by Phillip Minton; *The Healthy Chocoholic: Over 60 Healthy Chocolate Recipes Free of Gluten & Dairy* by Dawn J. Parker; *Chocolate And Cocoa: Health And Nutrition* by Ian Knight (editor); *Polyphenols in Green Coffee Bean and Chocolate* by Suzana Almoosawi; and *Chocolate: Food of the Gods* by Alex Szogyi (editor).

Part VII. Letting Logic Choose the Menu

Chapter 35. The Method of Doubt

Now this is the stuff of a philosophy course, but well, some readers may want to know where to read more about it. And why not try my own book, *Philosophical Tales* (Blackwell, 2008), which has a chapter on René Descartes putting his grand theory in both a philosophical and personal perspective. I do cite this book a few times here, but it is, I think, almost unique in its approach to the great philosophers— linking their high-minded interests to their mundane habits and everyday, practical concerns.

The original views of Descartes are set out in *Meditations on the First Philosophy* (1641).

Chapter 36. Correlation is Not Causation

This is a very valuable general principle! But for a quick introduction to logic, why not try my own *Philosophy for Dummies* (Wiley, 2010)? For more on linear and non-linear thinking, you might like to try my *Critical Thinking Skills for Dummies* (Wiley, 2014).

The strange, counterintuitive relationship between low-fat diets and putting on bodily fat has been explored by several studies, including one by a Finnish team of researchers led by Professor E. K. Hämäläinen, entitled "Decrease of serum total and free testosterone during a low-fat high-fibre diet," available at https://www.ncbi.nlm.nih.gov/pubmed/6538617. The researchers had their volunteers switch from a diet containing 40 percent calories fat (mainly from animal sources) to a diet containing a mere 20 percent calories from fat (mainly from polyunsaturated fats), and then back again to the 40 percent fat diet. They found that testosterone levels plummeted when the subjects switched to the low-fat diet and returned to higher levels when fat intake was increased once again to 40 percent.

Afterword: Existential Reflections in a Fast-Food Restaurant

Ah, McDonald's! For more of the same, and a ripping read (as well as a film), check out *Fast Food Nation: The Dark Side of the All-American Meal* (2001) by investigative journalist Eric Schlosser. The book examines the local and global influence of the United States fast-food industry and was adapted into a film directed by Richard Linklater in 2006. You can find segments of the film, and other McHorrors, on YouTube.

Possible allergic reaction to propylene glycol are discussed in a nice, balanced article by Thomas Rapp for Honey Colony, called "The Dark Side of Propylene Glycol: Side Effects And How to Avoid Them," March 7, 2017. It is online at https://www.honeycolony.com/article/propylene-glycol/.

Symptoms of MSG are set out by Katherine Zeratsky for the Mayo Clinic in an article headed "What is MSG? Is it bad for you?" It is online at https://www.mayoclinic.org/healthy-lifestyle/nutrition-and-healthy-eating/expert-answers/monosodium-glutamate/faq-20058196.

And then there's that perennial question about fats. Does the body consider saturated oils bad and unsaturated good? Harvard Health has a nice article on this issue with links to further sources:

https://www.health.harvard.edu/staying-healthy/the-truth-about-fats-bad-and-good.

But Denis Campbell, health writer for *The Guardian* (London) provides a summary of the newer ideas that the old consensus was wrong. The article, "Backlash after report claims saturated fats do not increase heart risk," was published on April 25, 2017, and is online at https://www.theguardian.com/society/2017/apr/25/saturated-fats-heart-attack-risk-low-fat-foods-cardiologists.

The original paper is called "Saturated fat does not clog the arteries: coronary heart disease is a chronic inflammatory condition, the risk of which can be effectively reduced from healthy lifestyle interventions," and was by Aseem Malhotra, Rita Redberg, and Pascal Meier in the *British Journal of Sports Medicine*, August 2017. You can read it online at http://bjsm.bmj.com/content/51/15/1111 .

The Canola Oil Question

First of all, McDonald's really does still use the oil, and in huge amounts. For example, see the story: "McDonald's to stick with canola oil," by Sean Pratt, published July 16, 2015, online at: https://www.producer.com/2015/07/mcdonalds-to-stick-with-canola-oil/.

Sarah Corriher makes a number of general criticisms of the oil, which she calls "a Frankenstein" food, but also some very specific ones in an article published for the *Health Wyze* report, May 11, 2009, online at https://healthwyze.org/reports/123-the-bomb-shell-truth-about-canola-oil.

Can canola help improve memory? The *Nature* study is called "Effect of canola oil consumption on memory, synapse and neuropathology in the triple transgenic mouse model of Alzheimer's disease," and was by Elisabetta Lauretti and Domenico Praticò. Published in *Scientific Reports* volume 7, article number: 17134 (2017). https://www.nature.com/articles/s41598-017-17373-3

The sceptical literature study was: *Nutrition Reviews* June 2013; 71(6): 370–385: "Evidence of health benefits of canola oil," article by Lin Lin, Hanja Allemekinders, Angela Dansby, Lisa Campbell, Shaunda Durance-Tod, Alvin Berger, and Peter JH Jones. Online at https://www.ncbi.nlm.nih.gov/pmc/articles/PMC3746113/.

Sally Fallon and Mary Enig were writing in "The Great Con-ola," July 28, 2002, for the Weston Price Foundation, online at https://www.westonaprice.org/health-topics/know-your-fats/the-great-con-ola/.

The scary story of canola oil for McDonald's trucks was covered by Reuters on July 2, 2007, in a story entitled "First fries, then vans: McD's to recycle oil," by Nigel Hunt. See: https://uk.reuters.com/article/environment-mcdonalds-biodiesel-dc/first-fries-then-vans-mcds-to-recycle-oil-idUKL0240836220070702

The claim that "Cooking oil in professional kitchens is usually a mix of 25 percent olive oil to 75 percent canola oil" I saw cited by John Moody in an article January 25, 2018, for *The Healthy Home Economist*. See: https://www.thehealthyhomeeconomist.com/canola-oil/

Rape seed oil, erucic acid, and illness is discussed in the journal *Annals of Nutrition and Metabolism* 1992; 36(5-6):273-8, in an article entitled "Fatty acid composition of blood lipids in Chinese children consuming high erucic acid rapeseed oil" by M.D. Laryea, Y.F. Jiang, G.L. Xu, and I. Lombeck. It is online at https://www.ncbi.nlm.nih.gov/pubmed/1492753.

About the Author

Martin Cohen has established a worldwide reputation as a radical philosopher and unconventional thinker. His two introductions to philosophy, *101 Philosophy Problems* and *101 Ethical Dilemmas,* have been translated into many different languages. Amongst his other books are an "anti-history" of great philosophers, *Philosophical Tales;* two Wiley *For Dummies* books, the UK edition of *Philosophy for Dummies* and *Critical Thinking Skills for Dummies;* a very different kind of *Encyclopedia of Philosophy and Ethics* (now available online); an illustrated *pot pourri* of philosophy called *Philosophy Hacks* (co-authored with Robert Arp) – and a guide to politically significant but otherwise pretty appalling travel destinations called *No Holiday: 80 Places You Don't Want to Visit.*

Martin lives part-time in the UK and part-time in southwest France with his wife and son, both of whom have been obliged (and occasionally delighted) to test out his recipes.

Index

recipe for (A Very Authentic Bread), 6–7

Thoreau on, 27

water content of, 103–104

white, behaving like sugar, 175–176

Breast milk and breastfeeding, 63–64, 120–121

Brecht, Bertolt, 131

Bromate, 18

Brumfitt, Taryn, 154

Buddhism, 159, 161–162, 313

Byron, George ("Lord Byron"), 248–249

C

Cadbury (company), 219, 220

Flake, commercials for, 223–224

Cadbury, George, 219

CAFOs (Concentrated Animal Feeding Operations), 190, 270

Calcium propionate, 11

Calcium sulfate, 10

Caloric intake at breakfast vs. dinner, 232

Caloric intake, relationship with body weight, 38–39

Calorie-controlled diets, 39–41, 77–78

Calories, kinds of, and weight loss, 42–43

Calories of stored energy, in human

body, 41

Canola oil, 271–272

Carbohydrates, 43, 71, 96. See also Low-carb diets

as energy source, 40, 70, 210

fat burning, effect on, 44–45

gut bacteria linked to cravings for, 110

pasta vs. white bread / rice, 175–177

in potatoes, 127, 176

Carrageenan, 17

Causation

vs. correlation, 260–265

Hume and, 41–42

Caveman ("Paleo") diet, 4, 29–35

Cheese, 17–18, 70–71, 109, 114. See also Dairy products

Chemicals, 12, 275. See also Food additives

artificial sweeteners, 209–213

farming, use in, xi, 189–190

obesogenic environment and, 199–203

Chicory (plant), 164

Chicory and Walnut Salad, 165

Chicory root extract, 163–165

Children, and obesity, 118, 142–143

Chili non Carne y Chocolate, 242–243